Teaching Higher-Order Thinking to Young Learners, K–3

To be truly educated today, students need more than knowledge; they need higher-order thinking skills. Critical and creative thinking is required to recognize and counter disinformation, to overcome thinking errors, and to be successful in school and life. To effectively teach these skills, we must start early, when young minds are still forming. While K–3 students are capable of higher-order thinking, most lessons engage only their lower-order thinking. In this comprehensive book based on sound science, Dr. Saifer offers many practical and engaging ways to develop students' logical, critical, and creative thinking skills within nearly every lesson, in all subject areas, and throughout the day. *Teaching Higher-Order Thinking to Young Learners, K–3: How to Develop Sharp Minds for the Disinformation Age* is key reading for any early childhood teacher, leader, or parent.

Steffen Saifer, EdD, a former teacher and administrator, is an international consultant and writer. He is the author of *Practical Solutions to Practically Every Problem: The Survival Guide for Early Childhood Professionals*, now in its third edition.

Other Eye on Education Books
Available from Routledge
(www.routledge.com/eyeoneducation)

Design Thinking for Every Classroom
A Practical Guide for Educators
Shelley Goldman and Molly B. Zielezinski

Everyday STEAM for the Early Childhood Classroom
Integrating the Arts into STEM Teaching
Margaret Loring Merrill

Universal Design for Learning in the Early Childhood Classroom
Teaching Children of all Languages, Cultures, and Abilities, Birth – 8 Years, Second Edition
Pamela Brillante and Karen Nemeth

Supporting Early Speech-Language Development
Strategies for Ages 0-8
Kimberly A. Boynton

Sparking Curiosity Through Project-Based Learning in the Early Childhood Classroom
Strategies and Tools to Unlock Student Potential
Elizabeth Hoyle Konecni

Teaching Higher-Order Thinking to Young Learners, K–3
How to Develop Sharp Minds for the Disinformation Age
Steffen Saifer

Teaching Higher-Order Thinking to Young Learners, K–3

How to Develop Sharp Minds for the Disinformation Age

Steffen Saifer

Routledge
Taylor & Francis Group
NEW YORK AND LONDON

Designed cover image: © Getty Images

First published 2025
by Routledge
605 Third Avenue, New York, NY 10158

and by Routledge
4 Park Square, Milton Park, Abingdon, Oxon, OX14 4RN

Routledge is an imprint of the Taylor & Francis Group, an informa business

© 2025 Taylor & Francis

The right of Steffen Saifer to be identified as author of this work has been asserted in accordance with sections 77 and 78 of the Copyright, Designs and Patents Act 1988.

All rights reserved. No part of this book may be reprinted or reproduced or utilised in any form or by any electronic, mechanical, or other means, now known or hereafter invented, including photocopying and recording, or in any information storage or retrieval system, without permission in writing from the publishers.

Trademark notice: Product or corporate names may be trademarks or registered trademarks, and are used only for identification and explanation without intent to infringe.

ISBN: 978-1-032-68340-9 (hbk)
ISBN: 978-1-032-64918-4 (pbk)
ISBN: 978-1-032-68342-3 (ebk)

DOI: 10.4324/9781032683423

Typeset in Palatino
by SPi Technologies India Pvt Ltd (Straive)

To the current generation of young learners and the generations to come. May you use your higher-order thinking skills to learn from the mistakes of the generations that preceded you to be
More responsible than we have been puerile,
More generous than we have been mercenary,
More respectful than we have been churlish,
More honest than we have been venal,
More erudite than we have been foolish,
More mindful than we have been thoughtless,
More kind than we have been heartless, and
More peaceful than we have been savage.

Contents

List of Figures ix
Meet the Author x
Acknowledgments xi

Introduction 1

PART 1   Thinking about Thinking **7**

1 An Educational Imperative 9

2 Types of Thinking Skills: The Tools in Our Head 21

3 Lower-Order Thinking (LOT) Skills: Functional… If
   Not Always Fun 31

4 Middle-Order Thinking (MOT) Skills: Only a Path,
   but the Only Path, to Wisdom 38

5 Higher-Order Thinking (HOT) Skills: Instruments of
   Insight, Innovation, and Invention .63

6 Thought Processes: Common Tasks, Uncommon
   Thinking 98

PART 2   Learning to Think, Thinking to Learn **135**

7 Higher-Order Thinking in Action: Supports and
   Challenges 137

8 HOT Teaching Precepts: Head, Heart, and Humor 163

viii ◆ Contents

9 HOT Teaching Methods: Context, Cognition, and
Creativity 183

10 HOT Instructional Supports: Sparks, Similes, and
Smiles 216

11 Teaching Reading and Writing with Higher-Order
Thinking: Yearning to Learn...........................241

Index...252

Figures

2.1	Saifer's Taxonomy of Thinking Skills (STOTS)	23
4.1	Art Cards Sample	44
4.2	Tree Chart	48
5.1	Same Words, Different Meanings	71
6.1	Map Evaluation Form	109
6.2	Family Groups	128
9.1	Math Playing Cards Sample	201
9.2	Game of Stones (and Shells)	208
10.1	Visual Cues	220

Meet the Author

Steffen Saifer, EdD, a former teacher and administrator, is an international consultant and writer based in Spain. He is the author of *Practical Solutions to Practically Every Problem: The Survival Guide for Early Childhood Professionals*, now in its third edition.

Acknowledgments

I am beholden to the many thought leaders whose wisdom has inspired me over the course of my career. Some are friends and colleagues, some are acquaintances, and some I know only through their higher-order thinking: Elena Bodrova, Barbara Bowman, Alicia Brandwine, Berry Brazelton, Sue Bredekamp, Nancy Carlsson-Paige, Margie Carter, Deb Curtis, Linda Darling-Hammond, Stanislas Dehaene, Daniel Dennett, Stephanie Feeney, Michael Fullan, Ellen Galinsky, Howard Gardner, Dan Gartrell, Stacie Goffin, Janet Gonzalez-Mena, Jim Greenman, Vivian Gussin Paley, Randy Hitz, Marilou Hyson, Elizabeth Jones, Daniel Kahneman, Lilian Katz, Herbert R. Kohl, Alfie Kohn, Jonathan Kozol, Cassie Landers, Elena Lenskaya, Deborah Leong, Joan Lombardi, Rebecca Marcon, Sam Meisels, Cari Olmsted, Bruce Perry, Robert Pianta, Daniel Pink, Steven Pinker, Jack Shonkoff, Daniel J. Siegel, James Wertsch, and Martin Woodhead.

And special thanks to my wife, Karen Ortiz, for her great editing and even greater support.

Introduction

Over the course of three decades, I have observed many teachers of young learners in dozens of countries, including in the U.S., spanning four continents. Nearly all of the teachers primarily elicited lower-order thinking from their students. They asked questions that have only one right answer, they gave information for students to memorize, they offered students tasks to copy or imitate, and they told students what to do and how to do it. In most of these classrooms, few students were attentive and interested and even fewer were enjoying the process.

So, it was very frustrating for me to see all the easy opportunities these teachers had to make their lessons more engaging and more challenging by eliciting students' higher-order thinking. Often, it was just a matter of rephrasing a question, asking an additional question, or encouraging students to ask questions. For example, I observed a lesson where the teacher held up pictures of various shapes, one at a time, while students drew each shape and wrote its name in their notebooks. Then, in unison, everyone said the name of the shape. At various points, the teacher could have asked students to think of objects that have the same shape as the shape in the picture. At the end of the lesson, the teacher could have asked students to draw a shape that was not shown to them, to draw a picture of a person or object using as many of the shapes as possible, or to put together two shapes to make a third different shape. The possibilities are almost endless. I wanted these teachers to teach higher-order thinking for two equally important reasons: to improve their students' cognitive abilities and to make the experience of learning more engaging and enjoyable. For me, these are two of the most essential qualities of good teaching.

The barrier to promoting higher-order thinking was not a matter of teachers lacking the time or having to change the subject or the curriculum. They did not consider higher-order thinking to be something they *should* teach (or even be allowed to teach), nor was it in their skill set to do so.

Nevertheless, I am hopeful that teachers can and will promote higher-order thinking. Whenever I suggested some easy, quick ways to prompt higher-order thinking, like those described above, nearly every teacher was excited to try it.

I strongly believe that the development of students' higher-order thinking skills is a critical strategy for improving the effectiveness of our system of education. In addition to helping students to sharpen their thinking and to identify and counteract disinformation, it engages students in learning and respects their feelings and intellectual capacities. This potentially makes it a strategy for improving the academic performance of disaffected students and for narrowing achievement gaps due to racial, class, family income, and other disparities.

Many of the countries with the highest student achievement scores, as measured by the Programme for International Student Assessment (PISA), prioritize higher-order thinking in their schools and embed it throughout their national curriculums starting in kindergarten or earlier. These include Singapore, Canada, Hong Kong, Ireland, Japan, and Finland (OECD, 2023). In addition, Finland has a media literacy curriculum that extends from kindergarten through college specifically to teach students how to recognize and distinguish among misinformation, disinformation, harmful information (even if true), and information that is true and informative (Gross, 2023).

Ultimately, the ideas in this book are aimed at ensuring students' current and future well-being—their happiness, mental and physical health, self-efficacy, empathy for others, and more. Educational attainment does not lead to well-being, although people who have well-being tend to get more education (Lee & Yu-Lin, 2022). Being "smart" (as measured by standard IQ tests) also does not lead to or correlate with well-being. But higher-order thinking abilities *do* strongly correlate with a number of factors of well-being (Grossmann et al., 2013).

My desire, which many other educators share, is that our students will be able to effectively use the full range of higher-order thinking skills to benefit all aspects of their lives and the lives of the people close to them. We want them to be adept at and to enjoy intellectual challenges to the best of their abilities now, throughout their schooling, and as adults. We want them to grow up to be a literate and wise generation who will create honest, compassionate, fair, and equitable societies.

I hope this book will help you to:

♦ Know a great deal about *all* thinking skills, including lower-order and middle-order thinking. This will provide contextual information needed to fully understand and value the educational purposes of higher-order thinking.
♦ Learn why, when, and how to teach higher-order thinking and hone middle-order thinking for maximum educational impact.
♦ Be adept at and motivated to facilitate students' middle- and higher-order thinking many times throughout the day, every day, and at increasingly advanced levels over the course of the school year.

This book is both practical and theoretical, based on recent social science and neurological research findings. The book starts with a "call to action," explaining the critical need to teach higher-order thinking, particularly to young learners. The remaining chapters of Part 1 describe in detail the full range of thinking skills, how they relate to each other, and their roles in five common thought processes. While more theoretical than the second part, it still includes many classroom and "real-life" examples. Part 2 of the book focuses on strategies and techniques for teaching young students to think logically, deeply, critically, and creatively. Throughout the book, the term "higher-order thinking" is replaced by its helpful, if prosaic, acronym, HOT. Lower-order thinking is replaced by the acronym, LOT, and MOT is used for middle-order thinking.

For most of the scenarios and activities in this book, the level of cognitive challenge can be easily adjusted for students from kindergarten through third grade or to individualize within a classroom of any grade. Many examples embed teaching HOT skills within the process of teaching subject matter content or provide the option to embed any content into the activity. There is at least one activity example for nearly every subject from music to math and science to social studies. The activities are engaging and enjoyable for both students and teachers and can be used with any curriculum. The activities use either no materials or materials that are free or inexpensive or that can be made from recycled items. There are four types of activities in this book:

- Small group activities that promote HOT, called *ThinkinGroups* (an oh-so-clever amalgam of "think in groups" and "thinking groups")
- Curriculum ideas and whole or small group activities called *Cognitivities* (a not-so-clever amalgam of cognitive and activity)
- Scenarios of teachers' lessons and interactions with students to promote their MOT, called *MOTivations*, and their HOT, called *Snap-sHOTs*
- Theme ideas that lend themselves to promoting HOT, called *HOThemes* and their related projects and inquiries

And there is a helpful website! There you can find downloadable materials, links to relevant articles and resources, research updates, new information, a blog in which you can participate, and more:

https://higher-order-thinking.com

References

Gross, J. (2023, January 10). *How Finland is teaching a generation to spot misinformation.* New York Times. https://www.nytimes.com/2023/01/10/world/europe/finland-misinformation-classes.html

Grossmann, I., Na, J., Varnum, M. E., Kitayama, S., & Nisbett, R. E. (2013). A route to well-being: Intelligence versus wise reasoning. *Journal of Experimental Psychology: General*, *42*(3), 944–953. https://doi.org/10.1037/a0029560

Lee, K. S., & Yu-Lin, Y. (2022). Educational attainment and emotional well-being in adolescence and adulthood. *Social Science and Medicine - Mental Health*. https://doi.org/10.1016/j.ssmmh.2022.100138

OECD. (2023). *PISA 2022 results: Volume I: The state of learning and equity in education*. Organization for Economic Co-operation and Development (OECD). https://doi.org/10.1787/19963777

Part 1
Thinking about Thinking

Graphic by Gwendolyn Rodriguez.

1

An Educational Imperative

Why is it important to teach higher-order thinking (HOT) in schools, especially in the early grades? Teaching critical and creative thinking benefits young learners in several ways:

- ◆ It motivates them to be eager learners because their intellects are supported and valued and their creativity is encouraged.
- ◆ It will help them succeed in school and in life by giving them the cognitive tools they need to plan effectively, make good decisions, overcome challenges, solve problems successfully, and more.
- ◆ It builds their capacity to reason before reacting emotionally or impulsively, so they can avoid common thinking errors and be able to recognize and deflect disinformation and other deceptions.

The Skills Students will Need... Sooner than Later

Good teaching prepares students for what lies ahead, not just for the challenges of the next grade but for the challenges they will face as adults. Although no one can predict the future, there is widespread agreement among educators and social scientists

DOI: 10.4324/9781032683423-3

that many current teaching practices are not adequately preparing today's students for tomorrow's world. So, they have identified some of the skills they believe students *will* need to meet those challenges, called *21st Century Skills*. Proponents urge curriculum developers, policy makers, administrators, and teachers at all grade levels and of every subject area to promote these skills. Twenty-first Century Skills include a number of important (so-called) soft skills—the ability to collaborate and get along with diverse people, to communicate effectively, and to be flexible and open to change, among others. But near the top of the list are the two HOT skills: critical and creative thinking (Chalkiadaki, 2018). However, it seems these skills are necessary to successfully navigate life in *today's* world. Perhaps the future has arrived earlier than expected.

It Is Now An Educational Imperative

We are living in a time when pernicious lies, outrageous claims, and dangerous deceptions are so quickly and widely spread and *so readily believed*! Even many authority figures are guilty of being both believers and perpetrators of lies. Millions of people all over the world are fooled by biased opinions pretending to be objective journalism, sales pitches disguised as helpful information, and propaganda masquerading as factual information. They believe outlandish and dangerous "conspiracy theories," which are not theories at all but lies meant to incite and spread hatred, distrust, and division. The negative consequences of this are very serious for societies and individuals. Trust, the ability to know what is true or not true, norms of civil behavior, expectations of fairness and morality (particularly from leaders), and a general sense of safety and predictability are the components of the glue that holds societies together.

Times of crises call for strong action. Teaching HOT is now an *imperative*.

People who have HOT skills are less susceptible to believing disinformation than those who lack or have weak HOT skills. The former are better able to recognize deceptions and find truths by thinking deeply. And they do not allow their base emotions to block their ability to reason (Lantian et al., 2021; Reboot Foundation, 2022; Tylor et al., 2023).

Higher-order thinking is a distinct ability unrelated to having an advanced college degree or to being "smart," at least in the traditional sense of having a high IQ. People with more years of education are *no* better at discerning disinformation than those with fewer years of education (Tylor et al., 2023). And people with high IQ scores are just as biased, impulsive, and easily deceived as everyone else; IQ tests do not measure HOT skills (Butler et al., 2017; Halpern & Dunn, 2021). Even students at Ivy League universities and history professors with advanced degrees have difficulty distinguishing between false and factual information online (Wineburg & McGrew, 2019). It is hard *not* to conclude from this that HOT skills are rarely taught in schools at every level of education and that, if they are, students are not learning them (Bouygues, 2018; Breslin, 2023; Wiggins, 2012). To be truly educated in the 21st century, it is necessary to have HOT skills. If schools are not teaching HOT, they are not fulfilling their duty to educate.

> **It is the capacity to think critically and creatively, not the possession of a high IQ score or an advanced degree, that gives a person the ability to recognize and reject disinformation and other deceptions.**

The Importance of Starting Early

Is it a realistic expectation for K–3 students to learn HOT skills such as critical thinking? This book is an affirmative response to that question. Not only is it realistic but it is *necessary* to start early, and this is for a number of important reasons.

Intuitive, but incorrect, ideas are formed early in life, particularly about natural phenomena such as "why it rains" or "what happens to the sun at night." Often the explanations children give of these phenomena are humorous and endearing in their naivete. But many students do not get accurate information until years later. At that point, the correct ideas do not always replace the incorrect ones but may be held simultaneously in a kind of mental competition with each other. For this reason, researchers who study this aspect of cognitive development urge early primary teachers to teach their students basic concepts of science, including causes and effects, questioning assumptions, and looking beyond surface appearances (Kelemen, 2019).

Teaching HOT skills can and should begin in kindergarten, if not sooner. Even parents and teachers of preschoolers can do much to develop their children's HOT. Because every thinking skill can used for tasks that are very easy (as well as very difficult), students of any age or ability can begin learning even the more conceptual thinking skills. Our young learners are capable of using many types of HOT skills at surprisingly advanced levels when teachers model them often, teach them explicitly and implicitly, and provide ample opportunities for students to practice using them.

Why Minds Need Sharpening

If students start early in life to develop HOT skills—when brain neurons and synapses are still forming, diversifying, winnowing, and strengthening—the skills are more likely to become automatic, to be used often and effectively, and to endure. It is much like learning a second language. The earlier in life it begins, the easier and more thoroughly it is learned, and the longer it is retained.

Promoting HOT skills often and regularly starting in kindergarten and continuing systematically up through middle and high school will ensure that HOT is internalized as a *mental habit*. This is important because the human brain tends to be naturally averse to critical thinking. The brain's default mode, it seems, is to stick to what is already known or believed (aka confirmation bias), to make quick judgments and stay with them even after shown evidence that they are wrong, to prefer the sensational over the reasonable no matter how ridiculous, to believe something because it is repeated often even if it is blatantly false, and to ignore information that is conflicting, complex, or counterintuitive (Kahneman, 2011, Kolbert, 2017). Furthermore, when the brain is under stress, base emotional responses like fear, anger, and disgust automatically kick in, and the ability to reason is suppressed (Schwabe & Wolf, 2013).

The reasons for this are complex and speculative, but it is likely because human brains in some ways have not evolved fast enough to keep up with a world that is rapidly and dramatically changing, increasingly complex, and more interconnected by the day. For hundreds of thousands of years, human survival depended on the ability to quickly distrust, fear, and objectify anyone who looked, sounded, and acted "differently" and to fiercely identify with an affinity group—a clan, tribe, sect, race, family, and so on. And during that time, our brains evolved to make this way of thinking automatic; quicker action against danger and stronger bonds with our clan improved the odds of living another day (Gorman & Gorman, 2021; Mercier & Sperber, 2017). But today, "us vs. them" thinking is a mental liability. It is the antithesis of the inter-cultural understanding, collaboration, and tolerance necessary for human survival in today's "global village." And extreme loyalty to fellow in-group members (aka nationalism) is a barrier to using critical and creative thinking to question the group's assumptions, beliefs, and behaviors. It promotes conformity, groupthink, and blocks openness to novel ideas and positive influences from outside the group.

In their 2017 book, *The Enigma of Reason*, authors Mercier and Sperber make a compelling case that human reason *has* evolved to a high level but primarily for navigating social relationships among fellow in-group members: the "us" in "us vs. them" thinking. However, intellectual reasoning (aka HOT) has not evolved to the same degree. This idea is supported by findings from experiments with preverbal infants. They show that babies as young as three months old have a strong preference for others who are like themselves and an equally strong, if not stronger, dislike for others they perceive as not like themselves (Hamlin et al., 2007, 2010; Mahajan & Wynn, 2012).

One "take-away" from Mercier's and Sperber's theory is to teach HOT skills within an enjoyable social context such as cooperative learning or group games and projects. This enlists students' advanced social thinking skills to help develop their nascent intellectual thinking skills.

> Without higher-order thinking skills, it is very difficult to overcome the brain's resistance for intellectual work. It is like trying to run a 10-kilometer race without ever having run a race before. However, when higher-ordering thinking is an established mental habit, the effort is minimized and intellectual work is an enjoyable challenge. It is like running in a 10-kilometer race as a conditioned marathon runner. No sweat!

What Should Schools Do?

The most common way that schools in the U.S. and many other countries are addressing this problem is by implementing media literacy programs. In 2023, California joined 18 other U.S. states to mandate that all schools teach media literacy. These programs typically focus on internet safety and responsible posting and on distinguishing fake news from real news, advertisements from information, and opinions from facts. While important and necessary, this information is insufficient for teaching students to avoid deceptions. According to Alice Huguet, an education researcher and policy professor at the Rand Corporation, media literacy programs do not address important issues, including how to avoid being emotional manipulated, ways to determine if important facts or relevant information has been deliberately omitted, and strategies to infer the intent of the author. She summarizes her critique by saying, "It's about being a critical thinker" (Buller, 2023). Because deceptive practices, enabled by advances in technology, keep morphing into ever more sophisticated and nefarious forms, they cannot be countered solely by teaching media literacy. It requires brain power and the desire and ability to keep learning that only a comprehensive approach to teaching critical and creative thinking skills can provide.

Conclusion

The theory posited by Mercier and Sperber (2017) that our social reasoning is more advanced than our intellectual reasoning helps explain a number of observable facts about the behaviors of many people today:

♦ Social media posts, shopping, internet influencers, and the lives of celebrities dominate the internet, while essentially all the knowledge in the world is just as accessible. In 2023, the English version of Wikipedia received about 2.4 billion worldwide visits per month, while YouTube received over 4.5 billion visits, and Facebook, Twitter, Instagram, and Amazon combined received about 5 billion visits (Hardwick, 2023).
♦ Of the 100 top-grossing movies in North America in 2023, none was a documentary and only two were based on actual historic events: *Oppenheimer* and *Napoleon*. Both viewed historic events through the lens of the personalities of the title characters (The Numbers, 2023).
♦ Most people prefer, and have more ability, to analyze, understand, and discuss other people and the complex details of their lives and relationships than to analyze, understand, and discuss abstract ideas, recent scientific advances, global politics, or the impact of technology.

Nevertheless, there are and always have been significant numbers of people whose intellectual reasoning is highly developed. While some of these people—Aristotle, da Vinci, Einstein, Stephen Hawking—were likely born with minds capable of very advanced HOT, there are many millions of people who have developed high levels of intellectual reasoning through effort and practice. Many millions more have the potential to think more critically and creatively, but they have not been developed in school nor supported by social norms. This is particularly true in countries that have strong anti-intellectual tendencies (Merkley, 2020).

A lack of HOT has a negative impact on democratic societies and their citizens. "Us vs. them" thinking is easily exploited by extremist politicians, many with autocratic tendencies. They win elections by telling citizens that immigrants are a dangerous threat to their shared and "superior" way of life. Creating a national-level threat allows a would-be autocrat to claim that "weak and inefficient" democracies need to be replaced by a "strongman" (Bartels, 2020, Norman & Fairless, 2023). The main tipping point that erodes democracies is when a small but significant minority of citizens lack or do not use their HOT skills and succumb to groupthink. Then there is insufficient pushback to their biases and unfounded, irrational fears and beliefs and more than sufficient support for them. This is an even greater contributor to the erosion of democracies than the strife caused by income inequality (Bartels, 2020; Haggard & Kaufman, 2021; Orhan, 2022; Stenner & Stern, 2021).

In autocracies, HOT is unwanted and feared, so, once in power, autocrats are quick to control what is taught in schools and, especially, what is not. But in democracies, HOT is welcomed and needed. While it is not possible to claim that democracies erode because HOT is not taught in schools, it is clear that schools can and should have an important role in shoring up democracies by helping students to make thinking critically and creatively a mental habit. In fact, providing this help is an imperative.

Key Ideas from this Chapter

1. Teaching HOT skills motivates students to be eager learners and helps them to make good decisions, overcome challenges, avoid thinking errors, and refute deceptions.
2. Higher-order thinking is considered to be among the most important of all the 21st Century Skills that today's students will need to be successful adults.
3. A lack of HOT skills has allowed millions of people to be easily deceived and to believe blatant lies.
4. Possessing HOT abilities is necessary to refute deceptions. People with high IQ scores or advanced degrees are just as gullible as anyone else.

An Educational Imperative ◆ 17

5. It is important to teach these skills while young brains are still developing so they can become mental habits.
6. For survival, the human brain developed the ability to automatically fear strangers and bond with an affinity group (aka an "us vs. them" mentality). This is counterproductive for survival in the world today.
7. Human brains may have evolved to have high social reasoning skills but not high intellectual reasoning skills.
8. The use of media literacy programs in schools, while important, is an inadequate approach to address students' inability to discern truth from fiction and to recognize and reject disinformation. Students need to learn HOT skills and to use them effectively to counter disinformation and deceptions of any and every form.
9. The lack of HOT by a significant portion of citizens can have serious negative consequences for democratic societies. To gain power, autocrats exploit the "us vs. them" mentality to stoke fear of immigrants and preach ultranationalism. Then they claim that democracies are weak and must be replaced by a "strongman."

Questions for Discussion

What experiences have you had related to the spread of conspiracy theories or other deceptions? What are the implications of your experiences for teaching HOT skills to young learners?

What are some examples of the use and impact of the "us vs. them" mentality? When, if ever, is it useful or helpful? What are some ways that its negative aspects can be mitigated or overridden?

What have you observed that supports or opposes the idea that the human brain can reason at a higher level about social issues than about intellectual issues?

What would a comprehensive schoolwide plan to teach HOT skills look like? How would you know that it is effective?

References

Bartels, L. M. (2020). Ethnic antagonism erodes Republicans' commitment to democracy. *Proceedings of the National Academy of Sciences*, *117*(37), 22752–22759. https://doi.org/10.1073/pnas.2007747117

Bouygues, H. L. (2018). *The state of critical thinking: A new look at reasoning at home, school, and work*. Reboot Foundation. https://reboot-foundation.org/wp-content/uploads/2022/05/The_State_of_Critical_Thinking_2018.pdf

Breslin, F. (2023, May 26). Three reasons why public schools don't teach critical thinking. *Medium*. https://medium.com/@frankbreslin41/three-reasons-why-public-high-schools-dont-teach-critical-thinking-90c475e98425

Buller, R. (2023, December 5). 'There's nothing more critical': California makes schools teach kids to spot fake news. *The Guardian*. https://www.theguardian.com/education/2023/dec/05/california-media-literacy-class-schools-misinformation

Butler, H. A., Pentoney, C., & Bong, M. P. (2017). Predicting real-world outcomes: critical thinking ability is a better predictor of life decisions than intelligence. *Thinking Skills and Creativity*. https://doi.org/10.1016/j.tsc.2017.06.005

Chalkiadaki, A. (2018). A systematic literature review of 21st century skills and competencies in primary education. *International Journal of Instruction*, *11*(3), 1–16.

Gorman, S. E., & Gorman, J. M. (2021). *Denying to the grave: Why we ignore the facts that will save us*. Oxford University Press.

Haggard, S., & Kaufman, R. (2021). *Backsliding: Democratic regress in the contemporary world*. Cambridge University Press. https://doi.org/10.1017/9781108957809

Halpern, D. F., & Dunn, D. S. (2021). Critical thinking: A model of intelligence for solving real-world problems. *Journal of Intelligence*, *79*(2). https://doi.org/10.3390/jintelligence9020022

Hamlin, J. K., Wynn, K., & Bloom, P. (2007). Social evaluation by preverbal infants. *Nature*, *450*(7169), 557–559.

Hamlin, J. K., Wynn, K., & Bloom, P. (2010). Three-month-olds show a negativity bias in their social evaluations. *Developmental Science, 13*(6), 923–929.

Hardwick, J. (2023, October 2). *The 100 most visited sites on the internet (US and worldwide).* ahrefs blog. https://ahrefs.com/blog/most-visited-websites/

Kahneman, D. (2011). *Thinking, fast and slow.* Farrar, Straus and Giroux.

Kelemen, D. (2019). The magic of mechanism: Explanation-based instruction on counterintuitive concepts in early childhood. *Perspectives in Psychological Science, 14*(4), 510–522. https://doi.org/10.1177/1745691619827011

Kolbert, E. (2017, February 19). *Why facts don't change our minds: New discoveries about the human mind show the limitations of reason.* New Yorker. https://www.newyorker.com/magazine/2017/02/27/why-facts-dont-change-our-minds February 19, 2017.

Lantian, A., Bagneux, V., Delouvée, S., & Gauvrit, N. (2021, January 13). Maybe a free thinker but not a critical one: High conspiracy belief is associated with low critical thinking ability. *Applied Cognitive Psychology, 35*(3), 674–684. https://doi.org/10.1002/acp.3790

Mahajan, N., & Wynn, K. (2012). Origins of 'us' versus 'them': Prelinguistic infants prefer similar others. *Cognition, 124*(2), 227–233.

Mercier, H., & Sperber, D. (2017). *The enigma of reason.* Harvard University Press.

Merkley, E. (2020). Anti-intellectualism, populism, and motivated resistance to expert consensus. *Public Opinion Quarterly, 84*(1), 24–48. https://doi.org/10.1093/poq/nfz053

Norman, L, & Fairless, T. (2023, November 25). As migration to Europe rises, a backlash grows: Anti-immigration parties are winning elections and surging in polls. *The Wall Street Journal.* https://www.wsj.com/world/europe/as-migration-to-europe-rises-a-backlash-grows-72a758fb

Orhan, Y. E. (2022). The relationship between affective polarization and democratic backsliding: Comparative evidence. *Democratization, 29*(4), 714–735. https://doi.org/10.1080/13510347.2021.2008912. ISSN 1351-0347.

Reboot Foundation. (2022). Science fictions: Low science knowledge and poor critical thinking are linked to conspiracy beliefs. *The State of Critical Thinking 2022*. https://reboot-foundation.org/wp-content/uploads/2022/09/Reboot-Science-Fictions-Final.pdf

Schwabe, L., & Wolf, O. T. (2013). Stress and multiple memory systems: From 'thinking' to 'doing'. *Trends in Cognitive Sciences*, *17*(2), 60–68. https://doi.org/10.1016/j.tics.2012.12.001

Stenner, K, & Stern, J. (2021). How to live with authoritarians. *Foreign Policy* online. https://foreignpolicy.com/2021/02/11/capitol-insurrection-trump-authoritarianism-psychology-innate-fear-envy-change-diversity-populism

The Numbers. (2023). North America (US and Canada) domestic movie chart for 2023. https://www.the-numbers.com/market/2023/top-grossing-movies

Tylor, J., Cosgrove, T. J., & Murphy, C. P. (2023, July 6). Narcissistic susceptibility to conspiracy beliefs exaggerated by education, reduced by cognitive reflection. *Frontiers of Psychology*. https://doi.org/10.3389/fpsyg.2023.1164725

Wiggins, G. (2012, October 19). Thinking about a lack of thinking. https://www.teachthought.com/critical-thinking/thinking-about-thinking/

Wineburg, S., & McGrew, S. (2019). Lateral reading and the nature of expertise: reading less and learning more when evaluating digital information. *Teachers College Record*, *121*(11). https://doi.org/10.1177/016146811912101102

2

Types of Thinking Skills

The Tools in Our Head

Because different tasks require different types of thinking, it is important to have the ability to think in many different ways. The great humanistic psychologist, Abraham Maslow, said, "I suppose it is tempting, if the only tool you have is a hammer, to treat everything as if it were a nail" (1966, p. 15). However, with a toolbox full of thinking tools, and the knowhow to use them, we can choose the most effective tools for the task at hand. And, if one thinking tool is not working well, we will have others to draw upon.

What *are* the thinking tools needed for our toolboxes? What purposes do they serve? How do we use them effectively? How do we teach young learners to use them? To answer these questions, it is helpful to start with a succinct overview of all the thinking tools, their main functions, their relationships to each other, and how they are used in thought processes.

Saifer's Taxonomy of Thinking Skills

Taxonomies are diagrams that capture the essence of a complex concept or theory by summarizing and organizing its main components visually using the fewest words possible.

DOI: 10.4324/9781032683423-4

They show the relationships among the components by categorizing and sequencing them. Taxonomies provide a common vocabulary, reducing the amount of miscommunication that can occur when complex ideas are shared, taught, discussed, and debated.

Terminology about thinking skills can be problematic. Terms, such as critical thinking, reasoning, meta-cognition, analytical thinking, and problem-solving, are often used by writers to mean higher-order thinking in general rather than distinct higher-order thinking skills or processes. Also, the term, higher-order thinking, sometimes refers only to critical thinking, not critical *and* creative thinking. Saifer's Taxonomy of Thinking Skills (STOTS) addresses these concerns by labeling the full array of thinking skills with precise terms that are clearly defined.

Because taxonomies are easily and quickly understood, they help create a shared understanding among stakeholders: teachers, administrators, university faculty, researchers, evaluators, curriculum developers, and others. A common vocabulary and a shared understanding improve the odds that the idea or theory will be broadly accepted, disseminated quickly, and applied with fidelity. This is important because the ultimate goal of education-related taxonomies, including this one, is to help teachers be more effective with less effort.

STOTS (Figure 2.1) shows the various types and categories of thinking skills on a continuum from practical thinking (at the bottom) to conceptual thinking (at the top). Logical thinking lies between. In addition, five common thought processes are listed, each of which entails the use of two or more thinking skills. All the terms, categories, and concepts in STOTS are explained fully in Chapters 3 through 6.

STOTS describes the array of thinking skills that people of all ages use in any situation for any purpose. Though broader than the field of education, it has important and direct implications for enhancing teaching and learning.

SAIFER'S TAXONOMY OF THINKING SKILLS (STOTS)

Higher-Order Thinking (HOT) Skills

Critical Thinking Skills
understanding and insight

Query
Infer
Deduce/Induce
Shift Perspective

Creative Thinking Skills
innovation and invention

Imagine
Generate
Reframe
Improvise

Middle-Order Thinking (MOT) Skills

logic and reason

Characterize
Associate/Differentiate
Categorize
Sequence/Pattern
Calculate
Connect Causes and Effects
Represent

Lower-Order Thinking (LOT) Skills

utility and necessity

Imitate/Copy
Follow Rules and Directions
Memorize/Recall
Know or Do by Rote
Identify/Quantify

Practical Thinking ---------- CONTINUUM ---------- Conceptual Thinking

Conceptual Thinking ---------- CONTINUUM ---------- Practical Thinking

---

Thought Processes

multiple thinking skills are used in each process

Analyses
Evaluations/Decisions
Solutions/Innovations
Plans/Strategies
Predictions/Theories

FIGURE 2.1 Saifer's Taxonomy of Thinking Skills (STOTS).

Graphic by Gwendolyn Rodriguez.

24 ◆ Thinking about Thinking

STOTS is designed to help teachers be intentional about promoting thinking skills. It is an aid for knowing every tool—all the thinking skills—their functions and how they relate to each other:

- ◆ Accomplish utilitarian tasks with lower-order thinking (LOT) skills
- ◆ Apply logic and reason to tasks with middle-order thinking (MOT) skills
- ◆ Make discoveries, gain insight, and seek truths with critical thinking HOT skills
- ◆ Produce something never seen or known before with creative thinking HOT skills

All the LOT skills and some of the more basic MOT skills are task-oriented, useful, and common. They are at the "practical thinking" end of the continuum. All the HOT skills and some of the more advanced MOT skills are process-oriented, concerned with ideas more than actions, and open-ended. These are at the "conceptual thinking" end of the continuum. Every thinking skill has value.

> **Conceptual thinkers may know that a tomato is actually a fruit, but practical thinkers know not to put it in a fruit salad!**

HOT skills are not necessarily more difficult than MOT and LOT skills. Every thinking skill can be done at a level that ranges from very basic or easy to very advanced or difficult. For most adults, memorizing a phone number is a relatively easy LOT skill, but memorizing all of Hamlet's lines in the Shakespeare play is a *very* difficult LOT skill. To imagine being the director of a science fiction movie is a basic HOT skill, but to imagine the complex fantasy world depicted in a science fiction movie is an advanced HOT skill. It is an easy HOT skill to infer the meaning of the phrase "there's a rat in this room" if it is shrieked by a person standing on a table or if it is whispered menacingly by a crime boss to his henchmen. However, it is a more difficult HOT skill if said in a neutral voice and the context is unknown or ambiguous. To know the inference would require first using

Types of Thinking Skills ◆ 25

other HOT skills, such as querying and deducing/inducing, if it can be determined at all.

We can also add HOT to tasks that require only basic LOT. This often leads to better results, deeper learning, and more enjoyment. But it may be *necessary* to use HOT for basic tasks if things go awry. Here is an example. The first time a main dish is prepared from a complicated recipe, it is best to use basic thinking tools such as following directions and quantifying—at least for those of us who are not professional chefs. If several attempts to make the recipe fail, then critical thinking skills are needed to determine the cause and find solutions, which may include determining that the recipe is faulty. In this case, more critical thinking skills can be used to fix the recipe or decide to abandon it. But, after successfully making the dish several times, the chef can use creative thinking tools to enhance the recipe. Ingredients and measurements can be adjusted to alter the taste or texture of the dish, hopefully for the better. There may be creative ways to reduce preparation time or to make it with less expensive ingredients. Vegetarian or healthier versions can also be created. Finally, its presentation can be embellished with fresh herbs or edible flowers to make it look as good as it tastes.

Lessons that typically engage only students' LOT and MOT are enhanced when activities that also engage HOT skills are added. Learning is deeper and stronger. An Aesop's fable will be better understood and appreciated by students if, after reading it, they learn about Aesop (who was a slave in ancient Egypt), act out the story, apply the story's moral to a contemporary and familiar situation, think of any circumstances where the moral would not or should not apply, create new characters and sub-plots to expand the story, and make up their own fables.

The five thought processes are common activities that everyone does almost every day. Each involves the use of many different thinking skills, often from all three categories. Thought processes are like building materials and methods, each of which needs a particular set of tools (thinking skills). They all can be done quickly if they involve relatively simple issues and time is of the essence, or they can be done slowly and deliberately if the issues are complex and time allows. Deciding which hat to wear is a quick decision (or should be), whereas deciding whom to marry or partner with is a slow and deliberate decision (or should be). The first two thought processes—analyses and evaluations/decisions—examine existing information and lean on critical thinking primarily. Solving problems and innovating are more of the moment; they examine dynamic information and use both critical and creative thinking. The last two thought processes—plans/strategies and predictions/theories—are future-oriented and lean on creative thinking.

One Activity, Many Types of Thinking

To help with understanding this taxonomy, here is a list of questions a first-grade teacher might ask students when preparing to make cards to send to a classmate, C.J., who has been absent with a prolonged illness.

1. "Are there five people at your table?"
2. "How many people are at your table?"
3. "How many papers for the cards do you need at your table?"
4. "How many marking pens does your table need for everyone to have three pens of three different colors?"
5. "What is missing from your table that you may need to make a card?"
6. "Thinking about C.J.'s personality and interests, what could you write and draw that will cheer up C.J.?"
7. "What should you *not* draw or say because it might unintentionally make C.J. feel bad?"
8. "In addition to the cards, what else we can send to C.J. that has no or a very low cost?"
9. "What can we do as a class to make C.J. feel welcomed when C.J. returns to school?"

How are these questions related? What pattern do they form? The list starts with a question that prompts LOT—there is only one right answer out of two possibilities (yes or no). Each subsequent question moves students towards more conceptual thinking.

Questions 2 and 3 also have one right answer, but there are more than two possible answers. Questions 4 and 5 require the logical MOT skill of calculating. Critical thinking HOT skills are required to respond to questions 6 and 7. The final two questions, 8 and 9, ask the students to imagine and generate new ideas, which are creative thinking HOT skills.

For all teaching and learning activities, not just questioning, it is important to determine if they elicit students' lower-order, middle-order, or higher-order (critical or creative) thinking. In many cases, one activity elicits several types of thinking.

There are certain positive attitudes and behaviors, called "thinking dispositions," that greatly support and enhance thinking skills and thought processes. They are not on STOTS, because they impact thinking rather than represent types of thinking. They are discussed further in Chapter 7 (on pages 137–141). Thinking dispositions include persistence, patience, curiosity, caution, attention, and flexibility.

The "construction" analogy for thinking skills has four components, with the addition of thinking dispositions. The finished "mental structures" are the results or outcomes of thinking and thought processes such as win/win solutions to problems, recognition and rejection of disinformation and deceptions, development of new theories, or the creation of new songs, artwork, and novels. Thinking dispositions are the many unseen supports and drivers behind the work that keep it moving—the funds, plans, coordination, deliveries, workflow, and so on. Thought processes are the "mental building materials and methods" used to construct the "mental structures." And thinking skills are the "mental tools" used to put them all together.

Construction Analogy
Thinking Skills are the *Toolbox of Tools*
Thought Processes are the *Building Materials & Methods*
Thinking Dispositions are the *Work Supports*
Results & Outcomes are the *Finished Structures*

With many tools, the right tools for the job, and good-quality building methods and materials (solid LOT and MOT skills), as well as adequate funding and workflow (thinking dispositions), the work can be done correctly and efficiently, and the final structure will be well built and functional. However, with specialized high-quality tools, excellent (even artistic) building materials, and highly skilled work methods, as well as generous funding and timely, efficient workflow (strong thinking dispositions), the final structures will be more than solidly built and functional. They will be unique and beautiful.

Conclusion

Saifer's Taxonomy of Thinking Skills is an aid for understanding all thinking skills by listing, organizing, and categorizing them. It also provides a visual representation of how they relate to each other on a continuum from practical to conceptual thinking.

All thinking skills—LOT, MOT, and HOT thinking, which includes critical and creative thinking—can be done at levels ranging from very easy to very difficult. Teachers can sharpen students' abilities to use all of the thinking skills effectively by incorporating many opportunities to practice them into daily lessons and activities. The types of questions teachers ask can promote different types of thinking, as shown in the example of a card-making activity. With this understanding, teachers can become more aware of their questioning strategies and vary them as necessary so that ultimately the majority of questions will engage students' HOT. Questioning is just one strategy for promoting HOT skills, but it is an important one because teachers ask many questions throughout the day.

Saifer's Taxonomy of Thinking Skills is a guide for maximizing the amount of teaching and learning that promotes HOT. Teachers can help students develop their abilities to think critically and creatively, to learn new conceptual thinking skills, and to move each thinking skill from its current level to a more advanced level. Possessing HOT skills at the most advanced levels possible not only provides cognitive and academic benefits but also is necessary for avoiding thinking errors and recognizing and rejecting disinformation, which is increasingly more sophisticated, ubiquitous, and pernicious.

Key Ideas from this Chapter

1. It is important to have the ability to use a wide range of thinking skills and apply them effectively.
2. Teachers can sharpen students' abilities to use all thinking skills effectively by incorporating a wide range of thinking skill opportunities into daily lessons and activities.
3. Taxonomies are useful as they explain complex ideas or theories visually and succinctly. They create a common vocabulary and a shared understanding among stakeholders.
4. STOTS describes three main categories of thinking skills: LOT, MOT, and HOT.
5. HOT is composed of two categories: critical and creative thinking.
6. STOTS also describes five thought processes: analyzes, evaluations/decisions, solutions/innovations, plans/ strategies, and predictions/theories. Each of these processes entails the use of a wide range of thinking skills.
7. Thinking dispositions such as curiosity, caution, attention, patience, persistence, and flexibility support and enhance the development and use of HOT skills.
8. All thinking skills can be done at levels ranging from very easy to very difficult.
9. LOT and MOT skills can form a foundation upon which HOT skills can be applied to make a task more enjoyable, meaningful, and successful.
10. Because teachers ask many questions throughout the day, it is important to use questioning strategies that elicit HOT.
11. Strong HOT skills are required to recognize and avoid thinking errors and recognize and reject disinformation and other deceptions.

Questions for Discussion

Describe some examples from your own school experience of tasks that you were asked to do as assignments and homework. Which types of thinking skills did they elicit?

What were you taught about thinking skills and the role of thinking in education in your professional coursework or training?

What are some of the specific barriers to promoting HOT that you face as an educator and/or, if you have children, as a parent? Discuss some ways that these barriers can be overcome.

What are some ways that questions typically asked of students can be worded, or re-worded, to promote critical and creative thinking?

A "construction work" analogy for thinking skills was presented. What other analogies could apply to developing and using thinking skills?

References

Maslow, A. H. (1966). *The psychology of science: A reconnaissance.* Harper Collins.

3

Lower-Order Thinking (LOT) Skills

Functional...If Not Always Fun

Lower-order thinking (LOT) uses and relies on information as it is. It is not applied, altered, manipulated, acted upon, or scrutinized. LOT skills are at the practical end of the "practical to conceptual continuum," as shown in Saifer's Taxonomy of Thinking Skills.

While they may appear to be inferior to middle-order thinking (MOT) and higher-order thinking (HOT) skills, it is more accurate to understand LOT skills as functional skills, as they are useful, necessary, and, of course, practical.

Lower-Order Thinking (LOT) Skills
utility and necessity

Imitate/Copy
Follow Rules and Directions
Memorize/Recall
Know or Do by Rote
Identify/Quantify

LOT skills are like a small toolbox containing just basic, essential tools: a hammer, wrench, drill, screwdriver, pliers, and tape measure. Each of their purposes is quite obvious and, for most

DOI: 10.4324/9781032683423-5

people, requires no special training. They are useful and effective for accomplishing simple tasks, such as hanging a picture, but not much more. Likewise, LOT skills are useful and effective for common mental tasks, such as making a shopping list or finding a lost set of keys, but are insufficient for understanding or addressing complex issues and problems or for avoiding thinking errors and refuting deceptions.

Tasks that use LOT are often the necessary first steps in thought processes that will require MOT and HOT to complete. For example, identifying/quantifying is used to collect information about a crime, which is then reviewed to find patterns, connect causes and effects, categorize, and characterize (MOT skills) as part of an analysis (a thought process). To solve the crime (finding solutions is another thought process) will require the HOT skills of deducing/inducing, querying, inferring, and shifting perspective.

Imitate or Copy

Imitating or copying is simply reproducing something that is already fully formed, known, and evident. The goal of such activities is usually to make the most accurate reproduction possible. Requesting that students repeat what a teacher says or does elicits this type of thinking. A basic form of imitating is an activity song like "Head, Shoulders, Knees, and Toes." Learning an intricate dance is a more advanced form of imitation. An example of basic copying is when students are given a paper with a letter or shape to reproduce. Creating a painting in the style of a particular artist is a more advanced form of copying.

Follow Rules and Directions

This is among the most common type of thinking that is asked of students, particularly in kindergarten. "Hang up your coat, pick out a book, and sit quietly in the group area" is an example of giving students directions to follow. As students become readers, written rules and directions start replacing or supplementing verbal instructions. An example of a more advanced level of following rules is knowing and complying with traffic safety rules related to crossing streets and riding a bicycle, which are challenges that many students take on between kindergarten and third grade.

Following rules and directions is the thinking skill used for tasks that involve organizing and arranging, such as filing papers alphabetically. This and similar tasks require only LOT because they are concrete and narrowly defined and the criteria are predetermined. Tasks in which the criteria are abstract or not yet developed require the MOT skills of characterizing and categorizing and the HOT skill of deductive/inductive thinking.

Following rules and directions is important for success in school: to track when assignments are due, how the assignments are to be done, and protocols for turning them in and responding to feedback. Later, they are important skills for success at work and in life, from following personnel policies to knowing the rules and procedures to vote to driving legally and safely.

Memorize/Recall

Memorizing is an important life skill. An emergency room doctor or nurse who forgets the triage protocols that everyone follows may endanger a patient's life. Not remembering to turn off the coffee pot simmering on the stove before leaving the house may cause a fire. Teaching students to improve their ability to remember by using reminders, making associations, contextualizing, and other techniques will help them academically.

As it relates to education, memorizing is the act of intentionally retaining particular information because it is important or useful. Recalling is bringing to mind the memorized information and expressing it verbally, in writing, or with actions. It is a common method for teaching multiplication tables, sight words, grammar rules, and so on, to young learners. Although it elicits only LOT, it can be a useful strategy when memorizing will save time and mental effort as long as it does not replace understanding. Recalling without understanding is just reciting.

When students respond to questions about what they did earlier in the day or over the weekend, or what happened on the playground to cause a conflict, they are recalling at a more advanced level because they have not intentionally memorized the events at the time they occurred. Students describe or explain the event, rather than recite, as they have to select aspects that are salient to them and formulate what they will say. Although this is often done automatically, it provides the opportunity for teachers to help students recall and describe the event in greater detail and more comprehensively. Recalling details is an important first step in thought processes such as analyses and finding solutions. Teachers can elicit more advanced thinking during a memory/recall activity by asking questions such as "What was the most challenging part of yesterday's assignment for you?" or "What was fair or unfair about the vote we took last week to elect the class representative? "How do you propose it could be improved to be fairer?"

Know or Do by Rote

When students give correct information or perform a skill correctly without understanding its purpose or meaning, they are only performing by rote. It is common for young learners to recite the alphabet without knowing the function of letters in creating words or to count to twenty without understanding that each number represents a unique quantity and that its value is relational to other numbers (called number sense). When students can decode words but do not understand what they are reading, they are only rote reading. It can appear that students understand a concept when actually they are just demonstrating rote knowledge. Solving math problems by relying only on algorithms is an example. Even some standardized assessments fail to distinguish between students' rote and actual knowledge, giving misleading information to teachers.

Identify/Quantify

Identifying involves naming or collecting tangible information, whereas *quantifying* refers to naming or collecting numerical information. Identifying and quantifying are the thinking skills used when the information is established, inherent, overt, or obvious. Listing all the characters in a story and stating how many there are involve identifying followed by quantifying. However, if the task is to identify the most interesting character, the logical thinking (MOT) skill of *characterizing* is needed to determine the criteria that make a character interesting.

Identifying tasks are very common in schools, particularly for older students. An example is reading books or articles in order to write a report about a famous person or to make a speech about how to care for a pet. Looking through a chapter in a textbook to find the answers to the questions listed at the end of the chapter is another example of an identification task. When students are asked to compare and contrast and are given the criteria (e.g., compare and contrast the shapes, colors, and textures of a maple leaf with an oak leaf), it is an identification task. When the criteria need to be determined, it is a MOT task (characterizing). As with the other LOT skills, identifying can be done at advanced levels using sophisticated instruments, such as an atomic force microscope to identify molecules or a giant optical space telescope to identify galaxies.

Quantifying—counting and measuring—is a mathematical form of identifying. Humans are hardwired, at least to some degree, to understand and learn math. However, in infants, these concepts are very general. They can only make distinctions that are overt and cannot, for example, sense that five objects are more than four objects (Brannon & Park, 2015). Quantifying can involve the use of instruments such as scales or tape measures. Even a sophisticated instrument that requires specialized knowledge and skills to operate, such as an x-ray machine, engages LOT if the task consists of calibrating the instrument, following protocols, and reading the results. *Evaluating* the results, however, would require the use of a wide range of MOT and HOT skills.

Identifying and quantifying are, nevertheless, important skills that everyone uses daily. Being good at these skills makes life easier. They are often the initial skills needed when using the five thought processes: analyses, evaluations/decisions, solutions/innovations, plans/strategies, and predictions/theories.

Conclusion

All LOT skills involve acquiring existing information and using it as is. The information is not manipulated, applied, or interpreted. Nevertheless, LOT skills are important and necessary. Everyone uses these skills every day, and being good at them is an advantage, particularly for certain tasks like learning to drive, studying for a test, following a map, or cooking from a recipe. In some cases, LOT skills are used to accomplish some very challenging tasks that few people can do, such as learning the notes of a Beethoven sonata or memorizing all of Hamlet's lines. Lower-order thinking skills are necessary but not necessarily easy or fun! Tasks that use LOT skills often initiate thought processes that later require MOT and HOT skills. Applying HOT skills, such as imagining, can make LOT tasks more engaging.

Improving students' LOT skills will help them to be more efficient at academic tasks and thought processes. Teaching LOT skills should be part of every teacher's job and every curriculum. However, it should be a relatively small part. In most classrooms, students spend much more time using LOT skills than HOT skills. Educators can reverse this by promoting **"A little LOT and a lot of HOT!"**

Key Ideas from this Chapter

1. There are five LOT skills: imitate/copy, follow rules and directions, memorize/recall, know or do by rote, and identify/quantify.
2. LOT skills involve acquiring existing information and using it as is.

3. LOT skills are important, practical, functional, and necessary.
4. LOT skills are insufficient for addressing complex issues and problems and for avoiding thinking errors and recognizing deceptions.
5. LOT skills are often required in the initial steps of tasks that use HOT skills.
6. LOT skills can be difficult and challenging, such as memorizing all of Hamlet's lines.
7. Currently, too many common teaching and learning strategies, particularly for young learners, elicit only LOT skills.
8. Helping students improve their LOT skills, particularly memorizing/recalling, will help them academically and improve their thought processes, such as making decisions and plans.

Questions for Discussion

What are some of the historical, social, and cultural reasons that LOT teaching and learning tasks predominate in most classrooms?

For some of the learning outcomes or standards expected of your students, how can you determine if students understand the concepts or just know them by rote?

What are ways that teachers can make necessary LOT tasks, such as memorizing facts or math algorithms, more meaningful and enjoyable to students?

For students who find certain LOT skills challenging (e.g., they are disorganized or have trouble remembering due dates), what can teachers do to help them compensate?

References

Brannon, E. M., & Park, J. (2015). Phylogeny and ontogeny of mathematical and numerical understanding. In R. C. Kadosh & A. Dowker (Eds.), *Oxford handbook of numerical cognition* (pp. 203–213). Oxford University Press.

4

Middle-Order Thinking (MOT) Skills

Only a Path, but the Only Path, to Wisdom

Middle-order thinking (MOT) is logical thinking in all its variations. Logical thinking involves making linear, objective, and systematic connections between objects, information, or quantities. Information is not just taken in, it is separated, connected, reorganized, and put to use. MOT skills are the mental tools used to reason. Reasoning, the application of logical thinking, shines a light on deceptions and scams and prevents or corrects many types of thinking errors (see Chapter 7 on p. 141).

> **Middle-Order Thinking (MOT) Skills**
> *logic and reason*
>
> Characterize
> Associate/Differentiate
> Categorize
> Sequence/Pattern
> Calculate
> Connect Causes and Effects
> Represent

DOI: 10.4324/9781032683423-6

MOT skills are useful and common. At a basic level, they are usually done quickly and almost automatically by adults. This is the case with turning a light switch on and off (connecting causes and effects thinking), driving cautiously when seeing a yellow triangle (representational thinking), or sorting laundry into darks and lights (associating/differentiating and categorizing thinking). Here, the information and the results are tangible, predetermined, and overt, and the tasks are more practical than conceptual.

MOT skills at an advanced level are needed for conducting research, such as evaluating the effectiveness of a new curriculum. Characterizing is used to determine and define the variables to be measured, sequencing is used to schedule the data collection activities in the correct order, calculating is used to get the results from the data (although usually a computer program will do this), and connecting causes and effects is used to determine whether the results are caused by the new curriculum, correlated to the new curriculum, or unrelated to the new curriculum. Here, the information and results are abstract and need to be developed, and the tasks are more conceptual than practical.

In *Star Trek*, Mr. Spock (played by Leonard Nimoy) is a half-human character who is an exemplar of logical thinking. In the 1991 film, *Star Trek VI: The Undiscovered Country*, Mr. Spock says, "Logic is the beginning of wisdom, not the end." This is an excellent description of both the limitations and the promise of logical thinking. It also explains why it is *middle*-order thinking. The seven MOT skills are more complex than lower-order thinking (LOT) skills but less conceptual or far-reaching than higher-order thinking (HOT) skills. Logical thinking can serve as a bridge between LOT and HOT skills, which is fitting because many logical thinking skills involve making connections and establishing relationships between two or more things or ideas.

Although the emphasis of this book is on promoting HOT, this should not overshadow the importance of middle-order logical thinking. Sound MOT skills are the bases for the strong HOT skills needed in all thought processes. Without accurate information obtained with MOT skills, the results from any analysis, evaluation, decision, strategy, solution, or prediction will be faulty.

Characterize

Characterizing is the logical thinking skill used to determine the salient aspects or main features of something (e.g., story, tree, city, and painting) when they are not predetermined, inherent, or obvious. Identifying is its lower-order cousin. Characterizing is an important skill because it is the thinking needed to accurately determine the criteria to use for applying most HOT skills and many other MOT skills, including associating/differentiating, categorizing, and sequencing/patterning.

One strategy to help young learners develop characterizing skills is through *ThinkinGroups* activities such as *Family Groups* (page 127) and *Don't Say the Word!* (page 209). In these activities, the core features are known, but the category or concept they describe is not. A simple example of *Family Groups* involves students hearing or reading a list of words that includes *dogs*, *cats*, *parakeets*, *goldfish*, and *hamsters* and determining that "pet" is their common attribute or the category to which they all belong. *Don't Say the Word!* entails describing an object without naming it, so students can guess what it is. For example, if the object is an umbrella, a student might say, "You put it over your head when it rains. It pops open and slides shut. It's usually black." This requires determining the key features of an umbrella, which is characterizing. This activity can be made more challenging by limiting the number of words that can be used in the description. The fewer words allowed, the greater the challenge.

The *ThinkinGroups* activity, *The Fine Art of Matching* (on page 44), offers many good opportunities for students to identify the salient features of artworks that characterize them. The attributes can be fewer and more obvious for younger students, such as the locale (two attributes: inside or outside), the subject (three attributes: people, food, and boats), and the style (three attributes: abstract, impressionist, and realism). For second and third graders, more conceptual features and attributes can be added.

Discussions about books usually include characterizing the book by determining its main theme and literary elements such as plot points, plot devices, settings, the protagonist, and the antagonist. But it is important to expand students' abilities to characterize beyond literature by providing ample opportunities for them to characterize the salient features of films, music, speeches, video games, historical and current events, and more.

Associate/Differentiate

Associating makes logical connections between two or more things, whereas differentiating makes logical distinctions. When used together, they describe the relationship between things more thoroughly. Why not just call this comparing? The term comparing is problematic because when it is paired with the word "contrasting," it means only associating. In common usage, however, it means *both* comparing and contrasting: "Let's compare notes" or "How does their performance this year compare to the one last year?" These statements assume that the responses will include contrasting (aka differentiating). For this reason, the term "associate/differentiate" (A/D) replaces the term "comparing" throughout the book. For young learners, the term "associated" (the adjective form of associate) can be replaced by the terms "same" or "similar," and the term "differentiated" (the adjective form of differentiate) can be replaced by the terms "different" or "dissimilar."

The following is an activity to help students develop A/D thinking skills through a modified memory matching game. Memory matching games typically involve identifying, memorizing, and recalling, which are LOT skills. Two cards are turned upright to determine whether they are the same (they match) or different. Each of the cards in a matched pair has exactly the same picture, and no other card has that picture. If the cards that are turned upright do not match, they are turned over again and placed back in the same spot. The focus is on remembering and recalling where the two cards that match are located. A memory matching game can be made very difficult by using many pairs of cards, but it is still a LOT activity involving identifying, memorizing, and recalling. However, when A/D thinking tasks are added, the game requires MOT. In the following *ThinkinGroups* activity, content learning in the area of art adds

42 ◆ Thinking about Thinking

another dimension to the activity, although this same type of memory matching game can be made for other subjects such as geometry, vocabulary (e.g., descriptive words and verbs), geography, famous people, and plants and animals. In addition, this activity can be easily adapted to provide any level of challenge. For kindergartners, the "deck" can consist only of cards with overt differences and similarities and contain fewer pairs of cards than for older students.

ThinkinGroups: THE FINE ART OF MATCHING

In this version of a memory matching game, the matching pairs of cards are similar, *not* the same. The cards are reproductions of artwork, although photos of diverse architectural structures (e.g., Eiffel Tower, pyramids of Giza, Brooklyn Bridge, and Taj Mahal) and of many types of sculpture can be added. In the basic version of the game, a matched pair consists of art of the same subject, genre, or style. The pairs range from very similar and easy to match (e.g., portraits by the same artist) to significantly different but clearly of the same subject, genre, or style (e.g., an impressionist landscape and a realistic landscape). There should be a sufficient number of cards and sets of cards so that all students can participate at the same time in small groups (of four or five).

Each set of art cards needs to contain a large number of pairs of artwork of the same genre and by the same artist. However, they should include many different genres, styles, and artists. Sets can be made more challenging by including multiple pairs of paintings of the same genre. A large set of cards can be separated into subsets for different levels of challenge and versions of the activity. There are tens of thousands of free fair-use images of paintings and photographs that can be downloaded from the websites of the National Gallery of Art, the Metropolitan Museum of Art, and many other museums.

One variation of the game is to include duplicates of the same card as well as cards that are similar. A matched pair still consists of *similar* works of art, not the same work. Adding such counterintuitive elements helps students develop impulse control and learn to avoid thinking errors. Once students are adept at the basic version, the criterion for what constitutes a match can be changed. However, this may require selecting certain cards to create a set that will work with the new criteria. For example, a matched pair can consist of paintings that have the same number of people in them, including zero, or cards of the same genre of art (e.g., abstract, impressionism, pop, Japanese prints, and realism) or the main subject (e.g., mountains, animals, flowers, food, and boats). Yet another criterion can be the media used (e.g., oil paint, watercolor, charcoal, ink, and pencil). The cards can also be selected to reflect a theme or content area in addition to art, such as basic geography, city/town/country life, types of houses (including nests, hives, caves, and other animal houses), and occupations. Figure 4.1 shows a small sample of art cards. The artworks in the figure were selected for their clarity when viewed as small black-and-white images, but full-color images should be used.

Associate/Differentiate thinking is used when the information is concrete, limited, or known and the results are ultimately knowable. Examples of this are estimating the square footage of a room, envisioning how the room will look when painted blue, appraising the value of the antique carpet on the floor of the room, and predicting the results of the football match on the TV in the room. Associating and differentiating are the middle-order cousins of deducing and inducing, which are the higher-order critical thinking skills required when the information or the results are abstract, unlimited, unknown, or unknowable.

Categorize

Categorizing entails grouping three or more similar things (called the element) by one or more shared attribute. This is also called classifying or sorting. In the *MOTivation* activity described on page 46, students categorize beads (the element) by three attributes: their color, size, and material. To categorize beads (or anything), each attribute must have at least two factors. In this set

Art Cards Sample

Breezing Up, Winslow Homer, ca. 1873

At Sea off Kazusa, Katsushika Hokusai, ca. 1831

Self-Portrait, John Faed, ca. 1850

Self-Portrait, Vincent Van Gogh, 1889

Irises, Van Gogh, 1853

Still Life, Henri Fantin-Latour, 1866

Mont Sainte-Victoire, Paul Cezanne, ca. 1895

Thirlmere, Paul Nash, 1914

FIGURE 4.1 Art Cards Sample.

Graphic by Gwendolyn Rodriguez.

Middle-Order Thinking (MOT) Skills ◆ 45

of beads, the material attribute has three factors: glass, ceramic, and wood; the size attribute has three factors: small, medium, and large; and the color attribute has four factors: red, blue, green, and multicolored. A factor can be further categorized by an additional attribute if the attribute has at least two factors. These are called sub-attributes and sub-factors. So, in this set, the wooden beads *can* be further categorized because they are made from three different types of wood. The additional attribute would be "wood type," and it would have three factors: pine, oak, and cherry. The chart below will hopefully make all of this a bit more understandable.

Element	Attributes	Factors	Sub-Attribute(s)	Sub-Factors
BEADS	Material:	Glass, Ceramic, Wood	Wood Type	Pine, Oak, Cherry
	Size:	Small, Medium, Large		
	Color:	Red, Blue, Green, and Multicolored		

In this example, the elements and all of its attributes, factors, and sub-factors are tangible, quantifiable, and stable. But categorizations can also entail elements, attributes, and factors that are abstract, unquantifiable and changeable. These require more advanced levels of categorizing. Many things are categorized by both tangible *and* abstract attributes and factors, such as architecture, religions, beer, and music. Trees also have tangible and abstract attributes, as shown in the *MOTivation, Free the Trees!* on page 47.

The concept of "happiness" is an *abstract* element that has quantifiable attributes. International surveys ask people questions such as how often they feel happy or depressed and how many times they laughed during the previous week. The results are given numerical values (aka scores), and the average score of the people in a country yields a happiness score for the country. On the other hand, flowering plants are *tangible* elements that have both tangible and abstract attributes. The tangible attributes include the shape of their leaves and petals, their sizes, and colors. The abstract attributes include threats to their habitat (if any), their natural history, their relative hardiness, their usefulness, and their current or potential value or worth. Factors of this

46 ◆ Thinking about Thinking

last attribute, worth, can be abstract and range from negative (an invasive species, perhaps, that is costly to control) to inexpensive (a petunia), to expensive (saffron from the saffron crocus), to almost priceless (certain rare orchids), with many points in between.

MOTivation: **BEADS**

A group of first-grade students is given a categorizing task to sort a set of about 150 beads by their size, color, and material in preparation for making name-badge necklaces for an upcoming field trip. In the set, there are small, medium, and large beads that are red, blue, green, brown, or multicolored and made of glass, wood, or ceramic. The students disagree about how to begin and are a bit stuck. The teacher suggests they start by sorting all the beads by color, and says, "But first figure out how many containers you will need. After you sort the beads by color, decide how you will sort them again. There are two more ways they can be sorted. But, before sorting again, figure out how many more containers you will need. I'll check in with you see how you are doing, but you can always ask for help." When they finish the task, the teacher asks them if the beads can be sorted by another category. One student suggests doing it by "what they feel like." During a brief discussion, the teacher supplies some new vocabulary: texture, quality, consistency, uneven, coarse, and jagged. Noticing that there are many wooden beads of various types, the teacher offers the students the option of sorting the wooden beads by their type of wood and shows them a website for learning the names of many types of wood from their photos.

As with all thinking skills, categorizing can be more or less difficult depending on the task and the ability level of the person categorizing. Usually, categorizing tangible elements, attributes, and factors is not as difficult as categorizing abstract elements,

Middle-Order Thinking (MOT) Skills ◆ 47

attributes, and factors. The following *MOTivation* involves categorizing a physical element with one tangible attribute and two more abstract attributes, each with multiple factors. For all three attributes, some of the factors are tangible and some are abstract.

MOTivation: FREE THE TREES!

To express their unhappiness about a plan to cut down trees around the school to make room for more parking spaces, third-grade students decided they need to learn as much as they can about the trees on the demolition list. Facilitated by the teacher, they made a large chart (see Figure 4.2) listing each of the seven trees (the elements) with three categories of information about them (their main attributes) and many factors that describe each:

Description: the type of tree, its origins, history, and main characteristics such as its size, the shape of its leaves, and texture of its bark.

Worth: the value of the tree when it's alive and growing, such as the fruits and nuts it bears, its role in counteracting air pollution, and the medicinal properties of its leaves, bark, seed pods, and flowers.

Benefits: the tree's contribution to the well-being and happiness of the students, staff, and people in the neighborhood, such as its shade, color and beauty, good smells, the habitat it provides for birds and squirrels, and its role in the local ecosystem.

To get this information about the trees, the teacher asked questions; facilitated discussions; provided relevant books, websites, and resources; and recruited two friends, an ecologist and an arborist, to help the students. The class made a display with photographs and a chart that summarizes the information they collected about the trees, which they presented at a joint meeting of the school board and the town council.

48 ◆ Thinking about Thinking

Tree Chart

	European Linden	American Beech	Northern Red Oak	Blue Spruce (x2)	Sugar Maple	Black Walnut
The Trees						
Leaves Nuts Flowers Sap						
Description	VERY BIG, leaves turn yellow and fall off, small yellow blossoms in spring	Grows slowly, branches spread wide, leaves turn gold and orange, makes nuts	VERY BIG, leaves turn red and fall off, grows fast, makes acorns in the fall, and catkins in the spring	Evergreen, silvery blue color, tall, big pine cones, sharp prickly needles	Big tree, bright red leaves in fall, "helicopter" pods with two seeds, sap makes syrup	Tall tree, spicy smell, leaves turn yellow, dark bark, walnut shells leave stains, toxic to other trees
Worth	Dried blossoms make tea for tummy aches, also smells good for airfreshners	Makes beechnuts which you can eat	Use acorns for math and science activities	Decorate for winter fest and not buy trees, cones for math & science, fire starters	Maple syrup	Walnuts, brown dye
Benefits	Shade, beauty, smells good, birds singing improves air quality	Shade, pretty in the fall, birds improve air quality, great for climbing	Shade, pretty in the fall, home to squirrels and birds, air quality	Pretty all year, festive in winter, shelter for birds and squirrels, blocks wind	Shade, beauty (especially in the fall), squirrels and birds, air quality	Shade, beauty, squirrels and birds, air quality, good smell

FIGURE 4.2 Tree Chart.

Graphic by Gwendolyn Rodriguez.

There is an important caveat about categorizing. The human brain is a meaning-making machine. It wants to find meaning and purpose in everything, even when none exists. One powerful way to make meaning is to put things into categories. Experiments with preverbal infants show that categorizing is hard-wired into our brains (Skelton et al., 2017). But automatic categorizing is a problem because it can too easily lead to categorizing incorrectly, over-categorizing, or stereotyping. "Us vs. them" thinking (discussed in Chapter 1) is an example of this. It is a narrow and problematic type of categorizing that puts every person into just two mutually exclusive and antagonistic categories. To counter automatic categorizing, teachers can provide many activities in which students practice deliberate and intentional categorizing, such as those described in the two *MOTivations*. Using a variety of HOT skills and developing many positive thinking dispositions (see Chapter 7 on pages 137–141) are two other effective ways to counter automatic categorizing.

Sequence/Pattern

Sequencing is a particularly important thinking skill for young learners. Reading comprehension requires the ability to track and recall key events of a story in the correct order. Sequencing is also central to mathematical thinking. Ordinal numbers—1st, 2nd, 3rd, etc.—define where something is in a sequence. Every math problem with more than one operation has a defined sequence for those operations, and every number has an implied sequence in relation to all other numbers (i.e., it comes before or after another number).

Prioritizing is an important type of sequencing skill. It is a main thinking skill for planning/strategizing, which is a thought process. Prioritizing is sequencing based on a criterion or several criteria, usually individually determined and subjective, such as importance, expedience, need, expense, effort, and timing.

Forming patterns is a special type of sequencing, although deciphering patterns is done with another logical thinking skill, *characterizing*. Patterning can be as basic as creating a necklace with the repeated pattern of two black beads followed by two red beads or as advanced as weaving a tapestry. As there are patterns in written and spoken language, mathematics, daily routines, human behaviors, life cycles, and so much more, having good thinking skills for patterning is a valuable cognitive asset. Patterning is the foundation of designing, which uses the creative thinking (HOT) skills of imagining and generating ideas.

Calculate

Calculating involves math computations: adding, subtracting, multiplying, and dividing. Adding single-digit numbers is the simplest form of calculation. The ability to calculate accurately, fluently, and consistently, even at this basic level, requires students to have numerical understanding or number sense. And having number sense is a prerequisite for understanding more advanced math. Number sense comes with the understanding that a number is more than a representation of an amount. There are logical relationships among numbers: a number has relative value to the numbers below it and above it, as described above in *sequencing*. This should be the focus of many math activities for young learners because it moves such activities from engaging LOT skills (rote counting and memorizing algorithms) to engaging logical thinking MOT skills.

Activities that involve "playing" with numbers (when done often, regularly, and with increasing levels of challenge) will develop math abilities, particularly number sense, at a deeper level and more effectively and enjoyably than activities that involve only pencil-and-paper tasks. For example, *Twins*, the math *ThinkinGroups* activity on page 203, and all its variations give students direct experience with the concept that the same number can be a high number or low number and a winning number or losing number.

Calculating is the purest form of logical thinking, as there is always one right answer and the process and results are unambiguous, though not necessarily easy. But, without any context, even basic calculating is abstract (by definition) and difficult for some students to grasp. Calculating is most effectively taught in the context of its applications. Two and two may be four, but what two things are added to what other two things and for what purpose? Why do we need to have four of these things anyway? Given how many people believe they are bad at math, dislike math, and have difficulty using math, educators need to make changes in how it is taught. A good place to start is by giving a reason that is understandable and meaningful to students for using every math operation they are taught.

Connect Causes and Effects

Infants experiment with cause-and-effect relationships when they intentionally drop things from their highchairs over and over. Children do this when they ask questions that begin with "What would happen if?" and "Would you still love me if I …?" In many cases, they are trying to determine whether their own cause-and-effect thinking is faulty.

Making meaning is a core mental activity for young learners, as they are actively trying to understand the world. Cause-and-effect relationships are a main source of information about how the world works, and children look for and find them everywhere. However, they often get it wrong. Sometimes, they assume a relationship exists when it is just a coincidence or an accident, or they assume there is no relationship when one actually does exist. (Of course, many adults make the same errors, particularly when it comes to complex scientific phenomena or abstract theoretical concepts.) For these reasons, it is important to sharpen young students' cause-and-effect thinking by providing many examples of sound cause-and-effect thinking and giving students many opportunities to practice it in different contexts and with different subjects.

Books and films are rich with examples of cause-and-effect relationships, as are major historical events. More hands-on learning about physical causes and effects include building a

52 ◆ Thinking about Thinking

tower with blocks until it falls over and then using the *same* number of blocks to build it in a different way so it won't fall over; creating a "Rube Goldberg"-type contraption from a drawn plan; engaging with software such as Crayon Physics (crayonphysics. com) with increasing challenges; and doing cooking activities to explore how changing just one variable or input (e.g. applying heat) can completely change the effect.

Cause-and-effect relationships also explain much of the dynamics of social interactions. When students understand the many ways their behavior affects others and how the behaviors of others affect them, they become more self-aware and better able to mediate their emotions. Even kindergartners can begin to gain these insights, particularly with the help of delightful and perceptive children's literature, as described in the following *MOTivation*.

MOTivation: LILLY

Each year in May, Ms. Cho-Klein, a kindergarten teacher, implements the theme "What Happens in First Grade?" Among the activities are reading high-quality children's literature with stories that take place in first-grade classrooms. *Lilly's Purple Plastic Purse* (Henkes, 2006) is always a favorite.

Lilly, the irrepressible mouse heroine of the story, adores her teacher, Mr. Slinger, so much that she wants to be a teacher when she grows up. However, when she shows off her musical purple plastic purse at inappropriate times, Mr. Slinger confiscates it for the day. Lilly's humiliation causes her to be angry, which she vents by drawing a mean picture of Mr. Slinger while deciding that she no longer wants to be a teacher. But a kind note and yummy snack from Mr. Slinger found in her returned purse cause her to regret the drawing and feel a deep sense of remorse. Fortunately, Lilly's sincere apology along with a nicer drawing of Mr. Slinger and gift of a yummy snack of her own have their intended effect. Mutual admiration is restored, and, once again, Lilly wants to be a teacher.

One of the follow-up activities to the story is to identify all the cause-and-effect relationships. To start the discussion, Ms. Cho-Klein uses four large graphics (mounted on stiff cardboard), each representing a different cause-and-effect relationship. The first is titled, *One Cause and One Effect*, and has a photo of the sun melting a snowperson. She has a similar graphic with a set of three photographs titled, *Two Causes and One Effect*, consisting of photos of the sun, rain, and the resulting rainbow. Another is titled *One Cause and Three Effects*. It consists of a photo of a rainstorm paired with photos of a wet dog, children jumping in puddles, and people walking with umbrellas. The last graphic, *Five Causes One Effect*, includes a photo of a child with a music trophy in one hand and a violin in the other (the effect) paired with photos of the child practicing at home, getting a lesson, attending a concert by a professional violinist, playing a duet with a friend, and performing in a competition.

Ms. Cho-Klein reviews the story with the children, asking questions such as, "What caused Lily to want to be a teacher?" "What did Lilly do that caused the effect of Mr. Slinger and Lilly being friends again?" "Did she do more than one thing?" "Was there more than one cause and, if so, what are they?" Ms. Cho-Klein uses the graphics to enhance her students' understanding and to reinforce the idea that causes and effects can happen physically (like rain causing puddles), socially with our actions and interactions with people, or emotionally with our feelings.

Most third graders are ready to understand more abstract and complex cause-and-effect relationships, including how one cause can have multiple effects and one effect can have multiple causes, as in the following example.

MOTivation: **DROUGHT**

In a third-grade classroom, a severe drought and its repercussions are hot topics among the students. They talk about not being able to swim because of the lack of water in the lakes and rivers, about neighbors who are not following the rules for saving water, and about the water fountains being shut off. The teacher, Mr. Garcia, elicits and supports their cause-and-effect thinking to deepen their understanding of the science and causes of the drought. He soon discovers that the students believe there is only one cause for not having enough water: a lack of rain. He tells them, "That is one cause, but there are others." On the whiteboard, he draws a cloud with rain coming down with a red line through it and writes, "1. Lack of rain." Underneath, he draws a picture of a hose faucet with drops of water coming down and a house with grass around it. "What might be another cause?" he asks. After a brief discussion, Mr. Garcia writes, "2. Using and wasting too much water," and says, "For the last ten years, a few years before you were born, until now, if everyone used just a little less water and if there were no lawns, which need a lot of water, we would probably not have a water shortage now." While drawing a picture of an apple, he tells the students, "Here's a hint for another cause. This one is hard." After no one can come up with an answer, he says, "Another cause is that we have many, many farms in our area and it takes a great amount of water to grow nuts, fruits, and vegetables." On the whiteboard, Mr. Garcia writes, "3. Farms."

"So, there are at least three causes for our water shortage: the lack of rain, using too much water at home and for lawns, and the large amount of water that farms need. A big, complicated problem, like not having enough water, usually has more than one cause. Also, the lack of rain has had many more effects than adding to a water shortage. It has caused many other problems, such as forest fires."

> Then, the students work together in small groups—with resources and assistance from Mr. Garcia—to determine why a lack of rain causes more forest fires and to identify as many other effects as they can.

It is important for young students to understand cause-and-effect relationships, particularly for those that are not immediate, in order to develop good social skills, communicate effectively, understand basic science concepts, delay gratification, and much more. Delaying gratification to achieve long-term goals requires an understanding that there is often a time gap between a cause and an effect. Teachers can help students make these connections by talking about them explicitly. "Putting effort into learning to read in first grade will make schoolwork easier for you in second grade. You will also be able to read wonderful books independently, like *Charlotte's Web* and *Harry Potter*. And reading well means you will get homework assignments done quickly, giving you more time to choose what you want to do."

Represent

Pretending is perhaps the earliest representational thinking in which human beings engage. When children pretend to be dogs, they use their bodies, actions, and voices to represent a familiar animal. When children pretend to drink water from a toy cup, they are representing the real activity with a simulated activity. The first drawings of objects that children create—typically a stick-figure person, the sun, a house, a tree, or a flower—shows they are able to represent familiar three-dimensional objects in two dimensions.

The level of representational thinking increases as children learn that a bunch of shapes strung together are individual letter symbols that together comprise a word; a special and important word that is their name and, therefore, themselves. At about the same time, young students grasp that another set of symbols, numbers, represent amounts.

A task that involves representation thinking can be relatively easy and straightforward—understanding that 2 is a symbol that represents a particular amount as well as the word *two*. It can also be quite challenging and uncertain even for adults—as in deciphering the allegory (which is a type of representational thinking) in Herman Melville's novel, *Moby Dick*.

Representing is a logical thinking skill because there is a direct relationship between symbols and what they represent—or at least that is the intention. Sometimes, what a symbol represents is not clear or easily understood. A sign with a large question mark inside a circle may lead a person to actually ask a question like, "What does this mean?" It is intended to represent an information kiosk, which is a bit easier to determine when seen in an airport terminal or train station.

Many symbols represent more than one thing. The letter *A* is a symbol that represents several phonemes and a word that means *one* or *the* in many Indo-European languages that use the Latin alphabet. It can also represent a score on a test, a rating of the quality of a steak, or the relative energy efficiency of an appliance. While decoding symbols is a LOT skill, coding with symbols or creating symbols entails representational thinking along with other thinking skills. (See pp. 198–199 for more information about teaching coding to young learners.) With the addition of imagining and other HOT skills, representing can take many compelling forms: clever minimalist set designs and props in theatre productions, beautiful metaphors in poems, and myths in which characters represent ideals (e.g., Venus representing the ideal of beauty). In some cases, entire books, such as the aforementioned *Moby Dick* are representational as allegories. Other allegorical books include *Animal Farm* by George Orwell and *Lord of the Flies* by William Golding.

Among the most recognized and impactful forms of representation are the symbols on signs seen in airports worldwide, also called *DOT pictograms*. (DOT is an acronym for the U.S. Department of Transportation; it is not another category of thinking skills!) Their purpose is to transcend language and literacy by communicating what and where something is, or what can and cannot be done, using the simplest and clearest visual representations possible. Although it may not be intentional, these symbols proactively create inclusion on a grand scale and show that there are commonalities among the great diversity of people in the world. However, if its main purpose is just to get people from Terminal 1, Gate 46 to Terminal 3, Gate 47 more efficiently, it's not working very well.

Graphic designers use representational thinking at an advanced level to create symbols for products (aka logos) that represent ideas, feelings, or qualities. The logos of automobile companies have been very carefully designed to represent how they want consumers to perceive their cars and distinguish them from other car brands. In general, logos with a few shiny diagonal lines are used to represent speed and modernity. Logos with complex designs and multiple patterns usually represent endurance, tradition, and luxury. Animals in logos are used to represent power. The logo of a British manufacturer of very expensive cars is a stylized, shiny chrome jungle cat (which is also the name of the company) leaping up diagonally in midair as if ready to pounce. This clever image manages to represent speed, power, tradition, *and* luxury. Representational thinking at the highest levels can be very impactful, such as getting some people to spend way too much money for a car.

An effective and enjoyable strategy to teach representational thinking is through the use of nonstandard symbols. Nonstandard symbols convey the *concept* of representation when they are arbitrary and refer to many different items and actions, including those that are not typically represented by symbols. For example, the following *Cognitivity* uses symbols chosen by students to represent musical directions.

COGNITIVITY: ORCHESTRA CONDUCTOR

Students make a set of cards with one or two shapes (symbols) on each card. The "conductor" shows the cards to the rest of the students (aka the orchestra) while they sing a familiar song. The symbols are unrelated to the directions they represent. A red triangle might mean sing a little faster, and a green circle might mean sing a little slower. Two red triangles would indicate sing *much* faster, and two green circles would indicate to sing *much* slower. Other symbols can indicate louder, softer, stop, start, higher, and lower. One student at a time takes a turn being the conductor, who starts by reviewing the symbols and the directions they represent to the "orchestra." The orchestra then sings, and the conductor holds up the symbols in the order and for the length of time of their own choosing. When students become proficient, new challenges can be added, such as holding up two or more symbols at the same time (if they do not conflict) and adding symbols that represent more complex musical directions and terms like crescendo (gradually getting louder), diminuendo (gradually getting softer), and staccato (choppy). Other variations are limited only by teachers' and students' creativity.

Scaffolded writing is another excellent example of using students' representational thinking to develop their reading and writing skills (Bodrova & Leong, 2019; Donovan et al., 2020; Scott-Weich & Yaden Jr., 2017). It is a very effective literacy strategy for kindergartners and first-graders in which students draw horizontal lines to represent words. This gives preliterate children the tools to "write" messages in sentences that carry meaning and are purposeful. They draw lines as they say the words, using basic writing conventions such as left-to-right sequencing, spacing between words, and starting the next line by moving the pencil down and to the left margin. The teacher then writes the words under the lines while students repeat the sentence. As students learn letter sounds, they write the letters on the lines, starting with initial sounds and letters. Starting sentences with "I," as in "I want a dog," helps children transition from representational writing to actual writing since "I" is a phoneme, a letter, and a word and is easy to write. Bodrova and Leong developed a system that uses the power of representational thinking to enable preliterate children to graphically record whole thoughts. Just as icons and symbols link people across languages and literacy levels, and sign language links people with and without auditory limitations, scaffolded writing links preliterate students with each other and with adults.

Conclusion

As there are seven distinct MOT skills, it is evident that a good deal of thinking involves logical thinking—or at least it should. Most people know when and why to think logically, know the importance and value of logical thinking, and are familiar with these seven skills, even if not familiar with their terminology. Nevertheless, most people have difficulty using them effectively and avoiding biases, distractions, mental laziness, and other influences that prevent or distort their use. Perhaps effectively using logical thinking would come easier for more people if, as students, they had received explicit instruction and more opportunities to practice it in a variety of contexts, for diverse purposes, and across all content areas.

Tasks that entail MOT skills are often the initial tasks in thought processes that require HOT skills. Grading students' assignments, which is a type of evaluation, relies on clear and objective criteria that characterize each grade, from A to F. Characterizing is a logical MOT skill. Strong characterizing skills will create accurate and complete criteria. Evaluations based on accurate and complete criteria will be fair, consistent, free of bias, and helpful.

Strong MOT skills can make a person competent and knowledgeable but not wise. That requires strong critical and creative thinking skills. But without strong logical thinking skills, it is not possible to develop strong HOT skills. Logical thinking is not just a "pathway to wisdom," it is the *only* path that goes there.

Key Ideas from this Chapter

1. MOT skills are logical thinking skills in all their forms.
2. There are seven logical thinking skills:

   Characterize: This is the thinking used to determine the salient characteristics or main features of something when they are discernable, but not predetermined or obvious, such as a story's plot, theme, protagonist, and antagonist.

   Associate/Differentiate (A/D): Because the term "comparing" has multiple meanings, it is replaced by the more specific terms "associating" (making logical connections between two comparable things) and "differentiating" (making logical distinctions between two comparable things). A/D thinking refers to the general thinking skill used to accurately and thoroughly describe the relationship between two things, their similarities and differences.

   Categorize: Categorization thinking is used to group things by one or more common attributes that are not predetermined or obvious. Each attribute can be comprised of many factors and sub-factors. Categorizing can be a complex activity when there are many attributes and factors that are abstract.

   Sequence/Pattern: Sequencing or patterning entails putting things in a logical order such as shortest to tallest, A to Z, highest value to lowest value, or, at a more conceptual level, most important to least (as in prioritizing). Patterning can be as simple as a pop song's verse–chorus–verse–chorus or as complex as the multiple recurring themes and variations in a Johannes Brahms symphony.

Calculate: This is thinking used to perform the mathematical operations of adding, subtracting, multiplying, and dividing.

Connect causes and effects: Cause-and-effect thinking involves understanding the relationship between an event and its impact(s). Young learners are developing the ability to recognize that some causes have delayed effects, some effects have multiple causes, and some causes produce multiple effects.

Represent: Representative thinking is the ability to make a connection between an object or concept and a symbol that conveys its meaning. Letters represent sounds, grades, or ratings. Icons at airports represent information to guide passengers, emoticons represent feelings, and numbers represent quantities.

3. MOT skills are useful and common, often done quickly and almost automatically by adults.
4. Tasks that entail MOT skills are often the initial task in thought processes that will also require HOT skills.
5. Strong MOT skills are necessary for the development of strong HOT skills.

Questions for Discussion

Discuss the many barriers and challenges to clear, logical thinking. How can teachers minimize these barriers for their students?

What are the positive and negative impacts of technology on the ability to think logically? Is the net effect positive or negative and why? Should technology be used to help young learners develop logical thinking skills? If so, how should it be used?

What are some of the common errors that adults make in regard to connecting causes and effects? (Errors are particularly common when it comes to explaining certain scientific and natural phenomena.) What are possible reasons why so many adults make these errors? How can teachers help students avoid making such cause-and-effect errors?

Students will spend many hours over many years quantifying (a LOT skill) and calculating (a MOT skill) as part of their math lessons. How can creative thinkings skills be introduced to make the lessons more engaging and challenging for young learners?

References

Bodrova, E., & Leong, D. J. (2019). *Tools of the mind: The Vygotskian approach to early childhood education* (2nd ed.). Pearson Education.

Donovan, C. A., Sekeres, D. C., & Kerch, C. J. (2020). Scaffolding background knowledge and emergent writing through conversations. *YC Young Children, 75*(5), 57–63. https://www.jstor.org/stable/26979189

Henkes, K. (2006). *Lilly's purple plastic purse*. Greenwillow Books.

Scott-Weich, B., & Yaden Jr., D. B. (2017). Scaffolded writing and literacy development with children who are deaf: A case study. *Early Child Development and Care, 187*(3–4), 418–435.

Skelton, A. E., Catchpole, G., Abbot, J. T., & Franklin, A. (2017). Biological origins of color categorization. *Proceedings of the National Academy of Sciences, 114*(21), 5545–5550. https://doi.org/10.1073/pnas.1612881114

5

Higher-Order Thinking (HOT) Skills

Instruments of Insight, Innovation, and Invention

All three of the main categories of thinking—lower-order (LOT), middle-order (MOT), and higher-order (HOT)—are important and necessary. However, educators must now make the development of students' critical and creative thinking a top priority. This is because the world is rapidly changing and increasingly complex. In addition, teaching students to recognize and refute deceptions and correct thinking errors is an educational imperative, as discussed in Chapter 1.

Higher-Order Thinking Skills	
Critical Thinking	**Creative Thinking**
understanding and insight	*innovation and invention*
Query	Imagine
Infer	Generate
Deduce/Induce	Reframe
Shift Perspective	Improvise

DOI: 10.4324/9781032683423-7

LOT skills use existing material and knowledge and apply them directly. MOT skills use existing material and knowledge and manipulate them to achieve a predetermined outcome. But HOT skills *scrutinize* existing material and knowledge and *develop* material and knowledge. The outcome of thought processes that use HOT is not predetermined and when creative thinking is applied, the outcome is something unique, innovative, or entirely new.

The difference between critical and creative thinking is much like the difference between non-fiction and fiction writing. Writers of historical non-fiction take known information and pull it apart and put it together to reveal new insights and understandings (deduct/induct). At the same time, they make complex events understandable to the lay reader (shift perspective). On the other hand, writers of historical fiction use the backdrop of a past event or time period to imagine how it might feel to have been there. This is often done with a contemporary sensibility and deliberate alterations of facts for dramatic effect (interpret, reframe). Although historical fiction can provide new insights and understandings, the primary purposes are to engage and entertain the reader.

While thought processes, such as finding solutions and developing strategies, primarily entail critical thinking, adding creative thinking will make the processes more engaging and productive. However, when there is an impasse during a thought process, creative thinking becomes a necessity. Combining critical and creative thinking often leads to more accurate, thorough, and effective results. And when high levels of critical thinking merge with high levels of creative thinking, the results can be extraordinary.

Albert Einstein embodied this idea. He considered his creative thinking skills to be more important in his work than his vast knowledge base and his exceptional logical thinking abilities. While artists and scientists are often considered opposite personality types, Einstein thought of himself as both. In a magazine interview, he said: "I am enough of the artist to draw freely upon my imagination. Imagination is more important than knowledge. Knowledge is limited. Imagination encircles the world" (Viereck, 1929).

Critical Thinking SKILLS: More than Meets the Eye

There are many purposes and goals for critical thinking, but four are vital:

- ◆ To look beyond what is apparent to what is actual
- ◆ To determine the veracity of information and refute disinformation and deceptions
- ◆ To not just know something but fully understand it and be able to apply it in different contexts
- ◆ To think clearly and accurately and correct common thinking errors

> **An ideal approach to critical thinking is to be skeptical but not cynical, and open-minded but not gullible.**

Query

To query involves more than just asking questions. It is the ability to ask relevant, helpful, and incisive questions to get a complete and accurate understanding of an issue, concept, event, person, and so on. It is used in all five thought processes, particularly for analyses and evaluations/decisions. Teachers can model this thinking skill for students by asking many different types of incisive questions throughout the day. "I noticed many of our indoor flowering plants are not doing well. I wonder why? I don't know enough about the plants to figure out what they need. Do they need more water or less water; more shade or more sun? Or is it something else? How can we find out? I also wonder if some of them are *annuals*, plants that must be replanted each year and naturally die in the winter. How can we find that out?"

Some of these questions serve a dual purpose. In addition to being examples of incisive questions, they provoke students to take their MOT skills to a more advanced level and use and practice their HOT skills.

66 ◆ Thinking about Thinking

There are good opportunities for students to practice asking incisive questions when they interview each other, older students in the school, family members, teachers, and school administrators. Each interview needs a focus or purpose. Students can ask adult family members to describe their own childhoods and how they differed from and were similar to the students' lives today. Teachers can be asked about why and how they became a teacher, what other jobs they have had, and what they might have been if not a teacher.

In the following *Snap-sHOT*, the teacher uses the opportunity provided by an upcoming visit to the school from a children's book author to develop his students' ability to ask incisive questions that will lead to a deep and comprehensive understanding about writing books, the work authors do, and about the books themselves.

Snap-sHOT: QUESTIONS FOR AN AUTHOR

In the weeks prior to a visit by a well-known author of children's books, Mr. Reese's second graders read several of her books and learn about her professional and personal life. They watch a short video of her working in her studio making illustrations for a new book. The day before the visit, Mr. Reese leads his students in a discussion to informally assess and, as necessary, sharpen their ability to develop incisive questions.

Mr. Reese: "Let's make a list of questions to ask the author tomorrow. Recall what we know from her books, the video that we watched, and her biography and think of questions that will give us additional information. Think of questions that cannot be answered in a word or two or whose answer can already be easily found, questions like 'Where were you born?' Instead, I might ask, 'What was your childhood like?' That would

	interest me, actually. I'll write your questions on the whiteboard."
Kim:	"'Is it hard to write a book?'"
Mr. Reese:	"If the author says, 'Yes,' what would you ask her then?"
Kim:	"'What makes it hard to write a book?'"
Mr. Reese:	"Yes, that will give us more information. Maybe you could just start with that question."
Rosa:	"But maybe she would say, 'No!' Maybe it's easy to write a book."
Mr. Reese:	"Good point, Rosa. What do you suggest?"
Rosa:	"Maybe asking, 'What makes it harder or easier to write a book?'"
Mr. Reese:	"What do you think of that, Kim? Of Rosa's change to your question?"
Kim:	"It's okay. But I think it's better to say, 'What makes it hard or easy *for you* to write a book?'"
Mr. Reese:	"Yes, I agree. And Rosa seems to agree, because she's nodding her head. If you will allow me, I'd like to suggest a slight rephrasing of the question. What does everyone think of, 'What part of writing books is easy for you and what part is hard?'" (*lots of nods*) "Another good way to really understand something well is to ask follow-up questions. These questions use the answers from the first question to learn more, to dig a little deeper. If the author says that it is easy for her to come up with story ideas, I might ask, 'Where do your best ideas come from?'"

Higher-order thinking questions are usually open-ended questions, but not all open-ended questions elicit HOT or do so with intent. Open-ended describes the form of a question, not the quality of a question. They are simply questions that do not have one correct answer and cannot be answered with a word

68 ◆ Thinking about Thinking

or two. However, some non-open-ended questions can be more compelling and have greater educational value than many open-ended questions. Closed questions can require using HOT skills to respond and at advanced levels of thinking. The set of questions from the *Snap-sHOT, Go with the Flow*, (page 224) are closed questions but elicit many HOT skills: "If we had lots of different funnels, which would you choose? How would it be different from this one?" They elicit imagining, associating and differentiating, evaluating, inducing, and more. Here's another example of a closed question that requires advanced levels of multiple HOT skills to answer: "Is this statement from the newspaper an opinion, an opinion presented as a fact, or a fact?" Open-ended questions can be vague and contrived ("What's happening here?" "What's that doing here?"), demeaning and rhetorical ("What's the matter with you?"), or prescriptive and still have only one correct answer or a very limited number of answers ("What is a safe way to cross a street?").

Yet, despite a lack of intentionality, the use of open-ended questions has been widely touted in the field for decades as a superior form of questioning, a key indicator of quality teaching, and a core strategy for scaffolding learning, particularly inquiry-based learning (Haden et al., 2016; Lee & Kinzie, 2012; van de Pol, Volman, & Beishuizen, 2010; Weisberg et al., 2016). Higher-order thinking questions, as a concept, redefine what constitutes a good question by basing the judgment on the quality of the question rather than its form.

Snap-sHOT: MY FAMILY FEEDS THE WORLD

All the students in Cruz's second-grade class at Chavez elementary (in a town close to the U.S.–Mexican border) were children or grandchildren of farmworkers. Cruz, who was a child of farmworkers, created a theme-based study of local crops, farming, and farmwork. Lessons based on state standards in math, science, social studies, reading, writing, and art were integrated into the activities. In addition, the students learned how wages and food prices are set and a few other basic economic concepts. Students interviewed and recorded family members and wrote their stories in English and Spanish, with photos and drawings. Prior to conducting the interviews, students practiced asking insightful questions and follow-up questions to elicit rich information and engaging stories. "What do you (or did you) like about farmwork and why?" "What is (or was) the hardest thing about farmwork?" Cruz then created a website hosting all the students' work, including the photos, drawings, and recorded and written interviews. Students proudly shared the website with their families on cell phones or on computers in the community library. The class also created a board game, *From Farm to Table*, that tracks crops from planting to consuming and presents obstacles like drought and frost, overplanting, shortage of workers, rising packaging and shipping costs, and fluctuating consumer demand.

Infer

Making inferences entails determining the meaning or drawing a conclusion from information that is indirect, implied, or incomplete. It is difficult to know much about children's ability to infer from developmental psychology research, as researchers define the term "inferring" in different ways. Many studies ask children to predict how a person or animal will feel in response to an event—an event that is usually overtly happy (opening a birthday present) or sad (losing a balloon) (Filiatrault-Veilleux et al., 2015). Predicting simple emotions from unambiguous information, however, is not a type of inference but a low-level form of connecting causes and effects, which is a MOT skill.

Nevertheless, almost all five-year-olds can infer that Little Red Riding Hood is in danger from the wolf, although she does not seem to know it, and it is not stated explicitly in the story, at least in most versions. It is a low-level form of inferring if the illustrations of the wolf make him look menacing or the storyteller makes him sound menacing. However, if the wolf looks and sounds neutral and the story is being heard for the first time, a higher level of inferring would be required, and the typical five-year-old may have difficulty making this inference.

70 ◆ Thinking about Thinking

Books are a great resource for promoting the development of students' inferential thinking. Teachers can ask students to infer as many things as they can about the book just by carefully examining the information on the cover. Then, as they (or the teacher) read the book, they answer questions that require inferential thinking, such as why a character did or said something unexpected, what may have happened before the story begins or after it ends, how one character feels about another character, and what messages the author is sending to the reader through the story.

Here is an enjoyable *Cognitivity* to promote inferential thinking.

COGNITIVITY: SAME WORDS, DIFFERENT MEANINGS

The teacher reads the following sentences emphasizing the word in italics and leads a discussion about the different meanings they infer (Figure 5.1).

> *"Ana* hears a little puppy." Inference: Do you or anyone else hear it?
> "Ana *hears* a little puppy." Inference: She can't see it.
> "Ana hears a *little* puppy." Inference: Not a big one.
> "Ana hears a little *puppy.*" Inference: Not a full-grown dog, nor a kitten or other animal.

Then the teacher reviews a sentence similar to the one above (without pictures), demonstrating how emphasizing a particular word and using body language can change the inferred meaning of a sentence. For example, cupping one's ear when the word *hear* is emphasized and pretending to hold something small when *little* is emphasized. After students have experience with this activity, they work in small groups to make up a sentence and demonstrate to the class how verbally and physically emphasizing different words changes the inferred meaning of the sentence.

Higher-Order Thinking (HOT) Skills ◆ 71

Same Words, Different Meanings

"**Ana** hears a little puppy." Inference: Do you hear it? Or, Khati doesn't hear it.

"Ana **hears** a little puppy." Inference: She can't see it.

"Ana hears a **little** puppy." Inference: Not a big one.

"Ana hears a little **puppy**." Inference: Not a full-grown dog, kitten, or other animal.

FIGURE 5.1 Same Words, Different Meanings.

Graphic by Gwendolyn Rodriquez.

Deduce/Induce

Deductive thinking involves separating or eliminating information, whereas inductive thinking involves combining and piecing together information. Their purposes are the same—to find solutions, get results, or gain a deeper understanding—so they are often used simultaneously. Deductive/inductive (D/I) thinking is required when the pieces of information or the results are abstract, unlimited, unknown, or unknowable. It is the higher-order cousin of associating/differentiating (a MOT skill), which is used when the information is concrete, limited, or known and the results are ultimately knowable. D/I thinking is the key thinking skill used by reporters, researchers, and police detectives to conduct their investigations. When detectives comb through clues and pieces of evidence to solve crimes, they eliminate those that are implausible or irrelevant, unravel evidence that seems connected but is not, and piece together those that seem plausible and relevant. If this is inconclusive, it is often necessary to go back or wait for additional evidence. Sometimes this process has to be repeated many times and over many years. The importance of persistence and patience, as well as other thinking dispositions, is discussed in Chapter 7 (on pages 137–141).

In his Sherlock Holmes stories, Sir Arthur Conan Doyle raised D/I thinking to a high level of intellect and entertainment. Although fictional and exaggerated, all of Sherlock Holmes's brilliant deductions and inductions are plausible, which is what makes the stories so compelling and enduring. The message to take away from the character of Mr. Holmes is "elementary": D/I thinking is a very powerful thinking skill. Doyle's stories can inspire educators to develop young learners' D/I thinking skills to the best of their abilities.

Activities that promote D/I thinking are, unfortunately, too rare in schools. This is likely because school curriculums overemphasize teaching existing content knowledge and underemphasize teaching how and why we know what we know, how to gain new or more knowledge, how to use the knowledge we have effectively, and what to do when we have limited or no

Higher-Order Thinking (HOT) Skills ◆ 73

knowledge about a subject. But there *are* ways to teach these concepts along with content knowledge even to our youngest learners—for example, asking students to create their own math word problems, to invent an educational game using elements from the games they already know, or to make up a story combining the characters or plots of two different stories.

The following *Snap-sHOT* illustrates a teacher and her students using D/I thinking and other critical thinking skills to understand a challenging concept. It is hands-on, interactive, and appropriate for young learners. It starts with the teacher going through a process of changing a mundane and unchallenging sink-and-float activity to a more challenging and complex activity that, nonetheless, is misguided and unsuccessful and does not involve HOT. Finally, she makes further, more substantive changes to the activity to engage more D/I thinking and other HOT skills. In addition, these changes give students a more accurate and thorough understanding of flotation.

Snap-sHOT: FLOAT YOUR BOAT

Flush with ideas from a recent workshop, Ms. Tamina sets up a new sink-and-float science workstation in her kindergarten classroom. Although she has done this activity many times before, this time she intends to make it more scientific. She adds a tally sheet for students to record their findings and some new items to test along with all the items she had previously used: small pieces of newsprint paper, which float at first but eventually sink, and a small bottle that floats when empty and sinks when full of water.

Before students test each item, they complete the tally sheet, which has four columns. In the first column, they write the name or draw a picture of the object they will test. Then they put a red checkmark in one of the other three columns to indicate if they think it will float, sink, or do both. After testing, they put a blue checkmark in the column that indicates what actually occurred. When they are done, Ms. Tamina asks probing questions, which is also a new addition to the activity. However, their responses surprise and concern her. While most students enjoy the activity, they all have difficulty predicting which items will sink or float or do both. Most are unable to explain the factors that make something float or sink. Tallying the findings was a tedious, if not meaningless, process; their enjoyment was primarily from dropping things into water and retrieving them. Ms. Tamina puts away the activity at the end of the day but is determined to get it right.

After several days researching, perusing science books, and talking with friends and colleagues, Ms. Tamina tries a different approach. She realizes that abstract and complex concepts such as buoyancy, density, and displacement are at play and if they cannot be made understandable to kindergartners, it is better to *not* do a sink-and-float activity because it can actually misinform them. Also, while she asked questions to elicit HOT, there was nothing in the activity that facilitated such thinking.

This time, Ms. Tamina starts with a short demonstration and discussion. "Here is a small plastic bottle filled with sand and here is a big glass jar filled with… what?" The children shout, "Nothing!" "Oh, there may be something in there. We'll find out, but first, which one is heavier, the bottle or the jar?" A few children feel them and say the jar is heavier. They put them on a balance scale, and the class sees that the jar is heavier. "So, which one will float and which will sink? Or will they both sink? Or will they both float? I want you to predict what will happen. Try to remember things that you have seen sink or float." Ms. Tamina records their answers after each one writes the word *sink* or *float* on a blue sticky note representing the small plastic bottle and on a pink sticky note for the glass jar. The most common prediction is that both will sink. Then she invites two students to place them in the container of water. "So, the jar floats and the little bottle sinks, even though there is actually something in the jar. It is something very light, much lighter than sand or water, and although we can't see it, we can't live without it." After a lively discussion about air, Ms. Tamina asks questions while demonstrating the concept of floatation. "What will happen when we replace most of the air inside the jar with stones? What will happen when we replace the sand in the bottle with air?" (She does both actions and places the jar and the bottle in the water.) "With air inside them, the jar and bottle can both float because of their form and structure. They have empty space inside of them filled with air. In the same way, big ships can float on water although they are very, very heavy because they have a lot of empty space filled with air inside of them. But big ships also float because of their shape and size. A very heavy ship needs to be very long and wide, or it will sink. If too many people get in a small boat, it will get too heavy for its size and will sink. If a boat gets a hole in it, and too much water gets inside, the water will make it too heavy for its size and also fill up the air space, and it will sink." Ms. Tomina further demonstrates this by putting a small piece of foil and a large piece of foil on the water. She puts two stones on the big piece and it floats, then puts the stones on the small piece and it sinks.

"Now, work in small groups to make a boat with one piece of foil that will float. You have pieces of wood, metal scraps, wire, and many other materials. You also have some stones. Make a boat that will hold as many stones as possible and still float. You have resources too. There are photos of different kinds of boats and ships, there are books that show the insides of ships, there are four buckets of water for testing your boats, and you can always ask for help."

During the work, one group asks why a square piece of wood floats when it's not shaped like a boat and has no place for air inside. Ms. Tamina interrupts the work of the class for a mini-lesson. "There is actually a lot of air inside a piece of wood, not in one big place, but in tiny pockets all throughout the inside of the wood. Stones have no pockets of air, so they sink. I will pass around a strong magnifying glass and you will be able to see some little pockets in the wood but not in the stone."

In addition to promoting D/I thinking, the activity in this *SnapsHOT* promoted querying, reframing, and connecting causes and effects at a more advanced level. The students (and the teacher) also engaged in several thought processes, including analyses and finding solutions to problems.

Shift Perspective

This is the ability to see things from another's point of view. It is the mental tool for understanding and empathy. Shifting perspective is necessary to prevent or de-escalate conflicts and clear up misunderstandings. The challenge is to determine other perspectives accurately, which can be difficult if they are unclear, in flux, or obscured, intentionally or otherwise. When diplomacy fails, it is usually because one or both parties have wrongly assumed, or incorrectly assessed, the other side's perspective related to their motives and goals. Diplomacy entails social shifting, which is one form of this thinking skill. Interpersonal shifting is the other, more common form, and is explained first.

Interpersonal Shifting

Shifting perspective interpersonally is the ability to accurately and objectively perceive how another person views the world, to achieve a mutual appreciation and understanding. Ideally, this includes their beliefs, cultural influences, motivations, and self-image. It is the thinking skill used by psychologists, counselors, and mediators to understand and connect with the people they are helping. To do these jobs well, a high level of this thinking skill is essential. These professionals are so adept at shifting perspective and spend so much time using this thinking skill that they need to be careful not to over-identify with their clients and lose the objectivity and distance necessary to be helpful.

Until recently, this ability had been viewed as something that was beyond the capacity of young "egocentric" children. However, we now know that even preverbal babies, starting at about seven months, are capable of shifting perspective, and perhaps even a basic level of empathy, when it comes to reading the overt feelings and emotions of others (Hamlin & Wynn, 2011; Hamlin et al., 2007; Hamlin et al., 2010). Smiling in response to a father making silly noises or smiling to coax a father to make those silly noises again starts even earlier, at about three months. This may not represent actual shift-perspective thinking or empathy, but such interpersonal reciprocity is likely their precursor.

Shift-perspective thinking is also used to develop strategies (a thought process). It is a great advantage in games, sports, commerce, law enforcement, and many other fields to be able to accurately "see" from the point of view of an opponent on the other team, a business competitor, or a perpetrator of a crime. People who have strong shift-perspective thinking can predict with uncanny accuracy what their rivals will do.

Characters in stories provide many good opportunities to help young students develop the ability to shift perspective. What would the story of Little Red Riding Hood sound like if told from the perspective of the grandmother or the wolf? *A Chair for My Mother* by Vera Williams (2007) is a heartwarming story in which a little girl expresses her concerns and hopes for her mother, who works long hours as a waitress, after they lose everything in a house fire.

Social Shifting

Another type of shifting perspective is the ability to adapt or change behaviors in response to prevailing social norms. It entails "seeing" the perspective of a group of people rather than of just one other person. A common euphemism for this is being able to "read the room."

Young learners use social shifting when they realize that they have to behave differently in different places or under different circumstances. Most of them understand this to a degree, though somewhat instinctively and unconsciously. They seem to naturally behave differently on the playground than inside the classroom and differently still at home. But they have difficulty—as do many adults—when behavioral norms and expectations are unusual, ambiguous, arbitrary, or just unknown and unstated. Parents find it amusing, and a little embarrassing, when children unintentionally violate an unstated social norm, such as singing loudly in the supermarket or showing all the dinner guests their new superhero underpants. These events suddenly remind us that there are many, many unstated social norms.

Usually, there are good reasons for particular social norms, but they can be hard for a young person to understand. "Why can I take my shoes off at home, but not at school?" "Why can I eat fried chicken with my fingers, but not a grilled chicken breast?" The knowledge and ability to act differently and appropriately in different environments are early and basic steps in the development of social shifting. The teacher's role is to make these differences explicit and clear and help students to adapt. Students benefit from knowing the reasons for different expectations. Although it can be challenging for teachers to come up with simple explanations that young learners can understand, it is an ability that teachers can learn with a bit of help and some practice. Here is an example: "Because there are many, many more people at school than at home, there are some things we can't do at school that we can do at home." Explaining first the overarching concept behind norms and then the reason for the norm helps students develop this thinking skill. "We keep our shoes on at school because if someone accidentally stepped on your bare toes, which is likely to happen with so many people here, it would really hurt. It would also hurt if you stepped on something sharp with your bare or stockinged feet."

WHOSE NORMS ARE NORMAL?

Whereas in most Western countries children cannot remove their shoes at school, in many other countries students are *required* to remove their shoes before entering the school building. In some of these places, they wear a type of indoor slipper, but in many, they are just barefoot.

There are other Western school norms that are not at all "normal" elsewhere. In elementary schools in an Eastern European country, classrooms are boisterous and lively and the teachers keep just enough control to prevent chaos. Students move about, argue passionately, shout out their ideas and opinions, and express their feelings and emotions, including their affections for their teachers. At any given moment, students can be heard, somewhere in the school, singing and dancing to traditional music with great skill and talent. However, the classrooms are tranquil compared with the chaos in the hallways during transitions. There are no prohibitions on running, yelling, or physically fighting in the hallways. It is not surprising then, that the politicians of this country are somewhat infamous for throwing punches at each other during parliamentary sessions and on live TV. Values and behavioral norms are transmitted by what is *not* taught as much as by what is taught. Not stopping physical violence nor teaching students how to resolve conflicts peacefully makes resolving conflicts violently an acceptable norm. Indirect messages often communicate more powerfully than direct messages.

Other than at a basic level, it is not realistic to expect most young students to shift perspective without assistance. However, they are often expected to. The expectations that a first-grade teacher has for students' behaviors, work habits, and capabilities may be quite different from the expectations held by the other first-grade teachers and are likely to be very different from the expectations of the second-grade teachers. And these differences may have little to do with age-related expectations and more to do with each teacher's personality and teaching style. To successfully make the transition to second grade, students have to first understand that teachers have different expectations, figure out what those expectations are, and then adjust their behaviors to meet those expectations. Wise second-grade teachers understand that shifting perspective is difficult, but emergent, for young students and make their expectations clear from the first day of school. By supporting students while they make the mental and behavioral shift during the first weeks of school, teachers can prevent problematic behaviors from developing, reduce students' anxiety (and their own), and increase students' positive engagement in learning.

Creative Thinking Skills: The Sky's the Limit

While the process of memorizing a Beethoven sonata entails (advanced) memorization skills, only a pianist with excellent creative skills can play it with the sensitivity and passion that will delight and move an audience. Only an actor with excellent creative thinking skills can take the words William Shakespeare wrote and bring the character of Hamlet to life. Higher-order creative thinking turns notes into music that breaks your heart, and turns mere words into a young prince whose anguish wrenches your soul.

To some people, creative thinking comes easily and naturally. Among them are a significant subgroup of people who are *compelled* to think creatively. They often have a difficult time as students because typical school activities give them few or no outlets for their creativity. In frustration, some of these students express their creativity in ways that are disruptive or inappropriate at school. It is important that the teachers and school administrators address the cause of these behaviors and not just react to them. With creative students, there are many ways to easily prevent and redirect these behaviors, and they are different from the methods that might be used to address disruptive behaviors by other students with different motives. Ideas for giving students acceptable outlets for their creativity, which will prevent disruptive behaviors, can be found throughout this section of the book.

Creative thinking and creativity are often misunderstood as rarified skills that only a few possess. Perhaps this is because they are not typically used as an instructional strategy or taught directly. They are mistakenly considered extracurricular, such as the art classes or music lessons taken after school. But creative thinking is an essential and common life skill used every day: when generating ideas at a work meeting, imagining a kitchen remodel, cooking a unique meal, making up a story to tell children, or transforming a dull mundane activity in a teacher's guide into one that is engaging, challenging, and suitable for a particular and unique group of students.

With guidance and practice, most people can think creatively with more intention for greater effect, at more advanced levels, more often, and in more situations. For example, conflicts and disagreements tend to get resolved either by someone winning and someone losing or by both sides reluctantly comprising. However, by using the creative thinking skill of reframing, the problem can often be resolved so that neither side loses nor is forced to compromise. As with all thinking skills, creative thinking can be improved upon, expanded, and sharpened with effective instruction, support, and practice. Strategies and techniques for doing this are provided throughout the book.

Imagine

Imagining is the ability to create a mental image of something that does not exist or has not been seen or an activity that has not occurred or has not been witnessed. It is the core creative thinking skill; imagining "what could be" underpins nearly all creative endeavors. A strong imagination is a great asset when engaging in many thought processes. When planning to decorate a room, a person with a strong imagination will be able to envision just how the room will look with various options. This will result in a satisfying final choice and will avoid wasting time, effort, and money purchasing items that do not look right or moving furniture over and over. Imagining is a vital part of solving problems, particularly for finding innovative solutions.

There are great academic benefits to having a good imagination and using it often. It should not be considered frivolous—daydreaming instead of working. It helps students to picture historical events, understand counterintuitive science concepts, visualize descriptive passages in books, and express original thoughts and ideas verbally and in writing.

Artists—whether painters, sculptors, designers, composers, writers, choreographers, and so on—create something tangible from what was first in their imaginations. People with strong imaginations are often drawn to the arts where they can express what they envision in their minds. Artists and creative people represent a significant percentage of any population, including students. As adults, they are represented in many careers, including some that are very lucrative. What can schools and teachers offer the future comedians, graphic artists, chefs, novelists, fashion designers, and movie directors in their classrooms?

Rather than relegating the activities that engage imaginative thinking to art, creative writing, special occasions, or breaks from academic work, it is important, and not difficult, to add creative elements to nearly every academic activity. This not only meets the needs of the young creatives and artists in our classrooms but gives the students who are not predisposed to using their imaginations opportunities to develop this important thinking skill.

With any assignment, students can be asked to add their own questions or create their own problems to solve. They can be required to solve problems at least two different ways or give two different opinions or make both sides of an argument. They can be offered the opportunity to draw a picture or set of pictures along with or instead of a writing assignment (similar to a short graphic or anime story). They can have the option of writing a joke, making up a riddle, or creating a game show for the rest of the class based on anything they are learning. Several students can work together to act out part of the story they are reading or a historic event they are studying.

In addition, teachers can *explicitly* teach imaginative thinking with activities whose primary purpose is to sharpen and expand this thinking skill. The following *Cognitivity* facilitates the development of imaginative thinking skills from more basic to more advanced. Students are given a challenge to invent or create something new. They can work individually, in pairs, or in small groups. The ideas for inventions can be amended to connect to a content area or for students to practice particular skills.

COGNITIVITY: INVENTORS INVENTING INVENTIONS

"Create" a new animal by combining parts of two or more existing animals. What are its diet and habitat? Can it be domesticated and, if so, for what purpose?

Invent a new musical instrument. It could be made up of parts of existing instruments or be something entirely original. Explain how it is played and demonstrate how it sounds. Play a song on it. Make up a song specifically for the instrument.

"Create" a new town or city that is very child-friendly. How can it be made safe for children to walk or bike to school? What kinds of play spaces can there be that are fun, challenging, and safe for children of all ages and abilities? For third graders, ideas for businesses, government services, restaurants, and so on can also be added. The end product can be a scale model, a drawing or drawings, a written report, or some combination of the three.

"Create" a new country. Describe its history, how it was formed and by whom, its language, food, music, geography, dress, celebrations, and so on.

Invent a new video game that will entertain as well as teach about a country, famous person, historical event, or a science or math concept. Describe and explain the game in detail along with drawings. Create a storyboard that will show how the game changes as it progresses. Identify its strong points and potential problems or weaknesses.

This *Cognitivity* helps to build the thinking skills needed to be good at solving problems, an important thought process, particularly for finding innovative solutions. It also helps to develop the type of imaginary thinking that is used in making predictions and developing theories, two other thought processes.

Generate

Generative thinking is imagining with a particular focus and purpose. Brainstorming is one common form of this type of thinking when the goal is to generate many ideas quickly rather than generating one or two "good" ideas. Generating ideas is an important aspect of solving problems. What might have caused the problem? What are some possible solutions?

When asked about his failure to get results after working for many months on developing a new type of battery, the prolific inventor, Thomas Edison, responded, "Results! Why, man, I have gotten a lot of results! I know several thousand things that won't work" (Dyer & Martin, 1910, p. 616). Generating many, many ideas to solve a difficult or unique problem or to create something completely new is a typical and often necessary part of the process. It took over 2,000 attempts before Edison figured out that a twisted strand of tungsten will transfer electrical energy into heat energy strong enough to emit a bright light without burning itself up. The result was the electric light bulb. Persistence is a key thinking disposition, as discussed in Chapter 7 (on pages 141–154).

There are two main circumstances in which teachers help students generate ideas. One is spontaneous, and the other is planned. Generating ideas spontaneously occurs when solutions are needed to resolve a conflict or to solve an immediate problem. Planned activities that engage students' generative thinking include brainstorming possible places to go for a field trip, ideas about a topic as part of a KWL (Know, Want to Know, Learned) lesson or similar activity, suggestions for project ideas related to a theme, and ideas about physical and scientific phenomena such as how airplanes fly, what makes the wind blow, or what happens to the sun at night. Asking students for their ideas about these complex but common phenomena, which many adults cannot explain accurately, gets them to think deeply and gives teachers insight into how they think. Their thinking skills can be challenged even further when several students who have differing ideas discuss and debate among themselves who is "correct." Of course, they may all be incorrect or only partially correct, which then requires a teacher's guidance and support.

The following activity is an example of explicitly teaching generative thinking. It can be done as a choice activity with a small group of students, during a break, or to reinforce concepts in geometry or other subjects.

ThinkinGroups: **SHAPE SHIFTING**

Sitting in a circle, students pass around a piece of stiff card stock in the shape of an equilateral triangle whose sides are about eight inches long. Each student holds it and says and shows what it could be, such as a hat, bib, mask, traffic sign, slice of pizza or pie, or other object. Students are encouraged, but not pressured, to come up with an original idea. Passing or delaying a turn is always an option. Each time the game is played, the shape is changed.

Challenges are added as students become proficient, such as using two shapes at a time, first the same shapes and then two different shapes. Solid shapes, such as cylinders, cubes, and pyramids, can be added. The game can also be played with objects such as a small cardboard box, long piece of yarn or rope, scarf, hoop, plastic tube, beverage coaster, small branch or stick, or large pinecone. Students can come up with their own ideas for objects.

Teachers should not start the activity as this often makes it harder for students to come up with their own ideas. But it is a good idea for teachers to take the final turn. This shows that there can always be another idea.

The ability to come up with effective solutions to problems is a thought process that utilizes the kind of generative thinking promoted in this *Cognitivity*. In addition, it is needed to make predictions or develop theories (one of the five thought processes).

The ability to generate *good* ideas—those that are relevant to the issue, realistic, positive, and likely to work—is an emergent skill in young students. The teacher's role is to help students become more proficient at generating good ideas by giving them many authentic opportunities to practice without judging their ideas. Students will learn how to form good ideas over time when they participate in many teacher-facilitated discussions about the merits of various ideas. Teachers can facilitate these discussions by keeping students on track and asking incisive questions: "Is there an easier or quicker way to do it?" "What about that idea would be more difficult to do and what would be easier?" "What can be done to make sure the idea will be successful?" "What complications or problems might come up?"

Reframe

Shifting *perspective* is a critical thinking skill, but shifting *perception*, or reframing, is a creative thinking skill. When shifting perspective, the other perspective or perspectives are extant and potentially knowable. But reframing can draw from multiple perspectives and lead to any number of new perceptions. Two types of reframing—interpreting and transferring—involve creating something unique rather than entirely new. These are explained later in this section.

One of the most effective ways that skilled mediators resolve problems is to reframe the nature of the conflict for their clients. The traditional view of mediation or conflict resolution—a particular type of problem-solving—is the use of logical and critical thinking skills to reach a compromise. But it can be much more effective with the addition of creative thinking skills, particularly reframing. In the *Snap-sHOT* below, a mediator works with the administrators of an elementary school and the parents who want to enroll their child in kindergarten in the fall.

Snap-sHOT: REFRAMING A PARENT/SCHOOL CONFLICT

Lorenzo's fifth birthday is one day after the eligibility date for kindergarten. The neighborhood school offers full-day kindergarten and has an excellent reputation as a science magnet school. But the administrators are adhering strictly to the rule and reject Lorenzo's parents' request to test his readiness for kindergarten. Lorenzo's parents have enlisted the help of their sympathetic state representative and a reporter from the local paper, both of whom are more than willing to shine a light on the "ridiculous inflexibility" of public schools. At this point, both sides agree to meet with a neutral mediator.

After separate discussions with the school staff and the parents, the mediator learns that the projected kindergarten enrollment is larger than usual mostly because of many out-of-neighborhood transfers, which were approved at the district level before the summer break. She also learns that Lorenzo's father was recently laid off from his construction job and is trying to start a painting business, and his mother might lose her job as a barista if she takes too many days off.

The mediator is then able to help reframe the situation as an unfortunate but necessary action to protect the incoming students and their teachers from overcrowded classrooms rather than as a rejection of a child or a case of insensitive bureaucrats being "ridiculously inflexible." Furthermore, she helps reframe the parents' issue as a plea for help rather than an unreasonable demand. They can't afford to pay for another year of childcare when the family income has dropped so dramatically. As a resolution, the school offers the support of their whole staff and the many community leaders with whom they have connections to help Lorenzo's parents find affordable, quality childcare and clients for his father's new business. They apologize for communicating so poorly and assure them they will be very happy and proud to have Lorenzo as a student in the school year that follows. Lorenzo's parents agree to tell the representative and the reporter that the situation is resolved, and they apologize for the problems they may have caused the school.

Innovative solutions are often necessary to solve problems for the long term by addressing the root causes of the problems. And it takes reframing thinking skills, along with all other creative thinking skills, to develop innovative solutions.

88 ◆ Thinking about Thinking

Reframing is one of the more sophisticated and complex HOT skills, so it is not a common thinking skill among young learners. Nevertheless, there are some students who are capable of reframing at a basic level. Also, when teachers use this skill themselves, students learn what it is and how it functions, which is an important first step in the process of acquiring it. Below is another example of a student reframing, which catches the teacher by surprise.

Snap-sHOT: IT'S TIME TO PARTY

The day before spring break, Mr. Ahmadi's third graders are looking forward to the party planned for the last half hour of class. But from the opening moments of class, the students are excited and restless, and Mr. Ahmadi, who is a first-year teacher, can't seem to settle them down to focus on schoolwork. Finally, he says to the class, "If you keep this up, I will cancel the party! I am drawing five boxes on the board. Whenever anyone talks when they shouldn't or is not doing their work, I will put an X in one of the boxes. If all five boxes have an X, then the party is cancelled."

While this seems to work for about fifteen minutes, it doesn't take long for all five boxes to have an X. After lunch, a grumpy group of third graders return to their seats. Immediately, Jonah raises his hand. "Mr. Ahmadi, it's not fair that we can't have the party because of a few kids who ruined it. Can't the rest of us have the party? We were good." Mr. Ahmadi replies, "No, because those were the conditions I set, and whatever we do or don't do, it has to be as a whole class." Again, Jonah raises his hand. "Okay, but can't we do something to get our party back? Do something good to you show we can be good and we should have the party?" After being rendered speechless for a few seconds, Mr. Ahmadi says, "Well, I guess we can try something. I will set the timer for ten minutes. If everyone does their work and pays attention the whole time, then I will erase one of the boxes. If you are successful, then we can try it again for another ten minutes. If you are able to erase all five boxes, then we will have the party." In the end, they *do* have the party.

Jonah reframed the situation from a loss and a big disappointment to an opportunity for redemption and a win. Although punishments and rewards are not the most effective strategies for managing students' behaviors, Mr. Ahmadi did learn that rewards generally work better than punishments. This is especially the case when students identify the reward they want because they will be motivated to earn it.

Interpret

Interpreting, a form of reframing, entails taking something that exists and making it uniquely one's own. It is a creative thinking skill because there are nearly unlimited ways that certain things, such as a piece of music, a style of architecture, or a literary theme or genre, can be interpreted. The expression "put your own spin on it" captures the idea. (The meaning of interpreting, as a thinking skill, is not to be confused with other meanings of the word, such as translating, deciphering, or decoding.) With interpreting, the starting point or basis is extant and tangible (e.g., a song, story, script, and character), the process is controlled by the artist (though sometimes with assistance) and ends with something unique rather than new or original. The focus of interpreting, unlike that of process-oriented thinking skills such as imagining and improvising, is on the final product.

For his plays, Shakespeare took well-known stories and bits of history and interpreted them to stunning effect. *Romeo and Juliet* is likely based on the tale of Pyramus and Thisbe written by Ovid in the year 8 CE. Leonard Cohen's "Hallelujah" and John Lennon's "Imagine" are among the most recorded pop songs by other singers, each of whom interprets these songs in their own unique style. Our greatest actors have the ability to interpret the dialogue they are given and the characters they portray in ways that are assured, unique, honest, and perfectly convincing.

These interpretations feel so "right" that it's hard to imagine that the characters could be portrayed any other way or any better. James Stewart in *It's a Wonderful Life*, Julie Andrews in *The Sound of Music*, Ben Kingsley in *Gandhi*, Jamie Foxx in *Ray*, and Meryl Streep as Margaret Thatcher in *The Iron Lady* are just a few examples of advanced interpreting by skilled actors.

Transfer

Transfer thinking, another type of reframing, is the ability to take a concept or idea and adapt it to work successfully in a different context or for a different purpose. Transferring is also called generalizing, but transferring is the preferred term as in certain contexts generalizing can mean stereotyping.

Architects use transfer thinking regularly. Every structure they design is unique but uses features, styles, and techniques that, in nearly all cases, have been used before. One such technique, the architectural cantilever, allows for a large, heavy structure to overhang or thrust out without structural supports underneath. It was made famous by Frank Lloyd Wright in 1935 with his Fallingwater House, which features two large concrete balconies protruding from the external walls over a waterfall. Now, cantilevers are more commonly used in the design of bridges and roofs over large stadiums. Because cantilevers eliminate the need for support posts or columns, they allow every spectator in a stadium to have an unobstructed view of the field. Although all cantilevers use the same principles of physics, they often look very different from each other and in some designs are not visible as they are embedded in the structure of the building. This is all possible because architects are able to *transfer* the concept of cantilevers and, with high levels of creative thinking, make it work using a variety of building materials, for many types and sizes of structures, and with a wide range of architectural styles.

One of the most effective ways to help young learners develop their ability to transfer is also one of the easiest: to name the action when it happens. "I just used transfer thinking when I had you use the same voting method to choose our next book to read as you used to decide who's drawing to use for the poster."

"We transferred the *idea* of making a graph from the graph we made to track daily weather changes to make a graph that shows everyone's favorite character from the books we read. We succeeded in transferring the idea to make a graph after we found a different type of graph to use because the two graphs had different purposes. We made the first one to show changes over a long period of time and the new one to show opinions at just one point in time." Transferring is an important thinking skill, and an important part of transfer thinking is being able to make adjustments to make the transfer work.

Improvise

Improvising is the ability to respond spontaneously to situations or people with relevant, unique, and effective ideas or actions. Improvising is often the only option when there is little or no time to plan or prepare. But, when it is freely chosen, it is a kind of art form. An improvisation is a process, much like a jazz session. The starting point or basis for a jazz improvisation is often simple, such as a drum beat or a basic melody line of a few notes. The musicians then create music that is new, unique, and significantly different from the starting beat or melody refrain. They create a process that is also a product, particularly if the music is recorded.

In most forms of improvising, the result is unknown until the improvisational process ends. Because no two emergencies or crises are exactly the same, rescue workers and hostage negotiators have to improvise, to some degree, to achieve the best possible outcome.

The 1997 film *Life is Beautiful* is a near perfect example of improvising as well as imagining and reframing. The protagonist, Guido, played by Roberto Benigni, reframes his son's perception of their experience as prisoners in a Nazi concentration camp to protect him from physical and psychological harm. Guido creates an elaborate fantasy that they are part of a game to test their fortitude and wits. He tells his son that they get points for completing "tasks" but lose points if they complain or cry. And, if they get a thousand points, they will win a tank. He continuously and brilliantly improvises to maintain the fantasy for his son until they are finally freed when the war ends.

Improvising is an advanced creative thinking skill, but through simple role-plays, young learners can practice improvising in a way that augments what they are learning and, for most students, it is enjoyable. The important thing is that they know what it means to improvise and begin to understand its purpose and value. Students can act out short scenarios based on historic events, famous people, and situations and characters from books. Teachers will need to help students formulate the scenario, identify the characters, and follow a short plotline. Within that framework, students improvise the dialogue and actions. For math concepts, students can create imaginary workplaces such as a restaurant, market, store, office, auto repair shop, and construction site. Then, as chefs, waiters, clerks, customers, mechanics, builders, and so on, they apply math functions in the process of improvising buying, selling, cooking, ordering, measuring, weighing, and more. During the role-play, teachers will need to support and help guide the improvision with suggestions, new vocabulary, adding props or more roles or just taking a role and participating. With any role-play, younger students will need more structure and support than older students.

By being given many opportunities to practice improvising in a variety of role-plays, some students will develop this thinking skill to a surprisingly high level. However, the more introverted students may find this activity uncomfortable. For these students, participation should be optional, and alternative ways to develop improvisational thinking should be explored. Role-plays can be done simultaneously in small groups, which eliminates an audience. Or two students can use a voice recorder and improvise an imaginary interview with a famous person, a character from a book, or a fictional person with an interesting job, such as an astronaut, a fossil hunter, an artist, an inventor, a detective, or—*drum roll please*—a teacher!

Conclusion

Whereas LOT and MOT involve information that is concrete, quantifiable, or known or knowable, HOT involves working with abstract, unquantifiable, or unknown information. Two tasks can have similar purposes or goals, but one will require MOT skills and the other HOT skills. For example, to answer the two questions below requires MOT skills (and LOT skills) for the first and HOT skills for the second. Nevertheless, both have the same goal: to better understand teachers' working conditions in the U.S.

1. *"Do teachers in the United States work more and get paid less than teachers in Canada?"* Finding the answer entails the LOT skill of identifying and the MOT skills of categorizing, associating/differentiating, and calculating. The question involves concrete information and has a definitive answer, which likely can be found in existing databases or reports.

2. *"Are teachers in the United States overworked and underpaid?"* This question is abstract, complex, and not directly verifiable or quantifiable, and the answer may be true in some places but not in others. In addition, it seems to be a "leading question" with an ulterior motive. To answer this question, the HOT skills of querying, inferring, and deducing/inducing are needed. An implicit bias, that teachers in the U.S. *are* overworked and underpaid, can be inferred from the question, depending on who is asking the question and why. If international data and research results about teachers' work hours, salaries, and feelings about their work do not exist, research studies would have to be conducted. And, in order to provide a complete, accurate, and nuanced answer, any differences *within* the U.S. and *within* other countries on these issues would have to be determined. There may be differences between inexperienced teachers and experienced teachers, elementary school teachers and upper-school teachers, teachers in rural schools and those in suburban and urban schools, and so on. Then the implications of those differences, if any, would need to be discussed.

The ten HOT skills—five critical thinking and five creative thinking skills—give us the ability to question assumptions, look beyond surface appearances (which are often misleading), make informed decisions, have insights, solve complex problems,

94 ◆ Thinking about Thinking

create original art and designs, develop new ideas, and so much more. Advanced HOT skills, honed over decades, are the tools of leaders, innovators, problem solvers, intellectuals, artists, scientists, and even some athletes.

The major stars of professional basketball are different from the typical professional basketball player (who are all exceptional athletes) because they excel at using HOT along with their physical prowess. Many of them are not taller, stronger, or faster than the more typical players, they just use more MOT and HOT skills and use them at more advanced levels. They use logical thinking before a game to determine how to exploit the other team's weaknesses and counter their strengths, particularly for the players they will guard and who will likely guard them. During the game, they use creative thinking to surprise their opponents with unexpected moves and shift-perspective thinking to determine what their opponent will likely do next, attempting to stay a step or two ahead of them—figuratively and literally!

While not everyone can achieve advanced levels of every type of HOT skill, nearly everyone can develop the full array of HOT skills necessary to be effective in all spheres of life. Yet HOT skills are too rarely called upon in typical school lessons and assignments, nor systematically developed in students, particularly young students. This chapter provides the initial steps for helping teachers remedy this problem: to understand the concepts and components of HOT.

Key Ideas from this Chapter

1. Higher-order thinking skills scrutinize existing material and knowledge and develop new material and knowledge. The outcome of thought processes that use HOT is not predetermined, and when creative thinking is applied, the outcome is something unique, innovative, or entirely new.
2. HOT is distinct from LOT and MOT because it entails working with information that is abstract or unknown and/or results in something unique or new.

3. The four critical thinking skills entail the ability to query, infer, deduce/induce, and shift perspective.
4. The four creative thinking skills entail the ability to imagine, generate, reframe, and improvise.
5. Querying is the ability to ask relevant, helpful, and incisive questions to get a complete and accurate understanding of an issue, concept, event, person, and so on.
6. Inferring is the ability to gain insights from partial, abstract, or non-explicit information.
7. Deducing/Inducing is the ability to separate or eliminate information (deducing) and to combine and piece together information (inducing). Their purposes are the same—to find solutions, get results, or gain a deeper understanding—so they are often used simultaneously.
8. Shifting perspective is the ability to see things from another person's point of view—interpersonal shifting— or from the point of view of the norms of another culture–social shifting.
9. Imagining is the ability to create a mental image of something that does not yet exist or a circumstance that has not occurred.
10. Generating is the ability to imagine with a particular focus and purpose. Brainstorming is a common form of this type of thinking when the goal is to generate many ideas quickly rather than generating a few "good" ideas.
11. Reframing is the ability to change perception, such as coming to a different understanding of an idea than was previously held. It is a key thinking skill for developing innovative solutions to problems.
12. Interpreting, a form of reframing, entails taking something that exists and making it uniquely one's own.
13. Transfer thinking, another type of reframing, is the ability to take a concept or idea and adapt it to work successfully in a different context or for a different purpose.
14. Improvising is the ability to respond spontaneously to situations or people with relevant, unique, and effective ideas or actions.

Questions for Discussion

Which HOT skills are you particularly good at and which do you find challenging? Why?

Do you have some students who show early signs of being adept at one or more HOT skill? How do they demonstrate it and how do you respond?

In the *Snap-sHOT*, *It's Time to Party*, the strategy for managing an overly excited group of students was reframed by a student from punishing misbehavior to rewarding good behavior. What are other ways it could have been reframed?

What are some ways that creative thinking can be promoted by altering existing assignments or activities or adding creative elements to them?

What personal experiences have you had in which you did not shift your social perspective to match prevailing norms? What were the consequences, if any?

It is a challenge to be skeptical without being cynical and to be open-minded without being gullible. What are some practical strategies that can help?

References

Dyer, F., & Martin, T. (1910). *Edison: His life and inventions. Vol. 2.* Harper & Brothers.

Filiatrault-Veilleux, P., Bouchard, C., Trudeau, N., & Desmarais, C. (2015). Inferential comprehension of 3–6 year olds within the context of story grammar: A scoping review. *International Journal of Language & Communication Disorders*, *50*(6), 737–749. https://doi.org/10.1111/1460-6984.12175

Haden, C. A., Cohen, T., Uttal, D., & Marcus, M. (2016). Building learning: Narrating and transferring experiences in a children's museum. In D. M. Sobel & J. J. Jipson (Eds.), *Cognitive development in museum settings: Relating research and practice* (pp. 84–103). Routledge.

Hamlin, J. K., & Wynn, K. (2011). Young infants prefer prosocial to antisocial others. *Cognitive Development*, *26*(1), 30–39.

Hamlin, J. K., Wynn, K., & Bloom, P. (2007). Social evaluation by preverbal infants. *Nature*, *450*(7169), 557–559.

Hamlin, J. K., Wynn, K., & Bloom, P. (2010). Three-month-olds show a negativity bias in their social evaluations. *Developmental Science*, *13*(6), 923–929.

Lee, Y., & Kinzie, M. B. (2012). Teacher question and student response with regard to cognition and language use. *Instructional Science*, *40*, 857–874. https://doi.org/10.1007/s11251-011-9193-2

van de Pol, J., Volman, M., & Beishuizen, J. (2010). Scaffolding in teacher-student interaction: A decade of research. *Educational Psychology Review*, *22*(3), 271–296. https://doi.org/10.1007/s10648-010-9127-6

Viereck, G. S. (1929, October 26). What life means to Einstein: An interview by George Sylvester Viereck. *The Saturday Evening Post*. https://www.saturdayeveningpost.com/wp-content/uploads/satevepost/einstein.pdf

Weisberg, D. S., Hirsh-Pasek, K., Golinkoff, R. M., Kittredge, A. K., & Klahr, D. (2016). Guided play: Principles and practices. *Current Directions in Psychological Science*, *25*(3), 177–182. http://journals.sagepub.com/doi/pdf/10.1177/0963721416645512

Williams, V. B. (2007). *A chair for my mother*. Greenwillow Books.

6

Thought Processes

Common Tasks, Uncommon Thinking

Each of the five thought processes engages a variety of lower-order thinking (LOT), middle-order thinking (MOT), and higher-order thinking (HOT) skills, but using HOT skills—critical and creative thinking—at a high level will get the most accurate and effective results from these processes. The first two thought processes, analyses and evaluations/decisions, work with information that already exists and entail mostly critical thinking skills. Current and evolving information is used when finding solutions to problems and both critical and creative thinking skills are used in this process. The last two thought processes, plans/strategies and predictions/theories, forecast information that does not yet exist and entail mostly creative thinking skills. If thinking skills are mental tools, then thought processes are the mental structures being built with those tools.

The five thought processes overlap and are often combined. Many evaluations and decisions are based on prior analyses. Before the decision to buy a car is made, an analysis is done to narrow down the number of cars to test-drive, which is the final evaluation. The analysis consists of reviewing finances, exploring loan options, reading reviews, talking to knowledgeable friends, considering one's needs and desires related to the size and type of car, scanning ads for bargains, and more. The results

DOI: 10.4324/9781032683423-8

of an analysis may spur the development of a theory, and any theory requires an evaluation to determine if it is valid. Solutions to many problems require analyses, evaluations/decisions, and predictions as part of the process of solving problems.

All the processes are common activities that most people do every day, usually quickly and at a basic level. Grocery shopping illustrates this nicely. First, the trip is planned by making a shopping list and finding some coupons. A strategy is developed to avoid traffic and crowds: go early and take backroads. Once there, the problem of which breakfast cereal to buy, Wheatee Loops or Funky Flakes, has to be solved. So, the available data are analyzed—their ingredients, nutritional information, and price—resulting in an evaluation: Wheatee Loops is healthy but expensive (even with the coupon), and Funky Flakes is inexpensive but unhealthy. Based on this evaluation, a decision is made to buy Organic Fruity O's instead, which is healthier than Wheatee Loops and, being on sale for 20% off, is only slightly more expensive than Funky Flakes. Finally, a theory about purchasing breakfast cereal is developed: stop purchasing the same brands over and over and think outside the (cereal) box!

There are also endeavors in which the five thought processes are done slowly and deliberately, using multiple and complex analyses, evaluations, and decisions that require advanced HOT skills. In criminal trials, first a plan is agreed to by lawyers on both sides, including evaluating and deciding who will serve on the jury. During the trial, jurors analyze statements, arguments, evidence, and documents for their credibility, relevance, and significance for deciding the case. Then the jury deliberates by evaluating the merits of each side of the case in relation to the law that has been allegedly violated. Finally, they make a decision: guilty or not guilty. If found guilty, the judge and jurors go through these steps again to decide the terms of the penalty. And, unlike choosing a breakfast cereal, making an incorrect decision can be very consequential. A dangerous felon may be set free, or an innocent person fined or sent to prison.

Young learners are just developing the skills used in these thought processes and are gradually learning to engage in them more deliberately. Unfortunately, these thought processes are not typically part of the curriculum for young learners, and when they are, they tend to involve activities that engage only students' LOT and basic MOT skills. In this chapter, there are a number of activity ideas to give students practice using these thought processes with HOT skills. Teachers can expedite this by naming the thinking skills and describing the steps involved in the processes as they guide students through them and when they model them for students.

Analyses

Analyzing involves an in-depth and detailed examination of something—an event, concept, theory, opinion, book, article, speech, movie, artwork, and so on. While all of these can be appreciated and enjoyed as they are, an analysis can lead to new insights, a deeper appreciation, and greater enjoyment. But there are many other reasons to conduct an analysis. A film editor analyzes a movie to find and fix errors and determine how to cut it and piece it together for maximum impact and enjoyment. Later, the same movie may be analyzed by a reviewer to evaluate how well it was edited. A children's book may be the subject of an analysis by a librarian, teacher, or parent to decide whether to buy the book based on its appropriateness and instructional value for their young learners. An academic book may be analyzed by graduate students to find research that supports their theses.

Other names for analyses, or for types of analyses, include diagnostic and data analyses, of which there are many kinds, critiques (or critical analyses), critical reflections (or self-reflections), and investigations. All analyses require the use of various LOT, MOT, and HOT skills.

Students need practice analyzing so they can develop all the thinking skills used in this process. After reviewing the elements and plot of a recently read story with third graders, a teacher might say, "With a partner, analyze the girl's behaviors and actions in the story. If you think she is pretending not to know who the visitor was, why would she do that? If you think she really doesn't know who it was, what might the author be trying to tell us?" It is helpful for students to start developing the ability to analyze with HOT skills by setting the parameters of the analysis rather than leaving it open-ended. Here, the primary thinking skill that students would use is inferring (a critical thinking skill). Their answers and explanations will provide ample opportunities for teachers to help them sharpen their ability to infer.

Investigating and parsing are two types of analyses for specific purposes. They can both lead to new insights that may change the meaning of an event, concept, theory, and so on. An **investigation** is often done for the purpose of finding information to answer a question, expose wrong-doing, or solve a problem, mystery, or a crime. In the case of investigating a crime, it would be followed by an evaluation and a decision. Evaluations/decisions is the second of the five thought processes.

Parsing, as a thought process, is a less formal type of analysis than investigating. It is a critical examination of information to uncover errors, falsehoods, contradictions, or hidden messages or meanings. (It is not to be confused with other meanings of the term parsing, such as diagramming the grammatical structure of a sentence.) Parsing often starts from the premise that something is questionable or amiss about the information and that an analysis will likely reveal it. "That thing *does* look like a UFO, but we should parse it. Maybe it's a satellite or spy balloon. We can check the National Aeronautics and Space Administration (NASA) and National Oceanic and Atmospheric Administration (NOAA) websites."

A critical reflection is a form of self-analysis. Whereas reflecting uses LOT skills (remembering, recalling), a critical reflection uses HOT skills. Helping students examine their own actions, behaviors, efforts, accomplishments, and mistakes with clarity and objectivity is a great service. This can be integrated into lessons, especially during reviews and as part of informal and formative assessments. Questions can include the following: "What worked well, and what did not work well and why?"

"What did you learn that you did not know before?" "How will you use what you learned?" "If you did it again (or if it happened again), what would you do differently?" "What would have helped you to do better?" Teachers can sharpen students' ability to critically reflect by asking follow-up questions in response to their initial answers and helping them to use the grammar and vocabulary needed to express their thoughts and ideas more clearly and fully.

The following *Snap-sHOT* is an example of analyzing in the form of a critical reflection. The teacher is attempting to help his students to critically reflect at a basic level when responding to "why" questions. There are two examples of critical reflection in this *Snap-sHOT*: one illustrates the teacher's advanced level of analytical thinking, and the other students' nascent and emergent level of analytical thinking.

Snap-sHOT: WHY IT'S HARD TO EXPLAIN WHY

Near the end of the day, Mr. Ortiz asks his kindergarten students to think about everything they did during the day. He then invites several students to name the activity they liked the most (recalling, a LOT skill, and associating/differentiating a MOT skill). This is something that nearly all the students do well. However, when he asks the question "Why did you like the activity?," which requires critical thinking (deducing/inducing), there are a few brief, vague, and general responses after a long silence. Although Mr. Ortiz knows his students' ability to analyze is emergent, he wants to learn ways he can support and nurture its development.

Fortunately, Mr. Ortiz' analytical skills are strong. Later that day, he thinks about why his students have so much trouble expressing the reasons for their choices (shifting perspective, a critical thinking skill). While reading an article on critical reflection, he is reminded that it first requires the ability to carefully and thoroughly review what occurred. But he had required only that his students name the activity—"going to the gym" or "the movie about the planets." So, Mr. Ortiz generates the idea (a creative thinking skill) to ask them to describe the activity and then to scaffold their thinking, as necessary, by slowing it down and expanding it through questions and brief discussions. He will help them describe the activity in as much detail as they can and, for now, stop asking "why" questions. (This is an example of how helping students use LOT skills at more advanced levels can scaffold the development of MOT and HOT skills.) When he implements this idea, he discovers that he can often determine why a student likes an activity by the aspects of it they choose to highlight and from changes in their voice tone and body language (shifting perspective, again). After a few more weeks of practice, Mr. Ortiz helps them identify the elements of their descriptions that indicate why they liked it. They do a little better, but their responses are still brief and rudimentary and less detailed and expressive than their descriptions.

Analyzing is often more effective when including the perspectives of others, particularly people with expertise and strong critical-thinking skills. Because it is difficult to "see the picture from within the frame," critical self-evaluation has its limitations. When Mr. Ortiz shares his story with a more experienced friend and colleague, Lena, he invites her to observe him in his classroom. Lena is able to see that the students lack the vocabulary related to describing complex or nuanced feelings (or, perhaps, they do not know how to use the words in that context)—words such as *satisfied, improved, capable, understood, fulfilled, excited, fascinated, unique, proud,* and *meaningful.* She suggests that Mr. Ortiz give them "lead-ins" such as "I liked it because it gave me...," "I liked it because I was able to...," or "I liked it because it was the most...." She also suggests that Mr. Ortiz model vocabulary by always taking a turn at the end to describe the activity that he liked the best and explain why. After Mr. Ortiz employed these strategies over the course of two months, more than half the students were able to explain—clearly, logically, and in more than sufficient detail for a kindergartener—why they like something.

> Note: Mr. Ortiz is admirable in his persistence and should be proud of the results of his labors, even if he was assisted by the rapid maturity of language skills that occurs between the ages of five and six.

Evaluations/Decisions

Every person makes hundreds of decisions every day. Many of these are basic, quick, and almost automatic, requiring little or no intentional thinking. But many other decisions are made deliberately based on an evaluation. All evaluations entail making associations and distinctions (a MOT skill) between what is actual, necessary, or desired and a predetermined set of criteria. Here are three decisions that are increasingly consequential and entail ever-more-complex evaluations, each requiring more, and more abstract, criteria:

1. Deciding whether to wear waterproof boots or regular shoes by evaluating the weather conditions with just one criterion: raining or not raining.
2. Deciding whether to stay home or go to work based on a health status evaluation with three criteria and on an evaluation of financial status with one criterion:
   Health status: (a) Having or not having a fever, (b) having enough energy or not having enough energy to make it through the day, and (c) likely or not likely to be contagious.
   Financial status: Having or not having any remaining paid sick days.
3. Deciding whether to get certification to become a school administrator or to remain a teacher by evaluating professional goals and financial needs, each with three criteria:
   Goals: (a) Wanting to have greater influence on school policies and practices or risking becoming a bureaucrat with little influence to shape policy and practice while missing teaching, (b) concern about getting burned

out as a teacher and having no other career recourse or possibly missing direct contact with students and getting little satisfaction from administrative work, (c) being in a position to make important decisions that will have a positive impact on teachers and students or possibly having no choice but to make decisions that will negatively impact teachers and students, such as cutting positions or reducing budgets.

Financial needs: (a) Having more money or possibly finding out that the income increase does not compensate for the increase in working hours, responsibility, and stress, (b) being able to afford a nicer apartment and a newer car or accepting a lower standard of living and finding inexpensive ways to make life more comfortable, (c) having the possibility of earning substantially more money by moving up the administrative career ladder or advocating for higher wages for teachers and adding income by writing books or magazine articles, doing consulting, teaching a night class to adults, starting an online business, and so on.

There are many terms that have the same meaning as deciding or a very similar meaning. These include preferring, selecting, electing, picking, determining, choosing, and opting. But there is one commonly used term for deciding—judging—that is also a distinct type of decision. A judgment is a type of decision that is formal and deliberate. Judgments imply a value assessment as in assigning a grade to a paper, rating a movie on a scale from one to four stars, or reaching a verdict in a court case.

Whereas intentional decisions are rarely made without an initial evaluation, evaluations can stand alone. A decision does not have to follow an evaluation. Students' writing is commonly evaluated on five criteria: (1) correct spelling, (2) grammar, (3) punctuation, (4) thoughts or ideas are clearly expressed, and (5) it is logically organized. While this evaluation usually leads to a judgment represented by a score or letter grade, feedback about how and why their writing met or did not meet each of the five criteria would be more helpful to students than just a letter grade.

Evaluation criteria can be straightforward and easy to determine objectively: "It must be between three and five pages" or "It has to have at least five paragraphs." They can also be complex, subjective, and abstract: "The idea has to be realistic" or "The answer must be thorough." To make these criteria work as the basis for an evaluation, the terms must first be assigned with their own criteria (aka sub-criteria) that clearly define the differences between unrealistic ideas and realistic ideas and between sparse answers and thorough answers.

A sound decision depends on a thorough and accurate evaluation. A thorough and an accurate evaluation depends on a complete and germane set of criteria. This is not easy for many reasons. Thinking errors, poor logical and critical thinking skills, lack of access to information, time constraints, limited resources, and many other obstacles can get in the way. The following scenario illustrates these issues.

Snap-sHOT: WHY CAN'T JORDAN READ?

Jordan reads slowly and sounds out some longer words. This is a fair and objective analysis of Jordan's reading skills, and on this basis, Jordan's teacher decides to put Jordan on the "low-reader" list for remedial instruction. This decision comes from the teacher's informal evaluation, weighing Jordan's reading ability against the criteria of what is typical and expected of students at Jordan's age and grade-level. As a young first grader, Jordan would be considered a good reader, but as a third grader, the teacher feels justified in this judgment, in part to ensure that Jordan will get much-needed extra help. This decision leads to a planned course of action: make a referral to the reading specialist.

However, a more thorough evaluation with more criteria would have revealed that Jordan reads slowly and with difficulty *and* has weak and blurry eyesight *and* has frequent ear infections. Therefore, a better decision would have been to schedule a multi-disciplinary team meeting with the reading specialist and the school nurse, who can connect the family to an audiologist, an ophthalmologist, and funds for eyeglasses.

Even when the results of an evaluation are complete and accurate, poor decisions are still made because the evaluation results are ignored, rejected, passed on, or deemed too difficult to act on. Too often, students like Jordan get help only with reading, although their vision problems and a potential hearing loss are known. Why? Perhaps the school has no reading specialist or school nurse, or no one takes responsibility to communicate with parents, or the school policy is that students' health issues are the obligation solely of the family. The decision is based on what is available and possible, not what is required or necessary. Although this is understandable, it is much like the man who is looking for his lost car key beneath the streetlamp. When a passerby asks where he might have dropped it, the man replies: "Over there where my car is parked, but this is where the light is!"

Even a decision based on the most careful and thorough evaluation should be made with the understanding that it might be wrong and one or many mid-course corrections may be needed. Making effective mid-course corrections requires creative thinking, particularly the ability to improvise.

Developing Students' Abilities to Evaluate

One way to support students' development of the thinking skills needed to evaluate effectively is to ask for their opinions about books that they read or that are read to them, a film or video that the class has watched, significant events, or shared experiences such as field trips. This way they will learn that there are many types of evaluations and that people can make vastly different evaluations of the same thing. When students give their opinions, teachers have the opportunity to sharpen their thinking skills by expanding their vocabularies and helping them to back up their opinions with facts and specific examples and to be clear and succinct. When teachers regularly model evaluating by giving their opinions (among other ways), students understand its purpose and value, hear the words and expressions associated with evaluating, and learn the types of thinking skills used to evaluate. Subjects that teachers can use to demonstrate evaluating that would interest young learners include popular family movies or television shows, a family trip along with photos and videos, and a recent large purchase such as a house or car. Teachers should model evaluating separately from students' evaluating activities so students will not be tempted to copy the teacher's ideas or feel too intimidated to express their own opinions.

Although evaluating is a common activity in schools, it is primarily done by teachers to students, not by students on themselves or other students. It is not often included as a student goal, addressed in curricula, or assessed, particularly for young learners. But such learners need many opportunities to practice developing evaluation criteria and applying them fairly and objectively. One effective way to do this is for students to evaluate each other's work in addition to their own. The following *Cognitivity* offers a method for peer evaluations that minimizes competitiveness and all but eliminates negative criticism and hurt feelings. The activity described below was preceded by two similar evaluation activities over the course of a month. Each activity was a little more complex than the previous one.

COGNITIVITY: WHAT MAKES A GOOD MAP?

As part of a project on geography and cartography, first-grade students work in five small groups to make a map of the school. Before they begin, the teacher facilitates a class discussion to develop a few criteria for making a good map. They come up with two categories of criteria: (1) Is it accurate? (2) Is it easy to read and follow? They brainstorm ideas for the sub-criteria that define accuracy and that make it easy to read and follow. Based on these ideas, the teacher develops a checklist that all students will complete to evaluate each of the maps made by the other groups. So, every student will get four checklists to complete (Figure 6.1).

After Group #1 presents their map to the rest of the class, the students in the other groups fill out the evaluation form. They check the box if they believe the map met each of the criteria. (When students become adept at this, the teacher adds a three-scale evaluation system in which students rate each criterion as (1) not met, (2) partially met, or (3) completely met.)

Map Evaluation Form

Group: 1   2   3   4   5   (circle the group number that you are evaluating)

Is the map accurate?

☐ Things are where they are supposed to be.

☐ Nothing major is left out.

☐ Nothing is on the map that should not be on the map.

☐ **The map is accurate.**

Is the map easy to read and follow?

☐ Things on the map are neatly drawn.

☐ The shapes of things on the map have similar shapes as the real things.

☐ Real things that are larger than smaller things are the same way on the map.

☐ **The map is easy to read and follow.**

FIGURE 6.1 Map Evaluation Form.

Graphic by Gwendolyn Rodriquez.

Following the presentations and evaluations from every group, the teacher collects the evaluation forms and shares the results with each group. The teacher helps each group figure out what they could do to improve their maps based on the evaluation results. The next day, the groups are given the opportunity to redraw their maps, and the presentation and evaluation process is repeated.

To adapt this activity for other grades, kindergartners can make a map of the classroom, second graders can make a map of the neighborhood that surrounds the school, and third graders can make a map of the broader community around the school. More criteria and sub-criteria, such as using symbols and adding a box at the bottom of the map that defines the symbols, can be added for second and third graders. Of course, the format of this evaluation process can be adapted to evaluate many other activities from writing assignments to group presentations.

Developing Students' Abilities to Decide

An effective way to develop students' decision-making skills is by offering many different kinds of choices many times a day. This provides the opportunities that young learners need to know how to make considered choices rather than arbitrary, instinctive, or reactive ones. Knowing why one is making a particular choice and having the skills to make it thoughtfully, but without too much deliberation, are important in life and have many potential benefits. Many students will need guidance from teachers to use HOT skills effectively when making choices, particularly at first and for younger students. Usually, just carefully worded questions are all that is needed. Using HOT skills when choosing makes it a more deliberate and intentional choice and can provide new insights, understanding, and appreciation in the process.

Giving students choices should be the default mode for assignments, daily routines, and activities. When students explain their choices, teachers can assess their ability to make decisions (a thought process) and can provide help as needed. Rather than all students reading the same book, they can be given a choice between reading either a fiction or a nonfiction book, both of which have been selected by the teacher to ensure they are appropriate and engaging. For science, students can choose between investigating the causes and consequences of earthquakes, hurricanes, or volcanoes. For social studies, every student can choose a different country about which they will all report on the typical street games played by children in that country and, for older students, what the choice of games says about the culture of that country. Younger students are given fewer and more limited choices than older students, and all choices are age-appropriate and feasible. Students are continuously challenged to advance their current levels of thinking in regard to choosing: "Are there any other options?" "Do you want to think about it a little longer?" "Do you need more information before you can make a choice?"

There are many naturally occurring opportunities to offer choices. For example, a second-grade teacher offers her class the option of going outside for recess even though it's raining lightly, playing in the gym, or staying in the classroom to work on projects or read independently. The teacher has the students form three groups based on their preferences and then makes a three-column chart, one for each option. Each group gets a chance to say why their choice is better than the other choices, and the teacher writes a few key words in each column to capture their ideas. In the process, the teacher scaffolds students' thinking skills and, at the end, states one additional pro and con for each choice to model more advanced generative thinking. Finally, the teacher brings the class back into one group, summarizes the information on the chart, and facilitates a vote.

Developing group decision-making skills is also important. Here is a *Cognitivity* designed specifically for young learners to make a group decision by voting. It is an extension of the previous *Cognitivity*, *What Makes a Good Map?*

COGNITIVITY: MAY THE BEST MAP WIN

While still in their small groups, one or two students from each group take a turn to briefly make the case for why their map is the best. For some students, the teacher may need to help them focus on the criteria they developed earlier in the mapmaking process. Then each group stands in turn. While one group is standing, all the other students who are sitting down either vote for that group's map by raising their hands or hold their vote for another group. This process ensures that students cannot vote for their own map. To help them avoid voting more than once, they put a sticky dot on the palms of their hands immediately after they vote. The teacher can readily see if a student tries to vote twice (accidentally, of course). The teacher tallies the votes, and the winning group receives appreciation and applause. Then a few willing students who are not in the winning group but voted for it are invited to say why it is a good map. Students in the winning group respond to questions about their process and their map. The map is posted on the wall or included in a documentation display about cartography and/or decision making.

For groups of students for whom this voting process is too difficult, the discussions can be curtailed, teacher-led, or eliminated. Also, the strategy for avoiding voting more than once can be made more concrete, if necessary, by having students fold their arms or hold a book after they vote.

Decisions made as a whole class or by groups of students are very valuable exercises but can be time-consuming. So, teachers need to give individual students opportunities to make choices for the group. A turn-taking chart ensures that all students get the same number of opportunities to make a choice. To create the chart, list all students' names vertically on a sheet of paper and attach it to a clipboard. Move a small black binder clip down the list of names to determine who will be next to have a turn to choose for the group. When the last student on the list has had a turn, move the binder clip back to the top. If a student is absent, put a small red binder clip next to the name and move the black one down to the next name. This serves as a reminder to give the student a turn on the first day back at school.

Making good decisions is key to success in school and life. For middle and high school students, on any given day, deciding whether, when, and for how long to play a video game, practice the piano, play basketball, study, do homework, watch a movie, or read a book may not feel consequential, but the impact of these daily decisions made over a period of months and years *will* be significant. Making good decisions as a student sets the stage for making good decisions later in life as adults, including

Thought Processes ◆ 113

very consequential ones such as deciding which career to pursue, where to live, and who will be your spouse or life partner. Giving young learners many opportunities to make acceptable, age-appropriate decisions is a great way to start developing their decision-making skills.

Solutions/Innovations

Solutions

Finding solutions to problems, or problem-solving, is another example of a common thought process that can happen quickly with relatively simple problems or over a long period of time with complex problems. It is also another example of a thought process that, though common, is often done poorly. Learning how to find good solutions and to innovate where possible is necessary because there are so many ways to come up with ineffective or counter-productive solutions: not taking enough time or putting in enough effort, not getting sufficient information or the right information about the problem, accepting a short-term temporary solution, down-playing the seriousness of the problem, assuming things will work out well eventually (aka optimism bias), addressing the effects of the problem rather than the causes of the problem, solving just one part of the problem rather than the whole problem, and many more. The following section explains problem-solving in general and is followed in turn by a section on innovation, a particular type of solution.

For problems of any type—simple or complex, concrete or abstract—finding solutions involves essentially the same set of thinking skills in the same sequence.

◆ Identify the problem (a LOT skill) and find out as much as possible about the context and nature of the problem and about possible cause(s). This entails the HOT skills of asking insightful questions (querying), deducing, and inducing, and it may also involve inferring. Complex problems may require conducting an analysis of this information (another thought process) before moving on to the next step.

114 ◆ Thinking about Thinking

- ◆ Evaluate the most likely cause(s) of the problem and decide on which to address (evaluations/decisions thinking process).
- ◆ Generate ideas of possible solutions (a thought process).
- ◆ Determine the criteria for what constitutes a good solution. For example, it must be a long-term permanent solution, and it cannot cost too much or take too much time (characterize, a logical thinking MOT skill).
- ◆ Decide on a solution based on how well it meets the criteria (the thought process of evaluating/deciding again).
- ◆ If the problem is solved, determine if the solution could be applied (with modifications if needed) to prevent or solve similar problems in the future (reframing, a HOT skill). If the problem is only partially solved, not solved, or made worse, then restart this process.

These steps constitute a broad and generic description of the problem-solving process. Each of the six steps can be broken down into smaller tasks. Some of these steps may be quite difficult and time-consuming, particularly the first step, but getting accurate and complete information about the problem is critically important. History is replete with examples of attempted solutions that failed, or made the problem worse, because they were based on faulty or incomplete information. In 14th-century Europe, the bubonic plague, which killed millions of people, was blamed on so-called "witches." Thousands of women accused of witchcraft were burned to death along with their cats. As the actual cause of the plague was a bacteria transmitted by fleas that live on rats, reducing the cat population made the problem worse. In the late 1950s, Chairman Mao of China addressed the problem of a grain shortage by having millions of sparrows killed. Sparrows were not eating the grain, but they were eating locusts. The rapid expansion of the locust population greatly exacerbated the grain shortage.

For technical support specialists, mediators, consultants, counselors, therapists, health-care professionals of every kind, and many others, finding solutions to problems is their main job. The *Snap-sHOT*, *Reframing a Parent/School Conflict* (on page 86), tells the story of a mediator who uses the HOT skill of reframing to solve a tricky problem that had the potential to escalate into a contracted legal battle. The mediator was able to get each side to see the problem from the other side's point of view (shifting perspective, a HOT skill). Conflict resolution is a particular type of problem-solving. It often entails using another HOT skill, improvising, to de-escalate emotions, keep the parties engaged, and move the process along in a positive direction. As conflicts among students are common, there are many opportunities for teachers to develop students' problem-solving skills in this area. Rather than viewing conflicts as a distraction or as a problem that students need to solve themselves, teachers can use them as teaching and learning opportunities.

Engaging in problem-solving often and with many different types of problems is a key teaching strategy for developing HOT skills because so many different thinking skills are used. Teachers can pose problems that can be solved relatively quickly: "How can we fairly choose who will go first?" Or they can pose problems that are more complex: "What can we do to welcome and comfort the new families and children who are coming here to escape the war in their home country?"

Innovations

Innovating is a process in which a problem is solved by developing something new or unique or by doing things a new way. An innovative solution implies that the problem was solved thoroughly and successfully by addressing the root causes of the problem. In some cases, innovations are widely adopted, particularly technological innovations ranging from cars to washing machines to laptop computers. All creative thinking skills are used in this process, particularly reframing.

Many innovations are possible because of breakthroughs in technology, but there have been many important innovations as the result of creative thinking. In 1982, computer scientist Scott Fahlman was frustrated that he could not communicate sarcasm or humor in the texts he posted to the message board on his university's network. So, to solve this problem, he invented the emoticon. :-)

So many solutions to address the problem of poverty have been tried and have failed. One innovative solution that has not been tried, until recently, is giving money directly to poor people. The assumption has been that they would spend it unwisely and *not* use it to pay off debts, purchase higher-quality food, save it, or invest it in a business or for furthering their education. But the research results from numerous pilot programs that give money directly to poor people show that these assumptions are not correct. Whether run by a state or federal agency or a non-profit organization in the U.S., the U.K. or Africa, this appears to be a successful innovation that could finally make a significant impact on reducing poverty (Acs & Dehry, 2020).

Some innovations solve problems most people did not know they had. Needing to heat food in seconds rather than minutes was not a problem many people lost sleep over, but microwave ovens solved it anyway. For nearly all of human history, the problem of not being able to watch hundreds of cat videos anywhere in the world on a wireless device that is also a telephone did not make life unbearable for most people. But, for those people who did find the problem unbearable, the solution (and the great relief it must bring) is now in their hands!

It is, of course, unrealistic to expect young students to be able to innovate, something that few adults can do. But with good problem-solving skills as a foundation, perhaps more students will grow up to be more innovate thinkers. Two activities in the previous chapter that promote imaginative and generative thinking also help to develop the creative problem-solving skills used to innovate: the *Cognitivity, Inventors Inventing Inventions* (on page 83) and the *ThinkinGroups, Shape Shifting* (on page 85).

Plans/Strategies

Planning is a basic form of strategizing, and strategizing is a more intentional and complex form of planning. Strategizing also implies planning to achieve a specific outcome or in response to the actions of another person. Planning uses more LOT skills,

Thought Processes ◆ 117

such as organizing and identifying, and more logical-thinking MOT skills, such as sequencing to prioritize tasks, than conceptual HOT skills. Strategizing uses more HOT skills, such as inferring and shifting perspective, than LOT or MOT skills.

Plans

Everyone plans often and regularly, though sometimes not as effectively as they could for the task at hand. While it's almost always a mistake to go to the supermarket without a shopping list, only 44 percent of shoppers bring one (Food Marketing Institute, 2016). Planning includes both students' and teachers' planning. Students learn a great deal when teachers think aloud about their planning and invite them to participate. This can be done informally as well as formally. When planning a field trip, for example, teachers can solicit students' ideas and invite their feedback throughout the planning process, which may happen over the course of several days. Planning something complex, like a field trip, involves using several MOT and HOT skills: generating ideas for where to go and weighing the options using associate/differentiate (A/D) thinking, listing the tasks chronologically (from booking the bus to follow-up activities for the day after the field trip), using sequential thinking, and calculating the costs. Naming the thinking skills when planning with students helps them learn what they are and how they are used. "Let's do some higher-order thinking and generate even more ideas. Let's sequence some of the things we need to do before the trip next month. What do we need to do first?"

Informal opportunities to explain plans often occur naturally and spontaneously. A kindergarten teacher might say, "Yesterday, we planned to go for a walk to the park today, but it is raining hard and is very windy. I can think of three options: we can go anyway and get wet, we can cancel the walk, or we can do activities in the gym. Can anyone think of another option? Let's evaluate the options and make a group decision about what to do."

Teachers of older students can support and help sharpen their emergent abilities to self-plan. They can ask their students questions like "How do you plan to finish the project by Friday? Make a schedule. Write down the tasks you will do each day until the project is finished. Track your progress by putting a check mark next to each task when it is completed. What might cause your plan to change? How will you amend your plan in response?"

Strategies

Strategies are intentional plans to achieve a specific goal. They attempt to predict obstacles that may get in the way of reaching the goal and propose ways to overcome them. Strategies can be carefully developed, reviewed, revised, and amended. Some are long-term and have many steps, like a novice runner's strategic plan to eventually win a marathon. But they can also be short-term and have just a few steps, like a strategy to ensure that a co-worker will not know about their surprise retirement party.

Strategizing entails advanced levels of the LOT skill of identifying; the MOT skills of sequencing and connecting causes and effects; the HOT skills of inferring, imagining, and generating; and the thinking processes of evaluating/deciding and predicting. When a strategy is in progress, the HOT skill of improvising may be needed to respond effectively to an unexpected glitch in the plan.

A good example of strategizing is how President Lyndon Johnson, a master political strategist, persuaded Congress to authorize and fund the Head Start program in 1964. Shortly after he became president (after John F. Kennedy was assassinated), he declared a War on Poverty, and Head Start was a key program for achieving that goal. It was just one part of a large antipoverty bill that funded many new programs, including Volunteers in Service to America (VISTA). In those days, politicians from either party would face criticism at home for opposing a program for young children from poor families. Unlike their parents, these children were widely viewed as the "deserving poor" because they were in circumstances beyond their control. Johnson knew this would make it difficult for many members of Congress to vote against the bill, although most opposed it. One strategic move was to keep the Head Start program relatively modest.

It started as an eight-week, half-day summer program and targeted just the poorest counties in each state. This kept the initial funding level low enough to deflect opposition because of its cost. The First Lady, Lady Bird Johnson, who was a persuasive speaker but soft-spoken and genteel, took the leading role in advocating for passing Head Start legislation. She provided a strategically smart counterpoint to her husband's gruffness and the hard-nosed way he lobbied members of Congress. And these are just some of the strategies that President Johnson used to make Head Start a reality.

The essence of strategizing in adversarial or competitive situations is to think several steps ahead of one's opponent. President Johnson was able to determine what members of Congress were thinking and feeling (infer, shift perspective) to predict the opposing arguments (induce) as well as determine what they would likely support. He then used that information to propose a program, Head Start, that would be difficult for them to oppose and included it in a bill with programs that many lawmakers would have otherwise opposed.

Can young learners strategize? Yes, and they do it more often than adults realize. However, most have difficulty developing a strategy with more than two or three steps, and they tend to do it reactively more than proactively. For example, six-year-old Luca develops a strategy for winning over a group of classmates who had rebuffed him on the playground. The next day, he brings to school a toy that he believes those classmates will want to play with. He chooses a toy car that is small enough to fit in his pocket so it will be inconspicuous until recess. While Luca is able to devise a strategy with two parts, he is unable to think far enough ahead to consider other options in case the toy is lost or is not attractive to his classmates. For most children, it is easier to strategize in the social or interpersonal realm than in other realms, including school and academics.

Strategies are unique thought processes. While Luca's social strategies are far from sophisticated or thorough, and his academic strategies are almost non-existent, he is able to strategize at a high level when playing his favorite video games and when playing soccer, as a budding star striker. How is this possible?

Unlike other thought processes and most thinking skills, the ability to strategize is not readily transferrable across activities, nor does it correlate with general cognitive abilities or academic achievement (Sala & Gobet, 2017). A person who is very good at one "strategy" activity, such as playing chess, is not automatically good at another "strategy" activity, such as playing poker or checkers or getting a bill passed in Congress against all odds! The word "strategy" is intentionally in quotes because many games and activities that *seem* to center on strategizing—some even purport to *teach* strategizing—actually involve little or no strategizing. Although chess was likely invented in India to teach war strategies (Kulke & Rothermund, 2010), changes to the game over time moved it away from that purpose. And in practice, the greatest chess players mostly rely on memorization/recall (a LOT skill), sequencing/patterning, and calculating (MOT skills). They tend *not* to approach a game with a comprehensive strategy nor improvise much during the game. Instead, they use a known sequence of chess moves that have proven to be successful previously in similar circumstances (Blanch, 2022; Giffens, 2013). Nevertheless, chess is strongly associated with high levels of strategic thinking: *"She outsmarted the competition like a chess master."* Essays on business and education internet blogs tout the great benefits of chess—usually without any evidence—for academic and business success because it develops a wide range of HOT skills and thought processes, especially strategic thinking. In their review of research, Sala and Gobet (2017) conclude that while "smarter people are more likely to be stronger chess players...there is little evidence that chess...instruction makes people smarter. Training (in) chess...capacity does not reliably enhance any skill beyond the skill (it) trains."

Rote strategizing, a form of strategizing, is often driven by strong basic needs. Hunger and survival spur animals of many species to strategize in ways that appear to be highly sophisticated. Popular videos on the internet show raccoons helping each other breach a wall, humpback whales working together to trap a school of herrings inside a net of bubbles, and crocodiles hiding silently and motionlessly under branches and twigs waiting for unsuspecting birds to alight. These are sets of behaviors that species have developed and honed over long periods of time, mostly serendipitously through trial and error. Some have become instinctual, and some are behaviors that each new generation of young animals learns from adults. Technically, rote strategizing *is* a form of strategizing because it involves intentionality to achieve a specific goal, planning, the use of several sequential and related tactics, and thinking dispositions such as patience, persistence, and attentiveness. (For more information about thinking dispositions, see Chapter 7 on pages 137–141.) But from an animal's perspective, it is a routine rather than a thought process. If the crocodile's hiding routine fails to provide lunch, it may try a completely different routine (if it has one) or the same routine again later. For people, there is a degree of rote strategizing in activities such as fishing, sailing, gardening, putting together furniture from a flatpack, and playing certain boardgames. Though not usually driven by strong basic needs, these activities involve planning, use similar established and predetermined procedures each time to achieve a specific goal, and involve thinking dispositions such as patience.

Because strategizing is highly context- and subject-dependent, students need to learn strategies specific to countering disinformation and deceptions, avoiding thinking errors, and achieving academic success. For academic success, they include generic test-taking strategies applicable to any test; reading, studying, and note-taking strategies applicable to any subject or text; and time management/organizing strategies related to schoolwork in school and at home. Students will be able to strategize academically, to the best of their abilities, if teachers provide the tools for it, offer many opportunities to practice it, expect it, and closely guide its development.

Predictions/Theories

Predictions and theories both make determinations of "what might be" based on existing information. This is also called abductive thinking. Estimations, speculations, prognoses, postulations, and hypotheses are all types of predictions. Predicting takes existing information and looks ahead to what is likely to be or to happen based on that information. Theorizing starts with an existing result and tries to determine what leads to or explains it. Predictions tend to deal with more concrete information and theories with more abstract information. The voracity of a prediction is determined by the *actual* result of the prediction. If the result will not be known—perhaps because it will happen far off in the future or because it is unknowable by nature—it is speculation. The voracity of a theory is determined by rigorous research investigations to test the strength and nature of the relationship between the proposed reasons and the result being studied. Some theories have been validated definitively such as the Heliocentric Theory posited by Copernicus in 1543 that the sun was stationary and the earth and other bodies revolve around it. Other theories remain tentative because they are difficult to validate, such as the Big Bang Theory of the origin of the universe. However, once a theory is thoroughly validated, it is no longer a theory but a fact or a law of nature. Nevertheless, it is not uncommon for new information to reveal that a proven theory, while still true, is not the only or complete explanation. The invention of the telescope revealed that the solar system revolves around the sun, not the entire universe (as Copernicus believed).

Predictions

Estimating (a type of predicting) the amount of time it will take to prepare for parent conferences entails remembering how much time it has taken in the past (a LOT skill). In addition, the number of current students must be considered (quantifying, a LOT skill), and the most important information to discuss needs to be determined (characterizing and A/D thinking, MOT skills). Then the students who are struggling must be identified (a LOT skill) because it will require more time to plan effective ways to enlist parents as partners in helping those students. Making plans is another thought process involving another set of thinking skills, which, to do well, can be quite time-consuming. Finally, a prediction of how much time it will take to prepare for parent conferences can be made: too much!

Practicing to estimate is a great starting point to help young learners to develop the ability to make accurate predictions. This can be done quickly and often throughout the day. How many days are left before spring break? How much time will it take to finish the book? How many pages are in the book? How tall is the school building? How long is the hallway? What is the temperature outside now? How many students are there in total in all three second-grade classes? How many books are there in the class library? In the school library? What year was the school built? What is your teacher's age? (This last one is optional!) Students can also predict what will happen next in a story, who will win a contest, the date it will snow for the first time (or if it will snow at all), and what would get the most votes if all the students in the class voted for their favorite movie, book, TV show, game, sport, activity, person, and school subject. Students need practice in making both long- and short-term estimates. Students should write down their estimates so they cannot change or forget them. After, teachers should have a short debriefing with students on the different ways they made their estimates or predictions. If most students are way off on a particular estimate or prediction, teachers can discuss the reasons for this and potential ways they could have made their estimates more accurate.

Hypotheses typically involve more abstract information than other types of predictions. They predict that a specific action or concept will have a particular result. They are often aspirational, made in the hope that they will prove to be true. To determine if they are true, hypotheses, like theories, need to be tested using sound research methods. Embedded in the premise of this book are several hypotheses. Four of them are listed below, each one more complex and more difficult to prove than the previous, in part because the desired results are increasingly further from the initial actions:

- ◆ Readers of this book will learn why and how to teach HOT skills.
- ◆ Teachers will accurately and effectively incorporate ideas from this book into their daily lessons.

- ◆ Teaching HOT skills will result in a significantly higher percentage of students using HOT skills and using more types of HOT skills than a similar group of students who did not receive instruction in HOT.
- ◆ Students who gain and use HOT skills in the early grades will have more academic and life success than if they had not gained or used HOT skills.

Hypotheses can be based on theories or contribute to the development of new theories, or the refinement of existing theories. The above hypotheses reflect theories of pedagogy that assert the efficacy of early learning. They also are in direct response to the theory that educational practices do not keep up with social, cultural, and demographic changes in societies. If these hypotheses were rigorously tested, the results would impact theories of early learning and theories about the relationship between school and society.

Theories

Some theories start with an observation and a question. In the following example, the question was not fully answered for many years. In 1666, Sir Isaac Newton observed an apple fall from a tree and questioned why it fell straight down and not sideways or up. Although the concept of gravity was well established by 1666, Newton defined it as a force and developed the theory that it was a *universal* force acting on and among all objects, even on earth itself. Based on this theory, he hypothesized (correctly) that gravity was the force that kept the moon in orbit around the earth. Although he could describe gravity and its effects accurately and in great detail, he was concerned that he could not explain why or how it worked. In his day, the tools and means did not yet exist to even formulate a hypothesis about the mechanics of gravity. Several centuries would have to elapse for this to happen. In 1905, Albert Einstein completed Newton's theory of gravity, determining mathematically that gravity is caused by a warping of space and time. He called this a General Theory of Relativity. More recently, multiple tests using advanced telescope and computer technologies have confirmed that the theory was correct and, as of 2024, it has not been disproven or amended.

Both Newton's and Einstein's theories involved creative thinking, as gravity is not tangible or visible and is evident only from its impact. Considering that Newton did not know what created gravity, his theory that gravity is universal reflects his high level of creative thinking. Einstein's creative thinking is even more extraordinary because his theory that explains gravity is counterintuitive and involves forces that are even more abstract, complex, and less evident than gravity itself.

Other theories are more uncertain and have changed numerous times. Many of these theories (no surprise here) deal with human development, behavior, and learning. Often these theories start with tangible or known phenomena and attempt to determine their cause or causes. The following example explores theories for why there are generational differences in behaviors and beliefs.

Researchers generally agree that there are clear, quantifiable generational differences among Americans, starting with the Silent Generation (born 1925–1945) through Generation Z (born 1997–2012) (Twenge, 2023). And, undoubtedly, there will also be differences between Generation Z and Generation Alpha (born 2013–2028). For many years, the prevailing theory has been that generational differences are the result of life experiences unique to each generation. The Silent Generation experienced the Great Depression, World War II, the birth of the Atomic Age, the Korean War, and the Cold War. The following generation, Baby Boomers (1946–1964), experienced post-war prosperity, the Vietnam War, multiple assassinations of leaders, the Civil Rights Movement, the height of the Cold War and the end of it, the Women's Movement, "The Pill," and the era of "Sex, Drugs, and Rock and Roll." As plausible as this theory seems, a new theory has emerged, based on mountains of data and sophisticated statistical analyses. This theory posits that advances in technology are the leading cause of generational differences (Twenge, 2023). According to this theory, what has made it possible and sensible for Millennials to delay careers and marriage and to have small families are all the labor-saving home appliances, conveniences like cell phones and ATMs, time-savers like online shopping and virtual meetings, and technology that prolongs life and makes life safer. These include smoke detectors, airbags in cars, and health advances like new medications, vaccines, diagnostic machines, and surgical procedures.

Jean M. Twenge, who developed this theory, used HOT—questioning assumptions, inducing, and reframing among others—to upend current widely- and long-held beliefs about generational differences. She let the data inform the theory rather than look for data that would support a theory she had already developed. Nevertheless, another researcher could come up with a different theory after analyzing the same data. Over time, new information and new analytical methods will develop that will alter many current theories about human behavior.

Not everything that is called a theory is a theory. Conspiracy theories are lies not theories, and actual conspiracies are crimes. The "theory" of evolution and "atomic theory" are proven laws of nature that began as theories. There are also many examples where activities and behaviors are consistent with a particular theory, but the theory is unstated, and the people involved are unaware of the theory. For example, teachers who use rewards and punishments as a classroom management strategy may not know that it reflects a theory of human behavior and learning called Behaviorism.

In education, there are many theories about effective teaching and learning. Each reflects a view of human development and the purpose of education that ranges from learning to follow rules and accepting the status quo (Behavioral Theory) at one end of the continuum to learning to think independently and questioning the status quo (Humanistic Theory) at the other end. The proponents of each theory cite research evidence that supports their theory. However, in many cases, they have not developed their theories from all the available information about student learning but have "cherry-picked" only the information that supports the theory to which they already subscribe. In this case, they are using not theoretical thinking but LOT skills like identifying and organizing, and they are succumbing to a common thinking error called *confirmation bias*.

It is important that students eventually have some ability to theorize in an intellectually rigorous way. This may not be possible until young students are older, but teachers can lay the foundation by being explicit about what a theory is and what it means to theorize and by encouraging nascent theorizing. Theorizing can be promoted by pointing out the theories behind actions and ideas. Another method is to have guided discussions with students from questions that do not have definitive answers and then to gradually increase the complexity of the topics, such as the following:

"Why do people have pets?"
"What does it mean to be smart?"
"What does it mean to be a good person?"
"What makes something fair or unfair?"
"What is friendship and what makes for a good friend?"
"What is happiness and how do you get and keep it?"
"What can children do that adults cannot and why?"
"What do you want the world to be like when you grow up, and what should be there that isn't here now or should not be there that is here now?"

The *ThinkinGroups* described below promotes theorizing, requires no materials, and can easily be adapted for a broad range of abilities.

ThinkinGroups: FAMILY GROUPS

The teacher first explains the concept of families of things, starting with human families, and represents it graphically (a logical thinking skill) with a flowchart as illustrated in the top part of Figure 6.2. Then she explains that the term *family groups* can be used to describe types of animals, such as insects, fish, and birds. With the students' input, she develops a Bird Family chart, similar to the one shown in the lower part of Figure 6.2.

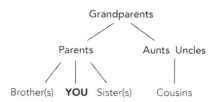

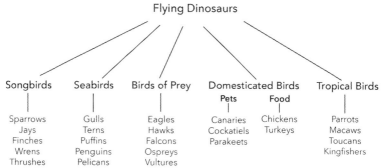

FIGURE 6.2 Family Groups.

Graphic by Gwendolyn Rodriguez.

The teacher then lists types of fish and sea mammals while the students try to identify the family groups to which they belong. She tells them that, in addition to animals, other things that are related can be in the same family group or category, and she challenges the students to name the family group for a set of items. For kindergartners, at first the items might be shirts, pants, dresses, hats, shoes, and so on. And, of course, the family group is "clothing" or "things that people wear." Later, they can be more challenging, such as "things that are green," "forest animals," or "things people eat for breakfast." For first graders, the family groups can include "things you can see at a construction site," "things that are loud," and "things that open and close." For second graders, family groups might be "things that melt," "things that smell good (or smell bad)," and "things that come in pairs." For third graders, "things that are found below the surface of the earth," "characters in books by Roald Dahl," "organs of the body," and "things that are timed."

As students become adept at the game, the categories can become more challenging to promote more advanced levels of theorizing, such as "things that people can't live without," "things that are ancient," "things that are microscopic," "excuses," and "parts of a piano." The last one is difficult because its main components are strings, keys, hammers, and pedals.

Another type of challenge is to include a mix of conceptual and tangible items in the list. "Things that you cannot hear" might include the voice of a giraffe, a baby crying in another city, silence, a television show with the volume on mute, and what someone is thinking. Curriculum content can be used to create family groups, such as "math terms," "animals that hatch from eggs," "names of seas and oceans," "parts of a plant," "languages," and "famous architectural structures." Of course, students can think up family groups and create lists to challenge their classmates.

Family Groups can also be played in the form of a game show, with teams that compete over time. Points can be won in several ways, such as determining the category before the other teams do, creating lists of items that stump other teams but are accurate, or some combination of the two.

Conclusion

When a range of critical and creative HOT skills are used to analyze, evaluate, make decisions, find solutions, develop plans, devise strategies, predict, and theorize, the processes are more thorough and the outcomes more effective and impactful. And when those HOT skills are sharp, the outcomes will be optimal. The five thought processes encompass most types of thinking that every person does daily. They are common but important, and too often they are not done effectively because of weak logical thinking skills and a lack of HOT skills.

Following are five ways to ensure that all thought processes are taught effectively and include HOT:

- ♦ The purpose of the process is clear and authentic. An analysis that is trivial or just an empty academic exercise does not challenge students to use HOT skills to their full potential, or at all, and therefore does not promote their development.
- ♦ While perfection may be the enemy of good, conventional is the enemy of excellence. Teachers cannot expect students to challenge themselves with HOT and strive for excellence if the problems they are asked to solve and the decisions they are asked to make are trivial or mundane. These processes are teaching opportunities. Mistakes are not problems; they are learning opportunities.
- ♦ The information used in thought processes is relevant, unbiased, complete, and accurate. The best way to help a student who is struggling with math depends on the cause of the problem. Is it due to a learning disability, uncorrected poor vision, difficulty concentrating, lack of opportunities to practice, not being developmentally ready, or some combination of factors?
- ♦ Offering many opportunities for students to engage in all five thought processes in a wide variety of contexts and for various purposes ensures that students will internalize them and use them effectively. Increasing the level of challenge of the processes gradually over time ensures that

Thought Processes ◆ 131

students will learn the benefits of using HOT skills to maximize the accuracy and impact of the results of the processes.

◆ Teachers examine and assess their own thought processes, know their areas of strength and weakness, and try to improve them as necessary. In addition, they model them for students and discuss them with students, as appropriate, including errors they may have made, the consequences of those errors, and how the errors were corrected.

Imagine how much better we all would be at understanding complex information, evaluating options to make major life decisions, solving complicated problems, planning large events, developing successful strategies, and making accurate predictions if these processes had been systematically taught to us and we were able to hone them starting in kindergarten (or earlier) and continuing through university.

Key Ideas from this Chapter

1. The five thought processes are analyses, evaluations/ decisions, solutions/innovations, plans/strategies, and predictions/theories.
2. Thought processes involve the use of a variety of LOT, MOT, and, when done well, HOT skills.
3. Analyses entail examining something closely and methodically to understand it well. Critical reflection is a form of self-analysis, in which events are recalled and examined in order to understand one's own behaviors or actions.
4. Most decisions are based on an evaluation, although evaluations do not necessarily require a decision. A sound decision depends on a thorough and accurate evaluation. The impact of daily decisions made over a period of months and years will be significant. Making good decisions is a critically important skill for success in school and in life. This includes group decisions as well as individual decisions.

5. All evaluations entail making associations and distinctions between what is actual, necessary, or desired and a predetermined set of criteria. Students should learn to make evaluations, not just be subjected to them.

6. Solutions to many problems can be addressed using a similar process: Identify the problem and find out as much as possible about the context and possible cause(s). Evaluate the most likely cause(s) of the problem and decide on which one to address. Generate possible solutions. Determine the criteria for what constitutes a good solution. Decide on a solution. If the problem is solved, determine if the solution could be applied to prevent or solve similar problems in the future. If the problem is only partially solved, not solved, or made worse, then restart this process.

7. Innovating is a process in which a problem is solved by developing something new or unique or by doing things a new way. The creative thinking skills of imagining, generating, and reframing are used in this process.

8. Planning is a learned skill that is essential for success in school and life. Teachers can help students develop planning skills by discussing their plans as they make them, giving students planning tools, and regularly asking them to describe their plans.

9. Strategizing is a more intentional and complex form of planning to achieve a specific outcome. Young students are capable of basic strategizing, but it tends to be intuitive rather than deliberate and involves only a few steps. Strategizing is a unique thinking process because the ability to strategize in one activity or domain does not usually transfer to any other activity or domain.

10. Predictions and theories both make determinations, based on existing information, of "what might be." Predicting takes existing information and looks ahead to what is likely to be or to happen based on that information. Theorizing starts with an existing result or phenomenon and tries to determine what leads to or explains it. It is important for teachers to know the theories that underlie their approach to teaching.

Thought Processes ◆ 133

11. Students need many opportunities to practice these thought processes and particularly to practice using HOT skills when engaging in them.
12. Teachers can help students learn to use thought processes effectively by honing their own thought processes, modeling them, and talking about them, including how they corrected errors.

Questions for Discussion

Recall a good decision that you made and a poor decision. Reflect critically on the factors that contributed to making the good decision and the poor decision. What lessons could you draw from these reflections to help students learn to make good decisions?

What types of problems do your students deal with on a regular basis? What types of curriculum-based problems do you challenge them with? Take one example of a problem and determine if it engages students' HOT skills. Which HOT skills does it engage and at what level of challenge in relation to students' abilities? How can the activity be amended to engage more HOT skills and/or more advanced levels of HOT?

Think of examples of predictions, either your own or ones that other people have made, that were accurate and some that were wrong. What were the thinking skills and specific thoughts that led to the successful predictions? What was faulty about the thinking and thoughts that led to the wrong predictions? How can you use this information to help your students make accurate predictions?

In the *Snaps-HOT, Why It's Hard to Explain Why*, on page 102, the teacher scaffolds his kindergartners' ability to reflect critically and articulate the reasons for their feelings. He gives them cues, helps them with vocabulary, and models ways to do it. What are some other strategies he can use to help his students reflect critically? How can these strategies be used to help students analyze stories and events?

References

Acs, G., & Dehry, I. (2020). *Using cash payments to reduce poverty*. Urban Institute. https://www.urban.org/research/publication/using-cash-payments-reduce-poverty

Blanch, A. (2022). Chess instruction improves cognitive abilities and academic performance: Real effects or wishful thinking?. *Educational Psychology Review, 34*, 1371–1398. https://doi.org/10.1007/s10648-022-09670-9

Food Marketing Institute. (2016). *U.S. grocery shopping trends, 2016*. Food Marketing Institute.

Giffens, G. (2013, November 30). Strategic thinking & the game of chess: Myth and reality. *Strategic Thinking Coach Blog*. https://strategicthinkingcoach.com/2013/11/30/strategic-thinking-the-game-of-chess-myth-and-reality/

Kulke, H., & Rothermund, D. (2010). *A history of India* (5th ed.). Routledge.

Sala, G., & Gobet, F. (2017). Does far transfer exist? Negative evidence from chess, music, and working memory training. *Current Directions in Psychological Science, 26*(6), 515–520. https://doi.org/10.1177/0963721417712760

Twenge, J. (2023). *Generations: The real differences between Gen Z, Millennials, Gen X, Boomers, and Silents—and what they mean for the future*. Atria Books.

Part 2
Learning to Think, Thinking to Learn

Graphic by Gwendolyn Rodriguez.

7

Higher-Order Thinking in Action

Supports and Challenges

Previous chapters provided detailed descriptions of the full range of thinking skills and thinking processes, explained the importance of teaching higher-order thinking (HOT) skills, and offered ideas for developing them in young learners. Throughout, there have been references to promoting students' thinking dispositions, using HOT skills to avoid thinking errors, and helping students to recognize and reject disinformation and other deceptions. This chapter covers these important topics as well as the impact of mental and physical health on HOT. While they are addressed separately, they are all connected. Thinking dispositions are helpful for recognizing and rejecting disinformation and avoiding thinking errors. Disinformation and other deceptions only fool people who do not have strong thinking dispositions and who do not have sufficient HOT skills to overcome the thinking errors that allow them to be deceived.

Thinking Dispositions

Thinking dispositions are the positive behaviors and attitudes that support and enhance HOT skills. They include being curious,

DOI: 10.4324/9781032683423-10

persistent, patient, attentive, cautious, and flexible. These dispositions are broad and general ways of interacting with the world, so having them, or not having them, impacts many important aspects of life in addition to thinking skills: relationships, study habits, career choices, job performance, and more. Possessing any, some, or all these dispositions makes it more likely that a person will use HOT skills often and effectively. For young learners, the more of these dispositions they have and the stronger they are, the easier it is for them to learn to use HOT skills and to internalize them as mental habits.

In the "construction" analogy presented in Chapter 2, "thinking dispositions" was one of its four parts. Here it is again, briefly: (1) thinking skills are the tools, (2) thought processes are the building materials and methods, (3) *thinking dispositions are the unseen supports and drivers behind the work that keep it moving—the funds, plans, coordination, transportation, and work-flow*, and (4) the results or outcomes are the finished structures.

People who are (even somewhat) curious, cautious, and attentive are better able to detect whether information seems odd or possibly incorrect. If they have patience, they will not rush to make a judgment or jump to a conclusion but will take the time to think about the information using HOT skills. Within the thought process of analyzing, they use the HOT skills of querying to learn more about the information, such as its source and context. From this, they *may* be able to infer and deduce/induce that the information is true, partly true, false, or intentionally false (disinformation). But they may not be able to make a definitive determination or may *only* be able to determine whether it is plausible or doubtful. Sometimes, a final decisive determination may not be possible for years, if ever. But being flexible, as well as patient and cautious, they are comfortable living with the ambiguity of not knowing. As long as there is no conclusive answer, they prefer uncertainty to an answer that may be wrong.

> Discomfort with ambiguity—the need for certainty—short-circuits higher-order thinking. It leaves little room for thorough analyses or time for generating and evaluating ideas. It too often leads to poor decisions, plans that go awry, and wrong or ineffective solutions. But there is much that teachers can do to help students develop patience, caution, flexibility, and other dispositions to enable them to accept uncertainty as a normal and common part of life.

There are many tragic examples where the need to have a quick answer has led to innocent people being convicted of crimes and guilty people found not guilty or not even charged with a crime. In the infamous Central Park Five case in 1989, New York City police, under pressure to quickly find the perpetrator of the brutal rape of a white female jogger, framed five innocent Black and Latino teenagers, just two days after the crime. In the 1995 case of athlete/actor O.J. Simpson, the opposite happened. His lawyers convinced a jury that the police "rushed to judgment" and planted evidence to frame Simpson for the murders of his ex-wife, Nicole, and her friend Ron Goldman. The jury acquitted him in just four hours. But, two years later, Goldman's father filed a civil lawsuit resulting in the jury's unanimous verdict that Simpson was responsible for both deaths and fined him $33.5 million.

Of course, the need or desire for closure has led almost everyone at some point to mistakenly jump to a conclusion or rush to a judgment (though hopefully about issues much less dire than the examples above). Who has never been too quick to cast blame and accuse the wrong person? Who has never made an incorrect assumption?

Here is a sample of statements to help students develop and hone a range of thinking dispositions. They can be integrated into the process of teaching and learning during any lesson on any subject or during daily routines:

Take your time.
Take time to think before you answer (or act).

140 ◆ Learning to Think, Thinking to Learn

Ask for more time to think or to find an answer if you need it.

If you don't know or are unsure, you can say, "I don't know, but I can find out."

You can ask questions before you answer (or act) if you need more information.

Talk about how you came up with your answer.

You can change your answer.

Talk about why you changed your answer and the different thinking you used.

There are several good answers to the question; think of another good answer.

Keep working at it and ask for help if you need it.

Mistakes can be good. We learn more from mistakes than from correct answers.

Think about all the possible results or outcomes—the good and bad—before you act.

The following *Cognitivity* helps students to accept uncertainty and be mentally flexible. There are two aspects of this activity; one is based on personal experiences and the other on history, science, and facts.

COGNITIVITY: WHO KNOWS?

For this activity, the teacher introduces a large wall chart similar to the example that follows.

It is displayed for the entire school year or for a significant portion of it. The teacher and students place sticky notes on the chart in each column. Once students understand the concept, it can be done informally and individually. During science, history, literature, and other lessons, ideas will be generated that can be added to the chart. Once a column is full, the notes are all removed so a new round can start. Variations of the chart include "Things Most People Do Not Know" (e.g. how huge cruise ships can float, the names of trees in a forest), "Things that Almost Nobody Knew 100 Years Ago But Nearly

Everyone Knows Now" (e.g., cigarettes are not healthy, movies can have sound), and "Things Many People Knew 100 Years Ago But Few People Know Now" (e.g., how to start a fire without a match, how to can vegetables).

WHAT **I** DON'T KNOW NOW			WHAT **NOBODY** KNOWS NOW	
Things I **Will** Know	Things I **Want** to Know	Things I Will Likely **Never** Know	Things Everyone **Will** Know	Things Everyone Will Likely **Never** Know
Who will be my next teacher	How to ride a horse	What it's like to walk on the moon	Who will be the next President	*The future!*
				What other people are thinking

For more ways to foster thinking dispositions, refer back to "Query" a critical thinking skill in Chapter 5 on page 65 and ahead to "Prompting" in Chapter 10 on page 222.

Avoiding and Correcting Thinking Errors

Much of our understanding of thinking errors comes from the work of Daniel Kahneman, whose book *Thinking, Fast and Slow*

(Kahneman, 2011) described the many ways that thinking is often biased, distorted, and faulty. Usually, people are not aware they are making these errors. Although he was a psychologist, Kahneman won the Nobel Prize for economics because prior to the publication of his work, theories of economics assumed that people acted rationally and in their own best interests.

Other common terms for thinking errors are thinking biases, behavioral biases, cognitive errors, cognitive biases, and cognitive distortions. Thinking errors are pernicious, not only because they happen automatically and there are so many of them but because they make us deceive ourselves *and* allow us to be easily deceived by others. Unscrupulous people exploit thinking errors to persuade people to believe their lies, to do something that is not in their best interests, to part with their money, or all three. Many people have lost their life savings to scams that took advantage of their thinking errors. These victims believed they could make a fortune from (unrealistically large) returns on investments that likely did not exist. "Optimism bias" led them to *want* to believe that the scam was legitimate, and "confirmation bias" led them to accept only the information that confirmed this and to ignore any contradictory information. In addition, "gratification bias" led them to downplay the risks involved in the transaction because a large short-term gain is more gratifying than a long-term, much less risky investment, even if it could bring a bigger gain. The scammers most likely used a number of verbal deceptions, which are discussed later in the chapter, to trick people into parting with their money.

Higher-order thinking is needed to avoid making thinking errors or to correct them. Thinking dispositions, such as patience, caution, and attention, are also very helpful. Even with good HOT skills, overcoming thinking errors is challenging for everyone, including most adults. Nevertheless, with modeling, guidance, and practice, even kindergartners can learn to recognize some of the more common and overt thinking errors, and most third graders will be able to catch some of their own thinking errors before or as they happen. There are two effective ways to help young learners do this, and they are quick and easy to implement. One is to prompt students before they are about to engage in a task in which it is common to make thinking errors. The second is to name and explain thinking errors just after they happen. For example, as students are planning tasks to accomplish a project or to complete assignments, teachers can remind them "A common thinking error is called the 'planning fallacy.' It means you probably think it will take *less* time to finish the project than it actually will. Projects usually take *more* time than you plan for. Let's talk about why and generate some ideas for avoiding this error so we can plan more accurately."

There are many types of thinking errors, but there are several that are common and consequential and that young learners are susceptible to or will likely understand. These include the previously mentioned planning fallacy and gratification, optimism, and confirmation biases, as well as the illusory truth effect, either/or thinking, and mental shortcuts. Mental shortcuts include assumptions, false associations, and stereotyping.

Optimism Bias

More commonly known as wishful thinking, optimism bias leads people to believe that things are better than they actually are or that things will turn out well regardless of what they do or don't do to affect the outcome. "Everything will be fine" and "Hope for the best" are two common expressions that reflect optimism bias. While having a positive attitude is a good thing, optimism bias often leads people to avoid dealing with problems and to not take the time and effort to think critically and creatively, resulting in poor decisions. Common types of optimism biases among young students include having expectations that are too high or unrealistic—how many friends will come to their birthday party, what presents they will receive, and how much fun it will be. This thinking error often gets played out academically when students do not study or prepare adequately, believing that they already know enough or that the test will be easy. All too often, optimism bias leads to disappointment.

Confirmation Bias

Confirmation bias is the tendency to attend to and believe only information that confirms already-held beliefs. It is what leads

144 ◆ Learning to Think, Thinking to Learn

people to be closed to different ideas or information and to be deceived over and over. Information that provides other perspectives, or contradicts what is believed, is conveniently ignored or dismissed. Many people will even believe a ridiculous claim or an overt lie if it aligns with what they believe. This makes confirmation bias particularly pernicious.

How does critical thinking moderate thinking errors such as confirmation bias? The following hypothetical conversation provides an example.

Adam: "I thought that administration's economist on TV was spot-on when she said inflation was too high. Something needs to be done!"

Eve: "Um, but she followed that by saying it's been cut in half in the past nine months and it's on a downward trend."

Adam: "Grumble, grumble."

Adam's response to the report was based only on the part he believed or wanted to believe. But had he used critical thinking skills, such as querying, inferring, and inducing, it would have nullified confirmation bias and led to a more nuanced and compelling response. This type of response is more likely to spur further discussion and a deeper understanding of the issue. Here is what that might sound like:

Adam: "The adminstration's economist on TV said that inflation is going down, but she didn't say why. I'm worried that it's just due to falling gas prices, not their policies. I want to know what they're doing to keep it going down because gas prices will go back up. I'm also worried we'll still be dipping into our savings a year from now."

Eve: "Good point. And *I* want to know what they're doing to make sure it doesn't keep happening over and over. It feels like we're stuck on an inflation roller coaster. By the way, you worry too much about everything."

Adam: "Grumble, grumble."

Note of warning: Using higher-order thinking does not necessarily improve one's personality.

Teachers can help students become aware of their confirmation biases by "confirming" their biases with a bit of fun teasing and sarcasm.

Student A: "I don't like science; it's boring."

Teacher: "Yes, I agree. I threw away my cell phone yesterday because there was so much boring science that went into making it. Who are you giving all your video games to?"

Student Z: "Girls like boys who are tough. They like guys who tell them what to do. I saw a bunch of videos on YouTube about it."

Teacher: "Really? I think you should try it, and I'll have the first-aid kit ready for your bloody nose! I also saw a video on the internet by a tough guy who said that most nine-year-olds will believe just about anything they see on internet videos if they like what it says! Many people believe things because they *want* it to be true or because it gives them an easy way out of making the effort that is actually required to do something hard, like connect with another person. That's a thinking error called 'trying to take the easy way out'."

The Illusory Truth Effect

This thinking error describes a category of thinking errors. Although the term is jargony, the thinking errors it names are basic and common. They all involve believing an idea or statement for reasons unrelated to its content. People tend to believe something that simplifies a difficult or complicated task or concept, or that is repeated many times, or because many other people believe it. Child-friendly terms for these are "trying to take the easy way out," "repeating a lie until even you believe it," and "jumping on the bandwagon."

146 ◆ Learning to Think, Thinking to Learn

This thinking error is complicated by the fact that many ideas or statements that simplify complex things, that are repeated often, and that many people believe are helpful, true, and accurate. MOT skills, such as characterizing, and HOT skills, such as deductive/inductive thinking and inferring, are needed to separate true ideas or statements from those that are (potentially) false.

Students can learn about these types of thinking errors when teachers name and explain them as they come up as well as in distinct lessons (spontaneously and planned). In the dialogue above between student Z and the teacher, student Z succumbs to the illusory truth effect about relationships, which the teacher describes and names. Other statements that can be used are "No matter how many times you hear a lie or wrong information, it will never be true or correct" and "If everyone in the world believed a lie or wrong information, it would still not be true or correct. Hundreds of years ago, almost everyone believed that the earth was the center of the universe and that blood-letting with leeches could cure illnesses."

Either/Or Thinking

The inability to see more than two options or to avoid thinking in terms like win-or-lose, yes-or-no, right-or-wrong, good-or-bad, or all-or-nothing is a major barrier to HOT, particularly creative thinking. It is also known as polarizing and dichotomizing. This is a difficult thinking error to overcome. It is so pervasive in competitive Western cultures, from sports, to business, to politics, to interpersonal relationships, that it can be considered a behavioral norm.

Intentionally claiming that there are only two solutions to a problem or offering only two options when there are more (which is almost always the case) is a common deceptive practice. It is even more pernicious when the options represent a false dichotomy or a false equivalent: "If you don't agree with me, you're not my friend," "If you don't support the war, you're on the side of the enemy." Sometimes, the message is indirect, which can be more impactful than direct messages: "If you buy this fancy car, good looking people will be attracted to you." (If you don't buy this car, good looking people will not be attracted to you.) "Buying this toy will bring you hours of fun and lots of friends." (If you don't buy this toy, you won't have fun or friends.)

There are many examples in the education field of the negative effects of either/or thinking. The "reading wars," which pit phonics and whole language approaches against each other, have been going on for decades. Given that (arguably) about half of the words in English are spelled phonetically (Hanna et al., 1966; Joshi et al., 2009), the case for a combined approach could not more clear or sensible. The unfortunate result of this either/ or thinking is that what may be the most effective approach to reading instruction is not reaching more students.

It takes HOT skills such as reframing, shifting perspective, and generating ideas to overcome this thinking error. The SnapsHOT on page 86 describes how a mediator was able to break free of either/or thinking by using the HOT skill of reframing. Students can learn to use these HOT skills to overcome either/or thinking when given examples with which to practice. It is helpful, as well as enjoyable, to start with obvious and exaggerated examples such as the following:

- ◆ "You have two choices now. You can walk silently down the hall or not run quietly down the hall."
- ◆ "You can be happy with our decision, or you can call the president and ask for a new teacher."
- ◆ "Only the students who have a dog named Cuddles will be allowed to go outside this afternoon."
- ◆ "If you get all the math answers correctly, you will definitely become a movie star one day."
- ◆ "Would you like to read the next chapter now or wait until next year?"
- ◆ "This book has a blue cover, so it must be a really funny book."

It also helps students to overcome either/or thinking by giving them a concrete alternative and naming it. This could be "both/and thinking," "yes-and-yes thinking," or "many possibilities thinking."

Mental Shortcuts: Assumptions, False Associations, and Stereotyping

Mental shortcuts (also called heuristics) often give wrong information when they are made quickly, intuitively, and without being mediated by MOT or HOT. However, when they are developed for a purpose and are made with intent, they are positive and useful. They reduce the amount of time and effort it takes to form an opinion or make a decision. A shortcut, after all, is a good thing if it gets you where you need to go more quickly and efficiently. Mental shortcuts are important tools in the application of math, technology, medicine, and ethics. They help emergency room staff make good decisions quickly.

Although there are many types of mental short cuts, three that are particularly problematic, common, and easy to make are "assumptions," "false associations," and "stereotyping."

Assumptions often come from internalized (and sometimes subconscious) beliefs, making them difficult to expose and examine. While a certain amount of assuming is necessary just to get through the day without becoming mentally exhausted from questioning every thought, wrong assumptions can be limiting and costly. These can range from "I could never learn to speak a new language" to "The more times I play the lottery, the greater my chance of winning." Assumptions expressed by other people may need to be questioned as they can lead to unhealthy self-criticism ("You'll never amount to anything"), to the spread of disinformation and biases ("You can't trust those people"), or to preventing positive change ("It's how we've always done it"). For these reasons and more, it is important for young learners to recognize assumptions, practice questioning their own assumptions, and learn to question assumptions from others.

Students can begin to recognize assumptions, whether internal or external, by listening carefully to the start of a statement. Assumptions often begin with phrases such as:

"That's just the way it is"
"It never…"
"It always…"
"Everyone knows that…"
"The best way to…"

Higher-Order Thinking in Action ◆ 149

"The only way to…"
"I can just tell that…"
"My intuition tells me…."
"While it can't be proven…"
"I heard somewhere that…"
"Someone told me…"
"It can't happen again because…"
"It will happen again because…"
"It happens… all the time/everywhere/to everyone/for no reason."

Students can also learn that using the word "they," without specifying who "they" are, is often a red flag that an assumption is coming.

Responses to statements that seem to be assumptions include:

"Who do you mean when you say 'they?'"
"Why do you say that?"
"Who exactly said (wrote) that?"
"Where is it written?"
"Did you check it out?"
"Do you have proof or evidence?"
"Where did it come from?"
"Shall we check it out?"
"Did you see it or experience it directly?"
"How do you know it's true?"
"How do you know that it's not a mistake/rumor/lie?"

Questioning assumptions does not necessarily require actual questions.

"It sounds like your opinion, not a fact."
"It doesn't seem… plausible, possible, likely, true to me."
"It sounds a lot like _____, which turned out not to be true."
"I'll have to think about that."
"I want to find out… more about it, if it's true, where it came from, who said it."
"Maybe there is another… explanation, perspective, point of view, opinion, idea, or way to do it."

False associations. In a study exploring one type of false association, researchers asked participants to rate the qualities of people by looking at photos of their faces. Adults and children alike rated attractive people as being nicer and more trustworthy than unattractive people, although males tend to do this more than females (Halpern, 2013; Hines, 2010; Kahneman, 2011). In this example of false associating, attractiveness, the ultimate superficial characteristic, is used as a mental shortcut for the more time-consuming and challenging task of analyzing to get sufficient and reliable information to make a reasoned evaluation.

Mental shortcuts use LOT skills where MOT and HOT skills are needed. The participants in this study used identifying and categorizing instead of characterizing, querying, and inductive thinking. Although the researchers did not offer the participants the option of analyzing (which is a bit misleading to the participants and may have skewed the results), a person with strong HOT skills would *still* respond to the task by saying "I can't do this because I can't determine a person's character from their appearance!"

Stereotyping is closely related to making false associations. Stereotyping entails assigning a characteristic to an entire group or class of people. Negative stereotyping based on race, skin color, religion, appearance, and so on is pervasive, often with tragic consequences. But even when stereotypes are positive (e.g., "Asian students are smart"), they are harmful because they are misleading and not true. This stereotype ignores other possible perspectives: they work hard, care about doing well in school, like to learn, want to make themselves and their families proud, are ambitious, work collaboratively with other students, or any or all of the above. Because the tendency to stereotype is strong and often automatic, the HOT skills to recognize, avoid, and counter this thinking error—intra- and inter-personally— must become mental habits.

One excellent resource for helping students avoid these thinking errors and learn to see beyond surface appearances is the animated movie, *Zootopia* (Howard et al., 2016). The main theme of *Zootopia* is that things are often not as they appear. It can be a great teaching tool by stopping at various points in the movie to help students recognize and understand the various thinking errors that are made, the consequences of those errors,

the HOT skills used to counter them, and the thinking dispositions of the characters and their impacts.

Zootopia is a bustling city of human-like animals; a utopia
of the future where all animals, predators, and prey live peacefully together. The protagonist is a fresh-off-the-farm, young
adult rabbit, Judy Hopps, who is a newly minted police officer.
*(Being among the smallest of the animals, she is a proxy for the chil-
dren watching the movie.)* Judy uses a full range of HOT skills to
outsmart animals much bigger and stronger and to recruit the
much-needed assistance of a street-smart fox, Nick Wilde. The
drama centers on a number of animals who have gone missing.
When Judy finds them, these otherwise-peaceful former predators have become savage. This creates trouble in paradise because
the animals that were formerly prey are starting to fear and mistrust *all* former predators, who are a small minority group living
among the far more numerous former prey. Their stereotyping is
exacerbated by overt differences in appearance between the former prey and the former predators. The predators are generally
much larger, and many have menacing-looking features such as
horns, tusks, and large sharp teeth.

Although Judy is hailed as a hero for finding the missing animals, the level of conflict and mistrust in Zootopia increases after
she publicly states that the predators are reverting back to their
natural state. *(She actually does not know why, so she repeats what
she heard others say—"the bandwagon effect"—rather than taking the
time needed to analyze and investigate using HOT skills.)* Amid the
chaos she helped create, Judy leaves Zootopia and goes back to
the family carrot farm to reflect on her failure. It is only when
she becomes calm and open to new information that she gains
the knowledge she needs to solve the problem of the predators
going savage. *(She demonstrates the thinking dispositions of patience,
attention, and persistence.)* By the end of the movie, we know the
predators were not returning to a savage state. It was all a deliberate plot by the ruthless, power-hungry mayor of Zootopia,
Dawn Bellweather. *(She knows that a state of fear inhibits higher-
order thinking and fosters lower-order thinking, making it easier for her
to control and manipulate her citizens.)* Turning a stereotype on its
head once again, this evil mayor is a sweet-looking sheep with a
meek voice. *(Lambs are common symbols of innocence.)*

Other examples of appearances and expectations being at odds with reality in the movie are that Zootopia is not at all a peaceful utopia; the crime boss, Mr. Big, is a tiny shrew; the source of an urban problem is in a rural area; and those "savage" predators are actually victims. Nothing is what it seems! To use critical thinking skills and look beyond surface appearances are important lessons that our students need to learn, and this film conveys these lessons beautifully and effectively, with humor and heart.

Disinformation and Verbal Deceptions

Young learners get most of their information from visual media rather than print. While visual disinformation exists—toys in commercials made to look bigger than they are, child actors showing exaggerated enthusiasm for their breakfast cereal— most of the disinformation from visual media is communicated verbally. Verbal deceptions, which both deliver and promote disinformation, are ubiquitous and powerful.

Also known as "logical fallacies," verbal deceptions include commonly heard phrases such as "This is the *worst* thing that ever happened!" or "*Everybody* knows that its true" or "You *always* do that!" These are all examples of one type of verbal deception, hyperbole, or exaggerating for effect. They are called logical fallacies because they can be unintentional mistakes in logic by the speaker. However, when they are used purposely to deceive and spread disinformation, which happens often, it is a mischaracterization to call them logical fallacies. Because they entail *illogical* statements to intentionally confuse or fool people, it is more accurate to call them verbal deceptions.

Although the verbal deceptions listed below sound sophisticated, it is not difficult to make them concrete and understandable to young learners. Many of these deceptions are commonly used in advertising and by politicians, salespeople, and opinion influencers on television, radio, and online. There are many activities throughout the book to help students recognize and parse verbal deceptions, including the *Cognitivity*, Brain Baits, near the end of this chapter.

Higher-Order Thinking in Action ◆ 153

Bandwagon effect: Appealing to a person's desire to belong, with statements such as "Everyone knows that…" or "Don't be the only one who…" or "Be part of the movement to…" A more child-friendly term is "Joining the crowd."

Scarcity effect: "Hurry before they run out," "Get them before they're all gone," and "There are only a few left" are common sales tactics. They work because they exploit the thinking error that something has more value if it is scarce. The scarcity effect also taps into FOMO (fear of missing out), which is also a good child-friendly term for this mental shortcut.

Hyperbole: Greatly exaggerating, including making statements that begin "You never…" or "You always… or claiming that an idea or belief is ridiculous or impossible without providing evidence. A more child-friendly term is "exaggerating."

Leading the witness: Statements or questions that attempt to get a particular response such as "Don't you agree?" or "Isn't it obvious that…." A more child-friendly phrase is "Think the way I think" or "Believe what I believe."

Shifting the burden of proof: Making a claim without evidence and requiring the other person to refute it. "I'm the most honest person in the world." (This is also hyperbole.) A more child-friendly phrase for this is "You can't prove me wrong."

Fallacy of composition: Claiming or implying that what is true of part of something must be true of the whole thing. An advertisement or sales pitch for a used car might say "Four brand-new tires" or "Ultra-low miles." The goal of these statements is to exploit buyers' inability to recognize and reject the fallacy of composition. The tires are likely the only thing that is new about the car, and many cars with low mileage have serious mechanical problems. A more child-friendly phrase for this is "Throwing away all the apples because one tastes bad."

Red herring: A statement that distracts from the topic or changes the subject to one that is more acceptable to the speaker. There are many red herring strategies, such as answering a different question than the one asked and attacking the speaker's credibility rather than the speaker's ideas (which is also called the "ad hominem defense"). A more child-friendly phrase for this is "creating a distraction" or "avoiding the question."

Non-denial denial: This is a specific type of red herring in the category of "avoiding the question." It is attributed to Ben Bradley, the former editor of the *Washington Post* during the Watergate investigation in the 1970s. When some of the people being investigated were asked directly about their involvement, they would respond with vague or misleading statements (rather than direct denials) such as "I was not aware that was going on" or "If you print that, I will sue you!"

Teachers can help students avoid making or being fooled by verbal deceptions by encouraging them to make direct statements, respond to questions directly, and avoid overusing words like "maybe," "sort of," "possibly," and "probably" and avoid the "passive voice" when speaking and writing. Students should also practice politely asking other people to clarify any statement that is ambiguous, whether intentional or not. "I'm sorry but I don't understand completely. Could you please explain it more?" "Do you mean _____, or did I not understand you?"

There are, of course, many other types of deceptive statements, but these are among the most common and impactful. The ability to parse them starts with the ability to recognize them. With teacher-guided practice, even the youngest learners can begin to recognize them and second and third graders can begin to parse them.

Stress and Other Obstacles to Thinking Critically and Creatively

The impact of stress on thinking and learning is well documented (Córdova et al., 2023; Yu, 2016). Stress and related negative emotions decrease the brain's ability to think clearly and rationally. Lower-brain functions are activated, which block HOT and negatively impact the ability to learn. On the other hand, positive emotions *increase* HOT abilities (Córdova et al., 2023). For this reason, many of the activities in this book are enjoyable and engaging, involving humor and games. Many adults, who might otherwise shun challenging cognitive activities, enjoy them in the form of games such as crossword puzzles, Wordle, and Sudoku.

Because fear causes high levels of stress and stress causes a decline in critical and creative thinking, instilling or fomenting fear is a powerful way that unscrupulous people attempt to manipulate and control other people. This is particularly effective with hard-wired fears, such as fear of people who are perceived as "different" or "the others," as discussed in Chapter 1.

Other factors that negatively impact the ability to learn and to use MOT and HOT include physical health, hunger, poor nutrition, and lack of sleep (Dubuc et al., 2020). Teachers may have to adjust their expectations for students' learning and thinking abilities when they do not feel well or are tired or hungry. While most teachers do not have much control over these factors, it is important to inform families, and everyone who works with families, of the direct connection between physical health and the ability to learn and to think.

COGNITIVITY: BRAIN BAITS

"This is the story of Goldilocks and the Three Gorillas." Brain baits, such as this one, help students to recognize and respond to verbal deceptions in a playful way. But brain baits can also be connected to content learning and be more subtle and complex as students gain HOT skills.

There is an example of a teacher using brain baits with the story of Henny Penny in the *Snap-sHOT, Is the Sky Falling?* on page 165. The story is essentially about the impact of fear and stress on rational thinking. Fear leads Henny Penny to jump to a (nonsensical) conclusion, which easily spreads to the other characters in the story when they see how frantic she is. Henny Penny doesn't do this intentionally; she really believes the sky is falling, which is one reason she is so convincing. The teacher reinforces the lessons of the story and helps the students to practice parsing with brain baits. When a paper falls from the wall, she shouts, "The ceiling is falling!" She then helps them identify the thinking error and refute it with incisive questions, visual evidence, and deductive thinking.

156 ◆ Learning to Think, Thinking to Learn

Following are two other examples of teachers using brain baits. The first takes place in a kindergarten class, and the second in a second-grade class.

Snap-sHOT: "CHEETAH'ED"

Teacher: "Here is a picture of my cheetah."

Students: "That's a dog!"

Teacher: "No, no, no. You can't trick me, I know it's a cheetah." *(shift the burden of proof)*

Students: "IT'S A DOG!!"

Teacher: "That's ridiculous, how can you possibly think it's a dog?" *(dismiss with hyperbole)*

Student A: "Cheetahs have spots!"

Teacher: "I know that! Look here on its back. There are spots." *(fallacy of composition)*

Student B: "They have spots all over."

Teacher: "Lots of things have spots all over. Like Dalmatians. Didn't you see that movie? And something else that has spots is…" *(red herring)*

Student C: "They don't have floppy ears."

Student D: "They're wild. They're not pets!"

Teacher: "That sounds like faulty thinking to me. A pet can be a wild animal or something that once was a wild animal. People have pet snakes" *(models parsing a false dichotomy and throws in another red herring)* "But my pet isn't a wild animal, so… she's really not a cheetah?"

Students: "NOOO!"

Teacher: "Well, they told me at the pet store she was a cheetah! But I think they 'cheetahed' me. HA! Do you think I can return it?"

In response, some students laugh, some look incredulous, some look skeptical, some look confused, and some look concerned about their teacher's sanity.

Higher-Order Thinking in Action ◆ 157

Teacher:	"Actually, I've grown to love my chee—my dog, so I guess I'll keep her. It doesn't really matter how her ears look or if she's a dog or a cheetah. She's a great companion with a sweet personality. *That* is what's important." *(models characterizing)*

Snap-sHOT: LINCOLN THINKIN'

Teacher:	"What to you is the most important thing about Abraham Lincoln or the most important thing that he did?" (Asks students to characterize as part of the thought processes of analyses and evaluations/decisions.)
Several students contribute ideas:	"He was poor but grew up to be a president." "He freed the slaves." "He won the Civil War."
Teacher:	"I agree with all of you. I really admire what a great speaker he was, too. He could really give a speech! And everyone loved him and his ideas. Our country wasn't divided like it is now, every person in America loved him, isn't that right?" *(leading the witness)*

There are a few nods but no responses. Silence for about 15 seconds.

Teacher:	"You let me trick you. I told you something that isn't true, but my question at the end fooled you. It stopped you from deep thinking, from parsing what I said. Or maybe it stopped you from telling me I was wrong. What was my question, and how did it trick you?"

During the discussion that follows, the teacher reminds the students that nothing they read about Lincoln said that everyone loved him and much of what they read were descriptions of the deep divisions between the North and South. A supporter of the Confederacy hated Lincoln so much that he assassinated him.

Then the teacher helps the students understand deceptive thinking in the statement.

Teacher: "Even if he was widely loved, it couldn't be possible that *everyone* loved him. That is a *gigantic* exaggeration. And I just said another one!" *(hyperbole)*

"Now I'm going to say 12 things about Lincoln. For each statement, write down the number 1 if you think it is true, 2 if you think it is false, 3 if you think it *could* be true, and 4 if it is an opinion not a fact. Don't let me fool you with distractions, exaggerations, or other verbal deceptions. Remember, if any part of my statement is not true, then the whole statement is not true."

'Lincoln was the sixteenth president.'

'Lincoln was the best president.'

'Lincoln didn't like using a computer to write his speeches; he wrote them with a pen and paper.'

'Lincoln believed in natural rights, like freedom, for everyone.'

'Lincoln preferred to read by lamplight to save money because lightbulbs were expensive.'

'Lincoln was born in a log cabin.'

'Lincoln was born in Kentucky in 1809 and died there in 1865, just five days after the end of the Civil War.'

'Lincoln liked the theatre; he liked to see plays.'

'Lincoln's mother wanted him to become a doctor.'

'Lincoln's father wanted him to be a pilot.'

'Lincoln's signature on the Declaration of Independence was the first and the largest.'

'If it wasn't for Lincoln, the South would have won the Civil War.'

The teacher facilitates a discussion about the statements and the types of deceptions they reflect. Then the students are given the challenge to write four different statements about Lincoln: one true, one false, one that could be true, and one that is an opinion. They do this working in small groups and then test each other.

Conclusion

This chapter is about deterrence and development. Deterring something negative from happening is almost always easier, and less costly in time and resources, than trying to fix it after. Once a person believes an overt and ridiculous lie, it is very difficult to convince them they are wrong. In the case of disinformation and of thinking errors and deceptions, this is particularly true. They would have to admit they were foolish and gullible, or worse—which goes against the strong human instinct for self-preservation and dignity. In addition, reasoning with that person using evidence and facts is often *not* effective because the beliefs are not rational.

Fortunately, teachers of young learners are in the deterrence/development business. Every day, teachers deter negative behaviors that range from unproductive to harmful, and they promote the development of positive behaviors that range from productive to beneficial. Now is the time to do the same with thinking. Teachers can deter students from making and being victims of thinking errors and deceptions, and they can encourage and develop students' thinking dispositions and HOT.

The ideas in this chapter delineate many specific types of thinking errors and deceptions and many ideas to help students use HOT skills to detect, expose, and deflect them. Some of the ideas are targeted and address particular thinking errors and deceptions, and some address the problem more generally. All of the ideas are suggestions and will require every teacher to use creative thinking to adapt them for their particular students. And, of course, what works this year may not work next year. Some of the ideas will be more useful and relevant than others, but, as it is difficult to predict which those will be, there are now more tools in the toolbox, more and better building materials to work with, more advanced methods, and more and better support to achieve the ultimate goal: young learners with sharp minds that will only get sharper as they carve a path to a more peaceful and saner world.

Key Ideas from this Chapter

1. Thinking dispositions support and enhance the development and use of HOT skills. They include being curious, persistent, patient, attentive, cautious, and flexible.
2. HOT skills help students avoid and correct thinking errors and to recognize and deflect verbal deceptions designed to fool or manipulate people and spread disinformation.
3. Thinking errors are usually made automatically and are very common. They include optimism bias, confirmation bias, the illusory truth effect, either/or thinking, and mental shortcuts.
4. Thinking errors are exploited by unscrupulous actors to manipulate and control people.
5. Optimism bias leads people to believe that things will turn out well, even when left to chance.
6. Confirmation bias leads people to believe only the information that they already agree with.
7. Either/or thinking leads people to believe that there are no more than two possible answers, solutions, or actions and to believe false dichotomies.

Higher-Order Thinking in Action ◆ 161

8. Mental shortcuts can be helpful and positive, but they also can lead to making assumptions, false associations, and to stereotyping.
9. Verbal deceptions, also called logical fallacies, are statements made to deceive people. Many of them do this by exploiting thinking errors. They include the bandwagon effect, the scarcity effect, hyperbole, leading the witness, the fallacy of composition, shifting the burden of proof, red herrings, and the non-denial denial.
10. Stress, negative emotions, poor physical health, nutritional deficits, hunger, and lack of sleep all negatively impact the ability to learn and to think. Stress, in particular, can block the ability to use HOT.
11. Positive emotions have a positive impact on the ability to learn and to develop and use HOT skills.

Questions for Discussion

After reviewing examples of fake news stories that have been believed by many people, discuss the question: What deceptive thinking strategies were used by the writers and what types of thinking errors were made by the readers who believed them? Repeat the discussion, focusing on advertisements (including those targeted at children), political speeches, and campaign ads.

What are some other types of thinking errors that were not discussed in this chapter that can affect and be understood by young learners?

What are some verbal deceptions targeted at young learners? Who does this and why? How are they different or similar to those targeted at adults?

Reflect on and discuss how thinking dispositions or the lack of them has affected your students' learning and thinking. What causes some students to have stronger thinking dispositions than others? What are ways that teachers can support and promote them within the curriculum and throughout the day?

References

Córdova, A., Caballero-García, A., Drobnic, F., Roche, E., & Noriega, D. C. (2023). Influence of stress and emotions in the learning process: The example of COVID-19 on university students: A narrative review. *Healthcare (Basel, Switzerland)*, *11*(12), 1787. https://doi.org/10.3390/healthcare11121787

Dubuc, M., Aubertin-Leheudre, M., Duval, C., & Karelis, A. D. (2020). Physical factors, cognition, and academic performance changes in adolescents. *Health Behavior and Policy Review*, *7*(3), 179–190. https://doi.org/10.14485/HBPR.7.3.2

Halpern, D. F. (2013). *Sex differences in cognitive abilities* (4th ed.). Psychology Press.

Hanna, P. R., Hanna, J. S., Hodges, R. E., & Rudorf Jr., E. H. (1966). *Phoneme-grapheme correspondences as cues to spelling improvement*. USDOE Publication No. 32008. U.S. Government Printing Office. https://files.eric.ed.gov/fulltext/ED128835.pdf

Hines, M. (2010). Sex-related variation in human behavior and the brain. *Trends in Cognitive Sciences*, *14*(10), 448–456. https://doi.org/10.1016/j.tics.2010.07.005

Howard, B., Moore, R., & Spencer, C. (2016). *Zootopia* [Film]. Walt Disney Productions.

Joshi, R. M., Treiman, R., Carreker, S., & Moats, L. C. (2009). How words cast their spell: Spelling is an integral part of learning the language, not a matter of memorization. *American Educator*, Winter 2008–2009, 6–42. https://education.ufl.edu/patterson/files/2019/04/JoshiTreimanCarrekerMoats2009.pdf

Kahneman, D. (2011). *Thinking, fast and slow*. Farrar, Straus and Giroux.

Yu, R. (2016). Stress potentiates decision biases: A stress induced deliberation-to-intuition (SIDI) model. *Neurobiology of Stress*, *3*, 83–95. https://doi.org/10.1016/j.ynstr.2015.12.006

8

HOT Teaching Precepts

Head, Heart, and Humor

The most effective way to learn to use a tool, particularly a specialized or power tool, is in the process of accomplishing a real task: hanging a picture, fixing a leaky faucet, or building a potting bench. And with the guidance of someone with experience and expertise, the new knowledge will be correct and learned more quickly and thoroughly—and safely! Then, with continued practice using each tool for different purposes and with a variety of materials, all the knowledge becomes a set of skills that gradually become internalized as the mental habits of the builder and the carpenter.

In the same way, the most effective way for students to learn to use the specialized set of mental power tools, called higher-order thinking (HOT), is by practicing them in the process of daily lessons, classroom routines, and all other educational activities. With quality instructional supports from teachers, students will learn to use them more quickly, thoroughly, and effectively. With ongoing practice and guidance, they become a set of mental skills that will gradually, over years, become internalized as the mental habits of the savvy and the wise.

In addition to active learning with expert support over time, there are many other ways to make learning "stick." Among them, there are four teaching precepts that uniquely align with

DOI: 10.4324/9781032683423-11

HOT, and, when taken together, they expedite the process of teaching and learning HOT skills.

1. Teach HOT skills explicitly, implicitly, and indirectly.
2. Teach HOT skills within activities that are *meaningful and relevant* for all students.
3. Teach HOT skills within activities that are *challenging and enjoyable*.
4. Teach students to use HOT skills to gain *insight, understanding, and appreciation*.

Teach HOT Skills Explicitly, Implicitly, and Indirectly

There is a great deal of controversary and disagreement about the best way to teach HOT skills, particularly critical thinking. There are three general approaches: explicit, implicit, and indirect. The premise of the explicit approach is that critical thinking skills, such as inferring and shifting perspective, are distinct abilities that can be taught and, once learned, can be applied to any subject area and for a variety of purposes.

The implicit approach is based on the premise that critical thinking skills are completely dependent on subject matter knowledge and are *not* transferable from one subject to another. It contends not only that critical thinking cannot be taught explicitly but that it *should* not be taught explicitly because doing so will negatively affect students' abilities to learn (Willingham, 2020). This idea is based on cognitive load theory (CLT), which posits that there is limited cognitive capacity in the brain's working memory and that too much information, particularly superfluous information, can overload it (Sweller, 2011). But ironically, there are many logical flaws and dubious assumptions in applying CLT to teaching HOT in this way (Ellerton, 2022), and the validity of CLT itself has been widely questioned (Leppink, 2020).

A hybrid approach that combines explicit and implicit approaches, called "infusion," entails explicitly teaching HOT skills within subject matter lessons and when teachable moments

HOT Teaching Precepts ◆ 165

offer opportunities (Swartz et al., 2010). This approach is reflected in most of the examples of activities—*Snap-sHOTs*, *Cognitivities*, and *ThinkinGroups*—throughout this book.

With the indirect approach, HOT skills are neither explicitly nor implicitly taught, but it is expected (or perhaps assumed) that students will learn them incidentally from the regular curriculum, daily lessons, teacher–student interactions, and possibly some modeling by teachers. This is likely the most ineffective *and* the most common approach. Nevertheless, when modeling by teachers is done often, intentionally and skillfully, and when it is combined with all the other approaches, it is an effective strategy. For young learners, it may be a *necessary* strategy.

The results from a large body of research on how best to teach thinking skills indicate that teaching thinking skills explicitly is important and necessary (Abrami et al., 2015; Collins, 2014; Ellerton, 2022). As Bryan Goodwin (2017) states in the title of his research review, "critical thinking won't develop through osmosis." Explicit teaching can entail the use of a commercial or prescribed "thinking skills curriculum" or of teacher-selected activities, whether commercial or handmade or both. Because they can be chosen (and modified if necessary) to align with the regular curriculum and to match the abilities and needs of students, teacher-selected activities tend to be more effective for teaching critical thinking than are set curriculums (Abrami et al., 2015).

Here is a *Snap-sHOT* of "infusion" in action. HOT skills are taught explicitly in the context of a well-known story.

Snap-sHOT: IS THE SKY FALLING?

After reading the story of Henny Penny (aka Chicken Little) to her kindergarten students, Ms. Das asks them questions about why Henny Penny thinks that the sky is falling when she is hit on the head by an acorn. A discussion follows about how being afraid and feeling panicky affect our ability to think clearly and reason and can cause us to make thinking errors. New vocabulary and concepts such as "jumping to a conclusion" and "cause and effect" are introduced. The students are asked for other examples of jumping to a conclusion, and Ms. Das provides several as well.

Later in the day, Ms. Das leads small groups of students to act out several alternative versions of the story. In one version, the other animals help Henny Penny calm down and ask her to explain how she knows the sky is falling and to think about other possible causes of something hitting her head.

Over the course of the week, Ms. Das takes advantage of some teachable moments, much to the students' delight. When a drawing falls from the wall during circle time, Ms. Das shouts, "The ceiling is falling! The ceiling is falling!" She encourages her students to try to convince her that the ceiling is not falling. At another time, when the class is outside on a warm day in late spring, a child slips and nearly falls. Ms. Das says, "Oops, I'm glad you didn't fall. Be careful of the patches of ice! LISTEN EVERYONE, WALK CAREFULLY THERE'S SNOW AND ICE EVERYWHERE. DON'T SLIP AND FALL!" The students try to refute her logic when she says, "Ice is slippery, Gino slipped, so there must ice on the ground." *(This logical thinking error involving causes and effects is also called a false syllogism: while the first two statements are true, the third, concluding statement is false.)* Several students take the time to look closely, and they notice a small spot of oil where Gino slipped. Ms. Das says, "Well I was wrong; thank you for correcting me. Well done. You thought about what I said and figured out it can't be true and then did an investigation and found the truth. You used lots of good thinking skills." Now let's use some more thinking skills and figure out what we can do about that oil patch. After generating some idea and discussing them, Ms. Das states, "I once was in an auto repair shop and saw someone put some dirt on top of spilt oil. Let's try that and see if makes it less slippery."

Several days later, Ms. Das reads the story again but focuses on the issue of the other animals believing Henny Penny's bad information, from which the fox correctly infers (a critical thinking skill) that all of the animals can be easily fooled.

Teach HOT Skills Within Activities that Are Meaningful and Relevant for All Students

There are many concepts about individual and group differences in the way people perceive the world and therefore think and learn (Celli & Young, 2014; Gardner, 2011; King & Mason, 2020; Pritchard, 2017; Saracho, 2017). A number of these concepts lack empirical evidence and have been subject to criticism, including some that are well known and widely used, such as learning style differences (Furey, 2020).

There is one concept, however, that has been proven valid over many decades: field-dependent and field-independent cognitive styles (Ansar & Ganesh, 2023; Witkin et al., 1962). Field-dependent thinkers perceive that a person's identity and the meaning and purpose of everything are primarily provided by their contexts, relationships, and connections. This type of thinking is also referred to as contextual or collectivist. Field-independent thinkers view each person, thing, idea, and event as primarily having an individual, unique identity independent of contextual factors, connections, or relationships. This type of thinking is also referred to as discrete or individualistic. The concept of contextual/discrete cognitive style differences is used here to illustrate how to teach HOT skills within meaningful and relevant activities to all students. The ideas, however, are responsive to *all* differences among students that may impact how they think and learn.

> Most contextual thinkers have stronger practical thinking skills than conceptual thinking skills, whereas the opposite is true of most discrete thinkers. Contextual thinkers tend to "see the forest but not the trees." Discrete thinkers tend to "see the trees but not the forest."

There is a link between contextual/discrete thinking and national cultures. The values, beliefs, and tenets of some national cultures, such as South Korea, strongly promote contextual thinking, whereas in other countries, such as the United States, they strongly promote discrete thinking. All national cultures can be characterized by the degree to which they promote one thinking style more than the other. This characteristic is thoroughly embedded within all aspects of society and has deep and ancient roots in the founding of every country (Hofstede, 2011). As a result, for most people, their thinking style is very solid and stable and resistant to change. But there are still individual differences within every culture on this cognitive style. There is a continuum from more field-dependent to more field-independent within the population of any and all national cultures.

Many students from immigrant families come to the U.S. and other Western countries from countries whose national cultures embrace contextual thinking more than discrete thinking. These students, as well as the students who are field-dependent but are not immigrants, will likely find it challenging to learn HOT skills and use them regularly. To make it easier for them, teachers can ensure that tasks and activities that promote critical and creative thinking skills have a meaningful context, a use and purpose, and have a strong social component. And when delivered with playfulness and humor, the learning process is enjoyed by everyone, as illustrated in the following *Snap-sHOT*.

Snap-sHOT: A SPECIAL LUNCH

The school kitchen staff has offered to make a special lunch every Friday. Each class is given the opportunity to choose the menu for one of these special lunch days. The students in each class will have to come to an agreement about the style of cooking, the main dish, a side dish, and the dessert they will request. Ms. Nguyen uses this opportunity to engage her first graders in a data-collecting, graphing, and decision-making activity. She starts with a whole class discussion and brainstorming activity, which she records on a whiteboard in four columns: Style, Main Course, Side Dish, and Dessert. The students easily agree on three styles of cooking that they like:

American, Mexican, and Chinese. Nearly all the students in the class have one or more of these three national cultures in their backgrounds, and one student has all three. For each style, they name two possible main courses and one side dish. They name two possible desserts (ice cream and brownies) and quickly and unanimously decide these desserts should go with all three styles. Ms. Nguyen then reminds her students that the whole class will need to decide on just one style, main course, side dish, and dessert.

She leads them in a lesson on sets and on determining the possible number of sets they can choose from. A set is a lunch comprising three items and one style, and each set is assigned a number and name. The students have fun working in pairs to make up names and arrive at "Bread, White and Blueberry," "Three B's: Burritos, Beans, and Brownies," and "Oodles of Noodles."

Later in the day, Ms. Nguyen leads them in making a bar graph of their choices. The graph has 12 numbers on the X axis, one for each possible lunch set. Using a secret ballot process, each student writes down the number and name of the lunch set that they like the best on a blue sticky note and their second choice on a yellow sticky note. Starting with their first choices, the students put their sticky notes in their appropriate spots to create a vertical bar graph. After Ms. Nguyen helps them "read" the results, they post their second choices and review the results again. "Reading the results" consists of determining which lunch sets have the most votes, fewest votes, the same number of votes, or zero votes.

Then Ms. Nguyen asks the question: "Set five got zero votes; does that mean that everyone in the class does not like the food in that lunch?" She guides a short discussion to help them understand that because the items in that lunch are also on other lunch sets that were selected as favorites, it cannot mean that no one likes it. "Also," she states, "you may like something just fine, but you chose something else that you like even more."

Ms. Nguyen offers alternatives to selecting the choice with the most votes. They include deciding by consensus after a discussion and (she jokes) letting the teacher decide. In the end, the students agree to select the one with the most votes.

Two of the lunch sets clearly have more votes than the others, but the one that has the most total votes has more second-choice votes and fewer first-choice votes. She asks the students, "Would it be more fair to choose the one with the most first-choice votes or the most total votes, or is there a way to count both?" After a lively discussion among the students, Ms. Nguyen describes how to count both sets of votes fairly by making first-choice votes worth more than second-choice votes, resulting in a total that shows which one has the most overall value. (She avoids the technical term for this, "weighting," as it would likely confuse first graders.)

To illustrate the concept, she makes two stacks of coins. One stack has ten coins: seven nickels and three dimes. The other has only eight coins: two nickels and six dimes. Together, they add up the amount of money in each stack and find that the smaller stack is worth more. Ms. Nguyen suggests that second-choice votes count as half a vote, so that two second-choice votes are equal to one first-choice vote, just as two nickels are equal to one dime and a nickel is worth half as much as a dime. When the votes are counted this way, the lunch set with fewer total votes but more first-choice votes has greater value. Some of the practical thinkers among the students still have difficulty accepting that the lunch set with the tallest bar was not selected. Ms. Nguyen reminds them, "Appearances can be misleading, so look beyond the surface and think deeply. Because something is bigger, it does not mean it's better or more valuable. Nickels are bigger than dimes." She then has the students congratulate each other on their hard work and higher-order thinking abilities.

Ms. Nguyen highlights the strengths of her contextual thinking students when they express personal preferences for food and see their cultures' cuisine represented and appreciated. The entire process involves a decision that requires sensitivity to the feelings and preferences of all the members of the peer group. They work in pairs to create a name for a lunch set, which also provides an opportunity for creative thinkers to shine. They are actively involved when they put their sticky notes on the graph. Ms. Nguyen knows that fairness is a concept all the students understand and care about, thereby putting the conceptual thinkers and the practical thinkers on a more equal footing during the discussions. Having students congratulate each other is a small but significant gesture to support the values of mutual respect and group harmony in the classroom. In addition, Ms. Nguyen embeds a few challenges in the activity for the contextual thinkers. The challenges are aimed at helping these students gain skills and feel comfortable thinking more discretely and conceptually, as future schoolwork will increasingly demand such thinking. The challenges include making an individual decision about their preferred lunch set and understanding that their teacher was not serious about making the decision herself. The final challenge was understanding that the tallest bar on the graph is not the one with the greatest value.

Among the many HOT skills that Ms. Nguyen promoted were representing a number and name for each lunch set (a logical thinking skill), generating ideas for naming lunch sets (a creative thinking skill), and calculating the number of lunch sets (a logical thinking skill). She engaged students in a simple analysis (a thought process) by inferring information from the graph (a critical thinking skill) and deducing information to respond to Ms. Nguyen's question about the lunch set with zero votes (a critical thinking skill). The students' used generative thinking to explore several different ways that the group can collectively decide on a lunch set (a creative thinking skill), and they had to infer that Ms. Nguyen was not serious when she suggested that she should make the decision (a critical thinking skill). Another analysis (a thought process) took place when they discussed the issue of fairness in determining which lunch set had the most value. Critical thinking was made explicit when Ms. Nguyen reminded them to look beyond appearances and think deeply.

The "*Snap-sHOT, My Family Feeds the World*" in Chapter 5 (on page 68) is another example of an activity that is meaningful and relevant as well as culturally responsive. In this scenario, a second-grade teacher develops activities to teach a variety of subjects in the context of a study of farmwork. All the students in the class are from families who are now or have been farmworkers. Like the *Snap-sHOT, A Special Lunch* above, it is also a good example of the infusion approach to teaching HOT skills.

Both *Snap-sHOTs* are examples of activities that are enjoyable and have a context relevant to students, a purpose they understand and with which they actively engage, and a strong social component. They make learning HOT skills easier, not only for contextual thinkers but for all students.

Teach HOT Skills Within Activities that Are Challenging and Enjoyable

What makes an activity challenging? In short, it engages students' HOT skills, and it is targeted near the top of their current ability level. This is also called "intellectual rigor." During the activity, teachers present many small challenges through their interactions with students. They pose questions, introduce new vocabulary, extend language, offer additional information and insight, clarify misunderstandings, and more. These are often referred to as "instructional supports" or, when done well and often, "quality instructional supports." If, in addition, they target the development of HOT skills, they are "HOT instructional supports." (Chapter 10 is all about HOT instructional supports, what they are and how they work.) While challenging activities or tasks may be difficult (more for some students than for others, of course), difficult tasks are often not challenging. Asking students to solve a problem that is beyond their capabilities or that just requires a great deal of time, are difficult but not challenging. They also can be frustrating and tedious.

Asking second graders to complete 25 problems subtracting three-digit numbers is difficult rather than challenging. It is also tedious because it only engages LOT skills and is needlessly repetitious. A similar assignment that is challenging might ask second graders to create and solve four subtraction word problems that entail subtracting three-digit numbers. Suggestions can be made, if necessary, such as, "Here are a few things that have three-digit numbers: the miles or kilometers traveled on long car trips, the number of days in a year, the number of pieces in a jigsaw puzzle, and the cost of a ticket to a concert or a professional football game. Can you think of others?" This is challenging because it requires the use of a several HOT skills. For most students, it will not feel tedious; for many students, it will be enjoyable.

When math is taught only through LOT skills, most of the advanced or quick-to-learn students are bored, and most of the struggling students do not learn it. Except for the most jaded, nearly all students want to engage with an intellectually rigorous curriculum, and they will eagerly rise to the challenges it offers. Also, when the curriculum is rigorous, there are fewer problematic and distracting behaviors for teachers to deal with because students are involved in learning and are neither bored nor "lost."

The positive correlation between challenging activities with quality instructional supports and student achievement is well documented (Teachstone, n.d.; Cadima et al., 2010; Fauth et al., 2019; Teemant et al., 2016). Unfortunately, it is also well documented that most teachers do not provide challenging activities and quality instructional supports that are in sufficient quantity or that are effective enough to impact student achievement (ECLKC, n.d.; Heppt et al., 2023; Katz, 2015). Many of the *SnapsHOTs* in this book showcase teachers challenging students with intellectually rigorous activities and providing quality instructional supports. They engage students' heads and hearts in equal measure.

Teach Students to Use HOT Skills to Gain Insight, Understanding, and Appreciation

This is potentially the most impactful teaching practice of the four. It is both a means for teaching and learning HOT skills and an outcome of using them. HOT skills are the tools that knock down barriers to reveal insights, build bridges to understanding, and pave the way to appreciation. These may seem too esoteric for young learners and daunting to teach, but they are developed over time and through many activities across all subject areas. They can often be promoted by enhancing an activity, as illustrated in the following *Snap-sHOT*.

Snap-sHOT: HARRIET 'ROUND THE MOUNTAIN

Jamaal, a kindergarten teacher, is also a talented musician. Among the many songs he has taught his students, "She'll Be Coming 'Round the Mountain" is a favorite. It has the fun challenge of repeating all the sounds and actions in reverse order ("choo-choo,""whoa back,""hi babe"), and Jamaal and his students enjoy making up silly verses. When developing lesson plans, Jamaal regularly searches the internet for background and contextual information that can enhance his activities. One day, Jamaal finds a version of the song with a verse he had never heard before: "We'll all sing hallelujah when she comes." This seems odd to him, so he reads more about the song and its history.

The next day, he shares what he learned with his class. He tells them, "Before singing 'She'll be Coming 'Round the Mountain' today, I want to read a book to you that will teach us something about the song. It's called *An Apple for Harriet Tubman*. It was written by Glennette Tilley Turner" (Turner, 2016). After reading and facilitating a short discussion about the book, Jamaal states,

"So, you probably want to know what a book about slavery and the Underground Railroad can teach us about our song

'She'll be Coming 'Round the Mountain.' Well, it is a very old song, and we don't know who made up the tune or wrote the words. But we do know that a long time ago it had different words. It was a religious song that people sang in church. Then the words and the name of the song were changed by slaves to make it a song that celebrates the Underground Railroad. Why do you think they didn't use the words 'slave' or 'Underground Railroad' in the song? Which words or phrases in the song could be about the Underground Railroad? We'll need to do some higher-order thinking to find out."

After a brief discussion in which Jamaal gives other examples of hidden messages and meanings in songs and stories, he tells them, "Now let's sing the song and think about slavery, Harriet Tubman, and the Underground Railroad. After, we'll talk about how we felt singing the song this time compared to how we felt singing it before."

Among the important insights and understandings that Jamaal gave his kindergartners, directly and indirectly, were the following:

- ◆ Things change and transform over time.
- ◆ Even the most powerless people can get a little power with creative thinking.
- ◆ Things are not always what they appear to be on the surface.
- ◆ Subject areas often overlap and enmesh—music, literacy, and history in this lesson.
- ◆ A single thing, such as a song, can have more than one purpose or meaning.
- ◆ There are many interesting and important things to learn from history.

Perhaps the most important aspect of the lesson is Jamaal's modeling of the value of intellectual pursuits. He taught students by example that obtaining more information and gaining a fuller

Conclusion

Here is a scenario that brings together all the major ideas in this chapter.

Pat, a new student teacher, stands in front of Riley's first-grade class with a bag full of vegetables from the farm the class visited the previous week. Pat's lesson plan addresses the content area of language and vocabulary development, specifically the names of vegetables. Pat asks the whole group the same question for each vegetable as they are drawn from the bag: "What vegetable is this?" Nearly all students answer each time in unison, although only a few students know some of the less common vegetables. Toward the end of the lesson, several students start whispering to each other and several others sneak books onto their laps and begin to read. The lesson wraps up when there are no more vegetables in the bag.

Riley, who had observed the lesson, noticed something interesting. At one point, Pat showed them a long red pepper and then later in the activity showed them a green bell pepper. It was a bit surprising that nearly all the students called out "pepper" for both.

In preparation for the unenviable task of giving feedback to Pat, Riley jots down a few questions:

Could there be more than one goal for the activity? What other goals, in addition to vocabulary, could be added? How would the lesson have been different with those additional goals? Did you notice that some students checked out? What do you think a teacher should do when that happens? How could the activity be modified to be more challenging and enjoyable? How can the same content be taught in a way that would elicit student's higher-order thinking?

HOT Teaching Precepts ◆ 177

Riley further prepares by writing down the following notes:

The activity could be more <u>thorough</u>. Show fewer vegetables and
explore each one in more detail. It would free up time to feel,
smell, and even taste them and for Pat to ask questions and
lead discussions that promote <u>HOT skills</u>. Remember: <u>insight</u>,
<u>understanding</u>, and <u>appreciation</u>.

Some question ideas:

How could these two very different-looking vegetables both
be peppers?

What do they have in common that makes them both
peppers?

What about this vegetable tells you it's a potato?

What are all the different ways to cook and eat potatoes
that you have tried?

Which vegetables do we have to cook to eat and why?

Which vegetables do we usually eat raw, and which ones can
we eat both ways, raw and cooked?

What makes a vegetable a vegetable and not a fruit or a
rock or a squirrel? Have a little fun with this, Pat!

A common problem with many activities and with the scope of
many curriculums is that they cover too much information too
quickly. They are more like a swamp than a lake—wide and shallow rather than confined and deep. Covering less information more
thoroughly is more meaningful and satisfying—much like how it
feels to swim in a lake as compared to wade through a swamp—
and provides many more opportunities to promote HOT skills.

It could be more meaningful to the students and more responsive to
contextual thinkers. Pat could pretend to be a farmer or a salesperson at a farmers' market or at a grocery store. The students learn
the names of the vegetables in the course of "buying" them. This
makes it more fun too.

Providing a context benefits more than just the contextual thinkers. At any age, most people learn better and retain information longer if there is a purpose for the activity—a reason for
taking the time and making the effort to learn something new.

It's the difference between learning to speak French sitting in a classroom in Montpelier, Vermont, or while living with a French family in Montpellier, France. Almost always, learning is more enjoyable and more effective when there is a meaningful context.

Teaching HOT skills explicitly, implicitly, and indirectly within challenging and enjoyable activities that are meaningful and relevant to all learners ensures that students will learn to use them effectively and to understand and value them. Using and improving HOT skills over time, they will gain the cognitive abilities for academic success and the mental habits for living well in the disinformation age. And if they can also use HOT skills to gain insight, understanding, and appreciation, they will very likely be self-motivated and inquisitive lifelong learners.

Key Ideas from this Chapter

1. There are four teaching precepts that expedite teaching HOT skills:
   a. Teach HOT skills explicitly, implicitly, and indirectly.
   b. Teach HOT skills within activities that are meaningful and relevant for all students.
   c. Teach HOT skills within activities that are challenging *and* enjoyable.
   d. Teach students to use HOT skills to gain insight, understanding, and appreciation.
2. The approach to teaching HOT skills reflected in the activities throughout this book primarily use the "infusion" approach, which entails teaching thinking skills explicitly but in the context of regular lessons and at teachable moments.
3. Modeling HOT skills by teachers can be effective when it is done intentionally, skillfully, and often and in combination with an explicit approach.
4. There are many individual and group differences in the way people perceive the world and think and learn. Field-dependent (contextual) learners may need additional supports to learn HOT skills.

HOT Teaching Precepts ◆ 179

5. Activities that are enjoyable and that have a context relevant to students, a use and purpose they understand and actively engage with, and have a strong social component make learning HOT skills easier, not only for contextual thinkers but for all students.
6. Challenging activities that elicit students' HOT engage them more when they are enjoyable. Using humor creates a positive, relaxed environment conducive to hard mental work.
7. Instructional supports entail a number of teaching techniques, including providing small challenges throughout an activity.
8. Challenging activities and quality instructional supports are associated with academic achievement, but their implementation tends to be an area of weakness for many teachers.
9. Many common activities can be enhanced to help students use HOT skills to gain insight, understanding, and appreciation of what they are learning, in addition to knowledge.

Questions for Discussion

Discuss teaching precepts that guide your teaching other than the four described in this chapter. Can those precepts be used to teach HOT skills? If so, how?

What is the role of modeling in the teaching/learning process? Use specific examples and any evidence you may have or know of to explain and defend your view of its effectiveness.

Choose a typical learning objective for your students from any subject area. What are some examples of activities to teach that objective that are difficult but not challenging and that are challenging but not difficult?

What are some examples from your life experiences of how gaining new information about an event, circumstance, book, artwork, idea, and so on led to new insights, a better understanding, and a greater appreciation of it?

Discuss the role of humor and playfulness in teaching and learning. What have been your own experiences as a student and more recently as a teacher? When, if ever, is it more of a detraction than an aide for learning? What types of humor are more effective for transmitting knowledge and teaching HOT skills than others? What are some ways that teachers who are not prone to using humor can still make learning enjoyable for students? Tell this "Dad joke" to someone right now: What's the difference between a fish and a piano? You can't tuna fish!

References

Abrami, P. C., Bernard, R. M., Borokhovski, E., Waddington, D. I., Wade, C. A., & Persson, T. (2015). Strategies for teaching students to think critically. A meta-analysis. *Review of Educational Research*, *85*(2), 275–314.

Ansar, M. R. U., & Ganesh, M. P. (2023). Cognitive styles research: A review of theory, assessments and applications. *International Journal of Indian Psychology*, *11*(1), 924–934. https://doi.org/10.25215/1101.094

Cadima, J., Leal, T., & Burchinal, M. (2010). The quality of teacher–student interactions: Associations with first graders' academic and behavioral outcomes. *Journal of School Psychology*, *48*(6), 457–482. https://doi.org/10.1016/j.jsp.2010.09.001

Celli, L. M., & Young, N. D. (2014). *Learning Style Perspectives: Impact in the Classroom*. Atwood Publishing.

Collins, R. (2014). Skills for the 21st century: teaching higher-order thinking. *Curriculum & Leadership Journal*, *12*(14). https://api.semanticscholar.org/CorpusID:141988538

ECLKC Early Childhood Learning and Knowledge Center. (n.d.). *A national overview of grantee CLASS scores in 2020*. ECLKC Data and Ongoing Monitoring. https://eclkc.ohs.acf.hhs.gov/data-ongoing-monitoring/article/national-overview-grantee-class-scores-2020

Ellerton, P. (2022). Critical thinking and content knowledge: what cognitive load theory gets wrong. *Scan: The Journal for Educators*, *41*(3), 4–9. https://search.informit.org/doi/pdf/10.3316/informit.391323994801034

Fauth, B., Decristan, J., Decker, A., Büttner, G., Klieme, E., Hardy, I., & Kunter, M. (2019). The effects of teacher competence on student outcomes in elementary science education: The mediating role of teaching quality. *Teaching and Teacher Education, 86*, 102882. https://doi.org/10.1016/j.tate.2019.102882

Furey, W. (2020). The stubborn myth of "learning styles". *Education Next, 20*(3), 8–12. https://www.educationnext.org/stubborn-myth-learning-styles-state-teacher-license-prep-materials-debunked-theory

Gardner, H. (2011). *Frames of mind: The theory of multiple intelligences* (3rd ed.). Basic Books.

Goodwin, B. (2017). Research matters: Critical thinking won't develop through osmosis. *Educational Leadership, 74*(5), 80–81.

Heppt, B., Henschel, S., Hardy, I., & Gabler, K. (2023). Instructional support in inquiry-based elementary school science classes: How does it relate to students' science content knowledge and academic language proficiency? *European Journal of Psychology of Education, 38*, 1377–1401. https://doi.org/10.1007/s10212-022-00653-6

Hofstede, G. (2011). Dimensionalizing cultures: The Hofstede model in context. *Online Readings in Psychology and Culture, 2*(1). https://doi.org/10.9707/2307-0919.1014

Katz, L. (2015). *Lively minds: Distinctions between academic goals vs. intellectual goals.* Defending the Early Years. https://deyproject.files.wordpress.com/2015/04/dey-lively-minds-4-8-15.pdf

King, S. P., & Mason, B. A. (2020). Myers Briggs Type Indicator. In B. J. Carducci & C. S. Nave (Eds.), *Wiley encyclopedia of personality and individual differences.* Vol. II. Measurement and assessment. John Wiley & Sons. https://online.vitalsource.com/#/books/9781119793922/epubcfi/6/116%5B%3Bvnd.vst.id.ref%3DAc123%5D!/4/2/2/2/6%400:0

Leppink, J. (2020). Revisiting cognitive load theory: second thoughts and unaddressed questions. *Scientia Medica, 30*(1), e36918. https://doi.org/10.15448/1980-6108.2020.1.36918

Pritchard, A. (2017). *Ways of learning: Learning theories for the classroom* (4th ed.). Routledge.

Saracho, O. N. (2017). *Cognitive style in early education.* Routledge.

Swartz, R. J., Costa, A. L., Beyer, B. K., Reagan, R., & Kallick, B. (2010). *Thinking-based learning: Promoting quality student achievement in the 21st Century*. Teachers College Press.

Sweller, J. (2011). Chapter two: Cognitive load theory. In J.P. Mestre & B. H. Ross (Eds.), *Psychology of learning and motivation*, pp. 37–76. Academic Press. https://doi.org/10.1016/B978-0-12-387691-1.00002-8

Teachstone. (n.d.). Effective educator-child interactions and child outcomes: *A summary of research on the Classroom Assessment Scoring System (CLASS) pre-K–3rd grade.* https://info.teachstone.com/research-summary-teacher-child-interactions-early-childhood

Teemant, A., Hausman, C. S., & Kigamwa, J. C. (2016). The effects of higher order thinking on student achievement and English proficiency. *INTESOL Journal, 13*(1). https://journals.iupui.edu/index.php/intesol/article/view/21254

Turner, G. T. (2016). *An apple for Harriet Tubman*. Albert Whitman and Company.

Willingham, D. (2020). *How to teach critical thinking*. New South Wales Department of Education. https://education.nsw.gov.au/content/dam/main-education/teaching-and-learning/education-for-a-changing-world/media/documents/How-to-teach-critical-thinking-Willingham.pdf

Witkin, H. A., Dyk, R. B., Faterson, H. F., Goodenough, D. R., & Karp, S. A. (1962). *Psychological Differentiation*. John Wiley & Sons.

9

HOT Teaching Methods

Context, Cognition, and Creativity

There are seven methods that, in certain forms, strongly align with the precepts discussed in the previous chapter. The methods include social learning, themes, projects and inquiries, case studies, role-plays and sketches, materials, and games. The forms of these methods described in this chapter are those that most effectively foster the development of students' higher-order thinking (HOT) skills and give teachers many natural opportunities to help students learn and improve them.

Social Learning

Learning with partners or in small groups should be the default mode, the rule rather than the exception. By requiring students to articulate and accurately communicate what they are thinking, social learning adds complexity to thinking tasks and fosters the development of more advanced levels of thinking. In addition, students need to be able to understand what others are communicating and their implications, which usually involve inferring, interpreting, shifting perspective, reframing, and other HOT skills. Of course, this can't be left to chance. Teachers may need to mediate these interactions to correct thinking errors and

DOI: 10.4324/9781032683423-12

184 ◆ Learning to Think, Thinking to Learn

help clarify any miscommunication or misunderstanding among students. Teachers may also need to assist if there are problems with group dynamics: a student dominates the group, some students do not participate, or the group is unable to agree. Partner or group work is also an opportunity to help students use a HOT skill at a more advanced level or to support their use of a new HOT skill. Negotiating roles and tasks, for example, often involves generating ideas and the thought processes of making decisions and solving problems. In addition, social learning methods support contextual learners as they engage in challenging mental work.

The *ThinkinGroups* activities that follow involve students working in pairs or small groups. It is a bit challenging, so it may require practice over time. It is designed to develop students' abilities to work collaboratively, communicate effectively, and think creatively. *Rhyme Time* addresses the content areas of art, drama, social skills, language and literature, and potentially more.

ThinkinGroups: RHYME TIME

Together with a partner or in small groups, students draw pictures that depict two words that rhyme. For example, they may draw a fat cat or a red bed. When all the groups are done, each group takes a turn to show their drawings for the other students to guess the rhyme. (*Creating the drawings requires imagining, generating ideas, planning, and representing; guessing the rhyming words requires inferring, deducing, and transferring.*)

The rhyming words can also be part of a short phrase, such as "pup in a cup" or "a mouse on a house." The mouse and the house can be drawn on separate pieces of paper, and the students can move the papers to show the mouse going on the house.

In another version of the game, students use physical demonstrations rather than drawings. For example, one student hops, and the other students in the group watch and laugh (a funny bunny). Props can also be used in demonstrations. Students might use brooms while their eyes are closed and their heads hang down (sweeping while sleeping).

The game can be noncompetitive, as described above, or can be made competitive in a number of ways. Points can be awarded to the group or pair that guesses the rhyme correctly before the others. Points can also be awarded for the funniest or most clever rhyme using a voting process like the one described in Chapter 6 (on page 111).

As they catch on to the game, the pictures can become more challenging. For older students who have become adept at playing Rhyme Time, the game can be extended to require more advanced levels of thinking by creating three-word rhymes and/or restricting the rhymes to a category, such as clothing (a blue shoe). It can also involve content knowledge such as math (the third bird, half of a giraffe, a square bear) and literature (the three bears go upstairs, Goldilocks's socks, the cat in the hat).

Themes and *HOThemes*

In this method, content knowledge in all subject areas, concepts, and skills are taught within activities that are based on a theme. Theme-based learning is an effective and powerful teaching method at every grade level, including postsecondary. College literature courses commonly assign books of various genres that address a theme such as justice, the immigrant experience, moral dilemmas, or coming-of-age. A theme creates a context, which is ideal for implementing the infusion approach to teaching HOT skills and which makes learning easier for contextual thinkers. It is more attuned to the way children naturally learn (Buchsbaum et al., 2011; Gopnik, 2016) and more like the way thinking skills are applied by adults in real-life situations. Also, it motivates students to learn, particularly if the theme is compelling to them. Themes also lend themselves to project-based learning, which is the next method discussed in this chapter.

A *HOTheme* is a theme that lends itself to activities that are intellectually rigorous, enjoyable, active and interactive, meaningful to students, and engage HOT. *HOThemes* address significant issues in children's lives, issues that all children grapple with almost every day.

Common themes in kindergarten and the early grades, such as seasons, weather, and special occasions like Thanksgiving (in the U.S.), Valentine's Day, and Halloween, lend themselves more to activities that engage LOT skills than MOT or HOT skills. However, themes like these can be enhanced by incorporating them under a broader, more compelling theme. For example, the theme "changes" (described below) can incorporate the themes of seasons and weather. Other *HOTheme* ideas follow.

Changes. Activities can involve differentiating changes among seasons, determining the cause of seasonal changes (connecting causes and effects), and investigating how the changes are linked and circular (inductive thinking), and how they impact students' lives (connecting causes and effects, self-reflection, and generating ideas). Changes happen to everything in nature, including people. Just as the tilt of earth over time—the year it takes to orbit the sun completely—causes the four seasonal changes, the course of time and events change people's lives. Births, marriages, new jobs, relocations, divorces, and deaths change families. For current students, turning five and starting kindergarten meant changing schools, teachers, friends, and activities and perhaps riding a school bus for the first time.

No Fair! This theme explores the issue of fairness and involves learning, inventing, and practicing different techniques to make sure that the pizza is divided equally, that everyone gets an equal turn on the swing, and that decisions are made fairly. It also involves understanding the various causes and types of unfairness, particularly those that are deliberately perpetrated or are covert. An important idea, but a bit abstract for young learners, is conveyed in this theme through many demonstrations: why *equal* treatment is not always what is most fair. For third graders, the theme can extend to social issues such as fairness in friendships and in sports.

Winning and Losing. This theme addresses the issue of competition in its many forms and ways to depersonalize losing and be gracious in winning. The roles that chance, luck, effort, skill, and practice play in winning and losing are explored. HOT skills that can contribute to winning, such as calculating, planning/strategizing, shifting perspective, and imagining, are practiced in the context of games and contests.

Skill or Luck? is a theme closely related to "Winning and Losing" and can be included in it rather than as a separate theme. In this theme, the issue of chance is explored in more depth. A number of the activities involve distinguishing between luck and skill. Students invent games and intentionally manipulate aspects of games to alter how much luck vs. skill is involved in winning. This idea is also embedded in the *ThinkinGroups, Twins* (on page 203).

Some are Better than Others addresses the issue of unequal innate abilities among people and the important role of effort in accomplishments. One goal of this theme is to help students understand and accept that some people have more ability or talent in certain areas than other people, although everyone has strengths and weaknesses. Activities for this theme help students to learn the concept of innate ability—talents, physical coordination and agility, and memorization capacity—but, more importantly, to learn that effort can bridge ability gaps and innate abilities will often dissipate without effort. Teachers model and encourage students to be happy for their classmates' achievements and be inspired by them rather than feel envious. Students are encouraged and supported to determine and share their own innate abilities and help each other identify the type of efforts that will strengthen their innate abilities. Students work in groups on multimedia projects about a person of their choosing who accomplished something great or who excels (or excelled) in some way. The projects highlight that person's efforts, the obstacles they faced and how they overcame them, as well as their innate abilities.

Brain Power addresses students' ideas and feelings about "good and bad" and power and control. Many children have misconceptions about physical power, which they learn from animated television shows and other media aimed at children. They internalize the false notion that "good guys" are always more powerful than "bad guys." This leads them to believe they can beat up or destroy anything or anybody who is "bad," no matter how big or strong, because they see themselves as the "good guys." This misconception logically leads to another misconception: violence is an acceptable solution to any conflict or threat because good will always defeat evil. The goal of this theme is for students to internalize the idea that brain power is mightier than physical power. The only way that a smaller and weaker animal or person can defeat or thwart a bigger and stronger animal or person is with brain power. Along with a variety of media literacy activities, there is an extended and deep inquiry of brain power in many forms through reading and analyzing stories (fictional and real) in which people or characters use cleverness (imagining and generating ideas), cunning, quick thinking, preparation, foresight, strategy, and similar tactics, rather than force, to solve conflicts or save themselves from danger. Stories with protagonists who are children or small characters are highlighted. Among these stories are fairy tales like "Puss n' Boots" and "Tom Thumb" and many of Roald Dahl's books.

Me and We deals with the tension between the individual and the collective, between self-identity and group-identity. Activities help students learn the many ways to be a good group member while still being a strong, unique individual and to think and act independently while respecting the needs and rights of others. Among many other activities, the books of Leo Lionni which address this issue—*Swimmy* (1963/2011), *Frederick* (1967/2017), and *A Color of His Own* (1975/2000)—are read and discussed.

Some of the most impactful theme ideas come from carefully observing children and listening to their conversations over time. Often an issue that concerns them emerges, as in the following *Snap-sHOT*.

Snap-sHOT: WILD AND TAME

A photo book about African animals is a favorite of the younger children in Drew's after-school program, particularly the photos of lions, cheetahs, and other big cats. The book is a large coffee-table type of book with sharp, colorful photos, some of which depict grisly scenes of big cats capturing and tearing apart impalas and other prey. The children find these photos to be both scary and irresistible. Small groups of children enjoy looking at the book together and having lively conservations, which include a good deal of squealing and "oohing," in addition to heated discussions about how to avoid being eaten by a lion.

In their play outside, children try to capture and "tame" other children who are pretending to be wild animals. Often, the "wild animals" let themselves be caught and tamed, but, after a short period, they go back to being wild. They repeat this cycle many times with slight variations and often switch roles. Drew believes that this provides a healthy way for children to act "bad" without consequences, to grapple with issues of impulse control, and to learn to manage their anger and other strong, negative feelings.

In response, Drew develops the theme Wild and Tame. The goal of the theme is to help the students gain a deep understanding of the concept of *control* and of their feelings and needs related to it. To accomplish the goal, Drew introduces several new and varied activities that promote the use of HOT skills in the process of exploring wildness vs. tameness and out-of-control vs. in control. These include reading and discussing relevant books, inventing stories, and using the stories as the basis for imaginary play scenarios that expand and add complexity to the stories.

During these activities, Drew jumps on the opportunities they present to engage children's HOT by asking incisive questions during discussions. Among the books they read and discuss are *Where the Wild Things Are* (Sendak, 1963), *The Lion and the Mouse* (Pickney, 2009), and *No, David!* (Shannon, 1998), and a few other books in the "David" series.

190 ◆ Learning to Think, Thinking to Learn

> Drew leads his students through a process for making up a story called Chain Stories (which is described later in this chapter, on page 211). One of the stories they create is about a tiger who is captured for the circus and is tamed and taught tricks to perform in a circus act. She misses her home and her family, but it takes several years and a few failed escape attempts before she has an opportunity to escape and return home. During those years, she had become a star of the circus with her amazing tricks. She is happy to be home and reunited, but it doesn't take long before she feels restless and bored. Life at home is a lot less exciting than the circus—there is no one to appreciate her tricks—and now she misses all her human and animal friends. Finally, she makes a deal with the circus manager that she will return to the circus if she can perform for half of the year and spend the other half of the year at home.
>
> Drew asks the children probing questions that initiate (guided) discussions:
>
> Can a real animal be both wild and tame? What would that look like? Can a person be wild? Tame? Describe a wild person. A tame person. What might cause a person to be wild? Can a wild person be tamed? How? Can a person be both wild and tame? What would that look like?
>
> As the children act out the story and improvise on the plot, Drew carefully observes changes to their thinking about control, the aspects of control that they focus on, and any new concerns that might emerge.

It can be challenging to develop activities that make the concepts addressed by themes concrete, interactive, and understandable to young learners. It is an additional challenge to develop activities that also elicit HOT to deepen students' understanding of the concepts. Therefore, *HOThemes* should be planned well in advance so there is ample time to research the topic, develop effective activities, identify resources, and obtain quality materials.

Projects and Inquiries

Projects and inquiries are ideal for implementing *HOThemes* and for facilitating all four teaching precepts. Both are types of investigations (a thought process). Projects take place over an extended period of time and involve multiple related activities, including inquiries. Often, the activities contribute to the creation of a final product or set of products—perhaps a mural, a scale model, or a set of student-made books on the theme of the project.

Inquiries are typically shorter-term and less comprehensive than projects and are employed for answering questions or understanding concepts or ideas. Inquiries are processes for discovering the answer to a question and coming to an understanding of an idea. Being given an answer or explanation involves LOT skills (identifying and memorizing). Inquiries engage HOT. Of course, not every question or idea can be, or should be, the subject of an inquiry. But teachers can occasionally initiate mini-inquiries by asking "What do *you* think?" in response to questions and at the start of a brief explanation of an idea.

Projects and inquiries are flexible and open-ended processes, and often the plans and activities, or even the original line of inquiry, change during the process. Even when the final product of a project is planned, exactly how it will turn out is not predetermined. The specific content or look of the product will be the result of the inquiry process.

Following are descriptions of projects previously referred to in the examples of *HOThemes*:

> This project for first to third graders relates to the *HOTheme, Luck or Skill?* It entails the development of games. There are four categories of games: those in which winning or losing is (1) entirely the result of luck, (2) mostly the result of luck and a little skill, (3) mostly the result of skill and a little luck, and (4) entirely the result of skill. Games can be of any type, such as board games, sports, and video games. Students study existing games of different types that fit into each of the four categories. They work in groups to invent a set of four games of any type, one for each category. Alternatively,

192 ◆ Learning to Think, Thinking to Learn

they can create one game with four sets of rules. Then they make the game or games, test them, revise them as necessary, and share their work during a whole-class family game night at the school.

This project for second and third graders, about people who excel, is an activity for the *HOTheme, Some are Better than Others*. Students work in groups to create multimedia presentations about a living person of their choosing who excels in some way and has achieved great things. It can be a famous person, like an athlete, actor, musician, scientist, or artist. The presentation must focus on information about the person's childhood and background and the story of how they came to be accomplished (not famous). After each presentation, there is a guided discussion about the challenges and supports, the type and amount of effort, and the role of innate ability and other factors that contributed to the person's success. Then students do similar, but individual, presentations about someone they know or are related to. The teacher assists them to develop good questions for interviewing the person.

Through **inquiries**, students learn and practice basic research methods within activities appropriate for young learners. Two types of inquiries are described below. The first one connects to the *HOTheme, No Fair!* It addresses a common concern about claims of unfairness: "Is it really unfair, or does it just feel that way?" It uses social science opinion research methods. The second example connects to the *HOTheme, Brain Power* and uses the literature review method of research adapted for young learners.

HOTheme: **No Fair!:** Using social science opinion research methods, this inquiry was initiated when a first-grade teacher overheard some of her students complain about having too much homework. They said that it isn't fair that they have more homework than their older siblings. The teacher agreed that it *is* unfair—if it is true. If the inquiry finds that her students do have more homework than older students, she promises them to reduce it. The inquiry starts with formulating the following research questions:

Do first graders have more homework than second and third graders?
How much more (or less) homework do first graders have?

Next the teacher leads them through the thought process of hypothesizing and eventually arrives at "First graders *do* have more homework: a half hour more than second graders and 15 minutes more than third graders." Data collecting entails first graders asking all second and third graders how much time they typically spend doing homework every day. In addition, the teacher examines two weeks of homework assignments from the second- and third-grade teachers to estimate how long it should take students to complete them. The teacher tallies all results (calculating) with the students, explaining what she is doing and why (modeling), and involving them as much as possible. Then they create a series of simple graphs to visualize the data (representing). After reviewing the data and doing a simple analysis—more/fewer, big differences/small differences/no differences, expected results/unexpected results—they could definitively answer the research questions, if only the bell hadn't rung to end the school day. The class heads home to do (too much) homework.

HOTheme: **Brain Power:** Using the literature review method of research, this inquiry for kindergarten or first grade is to explore the concept of brain power in general and, more specifically, how it can be used to thwart or defeat physical power or danger, especially for a small person or animal. The research method is a literature review of brain power ploys found in stories and to analyze the information. Stories include fairy and folk tales, contemporary children's fiction and non-fiction books, newspaper and magazine articles (summarized and retold by the teacher), and personal stories from students' family members and from other teachers and staff in the school.

In the process of collecting all the brain power ploys, the teacher guides the children to look for commonalities among them. This naturally leads to categorizing them (a logical thinking skill). The teacher guides brainstorming sessions (generating ideas) and discussions after each reading to describe and make associations and differentiations among ploys (a MOT skill). Identifying the categories is an ongoing process; they are added to and amended over the course of the inquiry. They come to realize that the ploys can be described in two main ways, by their type and by their purpose, although some ploys have more than one purpose and some are of more than one type. The four types of ploys are verbal (using words or sounds), physical (using the body or moving), visual (using small size as an advantage or using disguises), and assisted (using props or tools or getting the help of an ally). The three purposes are to avoid capture or danger, to help others, and to escape or defend or protect themselves. This gives the teacher and the class a method and the vocabulary to make the concept of brain power more concrete and understandable.

To help the students analyze the information, the teacher makes and posts a chart of the categories using symbols and graphics (representation). As new examples arise, they use the chart to associate and differentiate them from other ploys with similar characteristics. They play a simple game in which the teacher describes a conflict or a dangerous or scary situation (some are fantastical and some are plausible) and, referring to the chart, challenges the children to use their brain power to get out of it safely and peacefully. When appropriate, they act it out. The children also challenge the teacher with scary situations (many seem to involve dinosaurs), which are great opportunities for the teacher to model brain power.

Inquiry-based learning methods offer great opportunities to teach a range of subjects in an integrated way and within a meaningful context. They also allow teachers to observe students' cognitive styles and thinking skills authentically in action. The process and products of projects and inquiries are documented with photos, videos, and brief written explanations, observations, and students' statements. They capture how students found solutions to various problems, planned and strategized, and how they used and improved their thinking skills.

Case Studies

Case studies are not just for Harvard Business School students. They are as effective for third graders as they are for grad students. Case studies are short descriptions of real-life situations or dilemmas that are meaningful and relevant to young learners. Typically, students work in small groups to come up with responses and solutions. Case studies engage creative thinking because they do not have just one answer or a correct answer. Topics range from a new student entering the class who has mild autism to responding to a rumor that the school will be closing. Case study work elicits logical thinking, such as connecting causes and effects, and critical thinking, such as deducing/inducing. The *Cognitivity* below is challenging, but it deals with an issue that is relevant and compelling to young learners.

COGNITIVITY: THE CASE OF THE UNKNOWN BULLY

Someone is bullying the kindergartners and first graders on the playground and in the neighborhood. No one is willing to say who the bully is because the bully threatens to beat up anyone who tells. The bully knows what the kindergartners and first graders are saying and doing, so there must be a few of them that inform the bully in exchange for being on the bully's good side. No teacher or parent has been able to catch the bully in action.

What is the best way to solve this problem? Students try to come up with several solutions and then choose the one they think is best. For a solution to be considered among the best, it must ensure that no one gets hurt and the bullying behavior stops permanently. If the mean behavior can be transformed into kind behavior, that would be even better. The bully cannot be expelled or somehow removed from the school and neighborhood. Students are reminded that the bully does not necessarily have to be identified or dealt with directly and are given the suggestion to think about why someone would bully another person.

196 ◆ Learning to Think, Thinking to Learn

Role-plays and Sketches

In role-plays and sketches, students improvise (a creative thinking skill) the actions within the structure established by the teacher. Role-plays help students gain a deeper understanding of ideas and concepts. They also give students practice using new skills, behaviors, and vocabulary to apply their newly acquired HOT skills in a variety of situations and contexts (transferring). A popular idea for a role-play is to enact a talk show in which famous people from history are interviewed.

Another type of role-play focuses on resolving a conflict. This gives the role-play a bit more drama. Students practice applying HOT skills—generating ideas and shifting perspective—to resolve conflicts (the thought process of finding solutions) set in playful and sometimes fantastical situations. Some ideas for role-plays for resolving conflicts could be negotiating turns for taking the class Tyrannosaurus Rex for a walk; sharing equally the left-over half of an apple pie among three ants at a picnic; developing a process to decide which two of four astronauts will get to go to the moon; and determining how all the dogs in the pack can respond to the bossy and mean dog who won't invite them to her birthday party if they don't give her all their dog food.

Sketches are more prescriptive than role-plays and involve more sophisticated improvisation, so they are better suited to seven-year-old students and older. The subject of a sketch can be a scene from a book that students are reading (or being read to) or from a historic or current event that students are studying. Students are assigned to play the characters from the book or the people involved in the event. Additional characters can be added to include more students in the sketch as long as the roles are plausible and contribute to and do not detract from the story. By including nonspeaking roles, students who are introverted or who are language learners may be more willing to participate. The sketch begins with students acting out the scene as accurately as they can but without a script. Of course, the teacher provides instructional supports as needed. Then they are encouraged and assisted to improvise and expand the story or to go into more depth. Changing what actually happened is perfectly acceptable as long as students are intentional about the changes and the changes are plausible. Almost any content area can be addressed in a sketch. With practice, young learners can become surprisingly adept at performing sketches.

Materials that Matter

Materials include everything from math manipulatives, to worksheets, to books and texts, to computer software or apps. Some materials, "materials that matter," are better for engendering HOT than others, including some in the same category, as in the case of electronic materials discussed below. The "art cards" for the *ThinkinGroups, The Fine Art of Matching* (Chapter 4 on page 44) are examples of "materials that matter."

Electronic Materials: A Lot of LOT, Not Much HOT

Computers are great tools for teachers to facilitate teaching everything, including HOT skills. They can make learning lively and interactive and provide access to millions of resources and a world of information. In addition, utility programs are great for planning, organizing, preserving, and displaying student work and much more. They have become so essential that it is hard to imagine teaching without them. But as tools for young learners, there is little that promotes HOT; most "educational" software engages and reinforces LOT and low levels of logical MOT thinking.

Many websites with resources for young learners are too visually busy, commercialized, and not designed for nonreaders or even beginning readers. A delightful exception is the New York Metropolitan Museum of Art's website MetKids (www.metmuseum.org/art/online-features/metkids). While focused on art and creativity, it also has information about history, geography, and "big ideas," including inventions, mythology, fashion, and sports, as seen through the lens of the artwork in the museum.

There are some open-ended "art studio" software programs and apps, but drawing with real markers, pens, and colored pencils and painting with watercolors and other media using real brushes are much better options for creative expression.

There are, nevertheless, two software programs/apps that are cleverly designed to promote HOT, including creative thinking: "Crayon Physics" and "ScratchJr" or, for older students, "Scratch." Crayon Physics (www.crayonphysics.com) is a computer simulation game that somehow manages to engage and challenge both logical and creative thinking simultaneously. It is truly a *ThinkinGroups*. On the purely graphic interface, the player is given a task such as pushing a ball off a tall platform so it will land on a shorter platform. The task is accomplished by drawing freeform shapes and lines that, when completed, move in space and interact, accurately following the laws of physics. As there is an unlimited number of ways to accomplish each task, some of which are simple, the goal is to complete the task in a uniquely clever and creative way. The drawings can be done with a mouse or directly on a touchscreen. Unlike art studio software, these activities can be done only on a computer. In addition, there are tasks at many levels of difficulty, so kindergartners can use it and adults can be challenged. It is a commercial program but relatively inexpensive. This is a unique game. Available since 2009, it will hopefully continue to be available far into the future.

ScratchJr, for five- to seven-year-olds (www.scratchjr.org), and Scratch, for ages eight and above (www.scratch.mit.edu), are programs that enable students to use code (symbols) to write computer programs to create simple games and interactive stories. Because the possibilities are almost limitless, they have a strong creative component, though of a different type than Crayon Physics. While mostly logical MOT skills are needed to write a program using the command icons, inductive thinking, imagining, and generating ideas (HOT skills) are needed to create content for the program. Characters, actions, and typical computer commands (e.g., start a script or end one, repeat the previous command, go back to the start, and exit the program) are represented by simple icons. Students sequence the icons to create their stories and games. Some of the commands indicate what the user needs to do (touch an object and input a number or letter), which allows students to create games. Scratch, for older students, is closer to a complete programming language. Both versions are free to use and have abundant online resources for teachers. These are very helpful because most students will require some amount of instruction to use them. ScratchJr and Crayon Physics are two examples of activities that put the power of technology into the hands of young learners and are equal parts enjoyable and intellectually challenging. Similar programs and apps that provide coding tools and practice for young learners include Tynker (www.tynker.com) for ages seven and up; Kodable (https://www.kodable.com) for ages five to eight; Code & Go Robot Mouse Activity Set (www.learningresources.com) for ages five and up; and Pre-reader Express and other curricula from Code.org (www.code.org) for ages four to eight. Because technology changes rapidly, some of these resources may no longer be available and new ones will certainly be developed. Search for "coding for young learners" in your web browser to access the most current resources.

Books and Texts

All texts that students are exposed to—the ones they learn to read with, the ones they are read to by teachers, and the ones they read on their own—can contribute to developing their HOT skills. Fortunately, this is not hard to do. There is so much excellent children's literature at every reading level that the biggest challenge is to choose from among them. The qualities that define excellent children's literature are also qualities that engage and promote HOT. Qualities refer to both the structural elements of the story and the story itself. Structural elements that engage HOT include plot twists, subplots, flashbacks, characters who face and overcome challenges, humor to communicate serious ideas, and settings that are historical, foreign, or imaginary. Stories that engage HOT include topics and themes that are meaningful and relevant to students, messages that are subtle or allegorical, and characters who grow, learn, and change and who use their wits to overcome challenges.

Non-fiction books have somewhat different qualities. Good non-fiction books use clear, succinct language to accurately explain complex or abstract information and ideas without being condescending. Excellent non-fiction books do this and more. They make the information meaningful and enjoyable. Some contextualize the information by embedding it in an interesting event (e.g., a safari, a trip to the moon, a diving adventure, a fossil hunt). Some contextualize it by embedding it in a compelling narrative (e.g., the challenges that an arctic penguin faces to breed and feed their young or how an orphaned wild animal was saved, rehabilitated, and returned to the wild). And some give the information in rhyming verse with whimsical but accurate pictures.

Texts that do not have these qualities are like highly processed foods. They stave off hunger in the short term (reading happens and some reading skills may improve), but they do not provide enough nutrition to be healthy in the long-term (they do not contribute to student's ability to read more challenging and sophisticated literature later). In addition, eating bland food is not pleasurable, and a steady diet will make eating a chore and suppress one's appetite (they make reading a chore and suppress any desire or motivation to read). For more information about texts and learning to read, see Chapter 11.

Math Playing Cards

This is an example of a teaching/learning material that has multiple uses and is ideal for infusing the explicit teaching of HOT skills within a subject, which, in this case, is math. Math playing cards have the same characteristics as standard playing cards but have no picture cards (jokers, queens, or kings). Also, the four suits are shapes: squares, rectangles, circles, and triangles (rather than clubs, hearts, spades, and diamonds). The two suit colors are black and white, as shown in Figure 9.1, but they could also be black and red as with standard playing cards. The cards are referred to as "two of circles" or "twelve of rectangles." The cards should be the same size or a bit larger than standard playing cards, made with good-quality stiff card stock and laminated so they will last.

Almost any game that can be played with standard playing cards can be played with math playing cards, plus many more.

HOT Teaching Methods ◆ 201

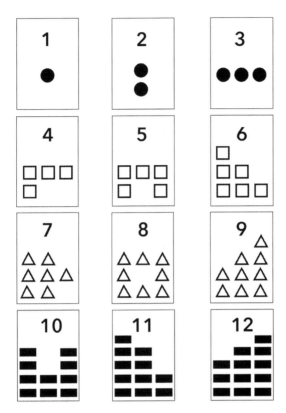

FIGURE 9.1 Math Playing Cards Sample.
Graphic by Gwendolyn Rodriguez.

The highest value card in the sample set illustrated in Figure 9.1 is 12, so the complete set would have 48 cards. But higher value cards can be added in sets of four, two of each suit. Also, blank cards with zero value can be added, as can "X cards." These are wild cards that can have any value or function the players choose before any game starts, such as the lowest, the highest, or always the same as the opponent's card. This introduces the algebraic concept that X represents an unknown.

For older students, cards can have additional suits in the form of shapes, such as ellipses, rhombuses, pentagons, and hexagons. For younger learners, higher-value cards can be removed; the highest card can be five, for example. However, more cards need to be added because most games require more than 20 cards. There can also be duplicate math cards, which are actually useful rather than problematic as with playing cards. The shapes on the cards should be randomly scattered or grouped in different ways as in the sample.

There are many other possible variations of math playing cards. For seven- and eight-year-olds, a set of cards could just have the black and red number symbols with only one shape on each card to indicate the suit. Every classroom should have multiple sets of several versions so groups of students can play at the same time and a range of ability levels can be accommodated. These cards are used in the *ThinkinGroups, Twins,* explained in the next section.

Games and *ThinkinGroups*

Games are terrific teaching and learning methods. And when they facilitate the acquisition of content knowledge with HOT, they are *ThinkinGroups.* These interactive, enjoyable activities can address any content area and facilitate the development of any and all MOT and HOT skills. *ThinkinGroups* often require students to use two or more types of thinking at the same time or in quick succession. They also promote social skills, such as taking turns, and build thinking dispositions such as attention, patience, and persistence. When playing in teams, *ThinkinGroups* can help students learn to collaborate.

While many games are competitive, and losing can be difficult for some students, when they play games of different types often and regularly, they come to understand that everyone sometimes wins and sometimes loses, especially when there is a large element of luck. This understanding can be further facilitated through the previously discussed *HOThemes,* projects and inquiries that explore the concepts of luck, ability, practice, effort, and skill as they apply to winning.

Existing games can be modified, or new games can be created, that require students to use HOT skills in the process of

HOT Teaching Methods ◆ 203

playing. One quick way to modify games that involve points or numbers is to make a new rule that lower numbers beat higher numbers. Also, winning could mean having the fewest cards or no cards, having the lowest final score, or finishing last (outlasting one's opponent). Using such counterintuitive rules in games gives students practice applying HOT skills that can help thwart thinking errors.

Game rules can change periodically, followed by discussions about the ways the changes impacted the game. Students can contribute ideas for changing rules (generative thinking) and predict what will happen (a thought process). Playing different types of games that require similar capabilities and use the same game principles helps students understand the abstract concepts and transfer them to other activities (transferring is a type of reframing HOT skill). For example, to wait and watch for an opportune moment is an important ability and effective strategy in many games. Skilled players have the patience to wait for a good pitch in baseball, a good card in a card game, a good opening to run back to the base in a game of tag, and a good opportunity to capitalize on an opponent's mistake. While patience may still be a virtue, there seem to be fewer and fewer exemplars of patience in popular culture for young learners to emulate. Another way to help students transfer concepts is to provide multiple variations of the same game, as in the example below.

ThinkinGroups: TWINS

The basic version of **Twins** is the same as the card game "War" but uses math playing cards (as previously described on page 201). For two players, the deck is divided in half with the cards face down. Players turn over the card on the top of their stack and place it face up on the table. The higher-number card takes the trick. When the cards are the same number, they say "Twins!" They place two more cards face down and play the third card. The player with the higher-number card takes all four of their opponent's cards. If the deck includes duplicate cards, a hand could result in "Identical Twins." In this case, three cards are placed face down and the fourth card is played. The winner of the game is either the player with all the cards or the one with the most cards after a preset time period. There are an unlimited number of variations of Twins. Below are just a few.

Twins Upside Down. In this variation, the lower-value card beats the higher-value card.

Twins: What's the Difference? Players each overturn two cards and subtract the lower number from the higher number. The same numbers equal zero. The values of the difference determine the outcome. Before the game starts, or even before each hand, students decide if the higher-value or the lower-value difference wins the trick. A more challenging variation entails playing three cards.

Twins: Limited Addition. This is the same game as Twins: What's the Difference? except card values are added together. Older students can multiply or divide the values.

Twin Teams. There are two players on each team. The deck is divided into fourths. Each player overturns one card. The two players on the same team subtract, add, multiply, and so on their cards (depending on the version of the game being played). The team's results are then played against the other team. Using a large deck or two decks will make the game last longer.

Twin Teams Plus. Each player picks up two cards from their deck. The two team members look at the four cards together without revealing them to the opposing team. They arrange the four cards into two sets of pairs that will give them the best chances to win the next two hands. They put the cards back on their stacks so that the pairs they created will be played correctly. This process repeats after the two hands are played. The game can also be played with each player picking up three cards and strategizing the next three hands.

Twins II. Twins II is a different version of Twins, not just a variation. Except for Twin Teams Plus, winning is a matter of luck in the previous variations of Twins. Twins II introduces strategizing (a thought process), although luck still plays a major role. This basic version of Twins II is a two-player game. Each hand begins with the two players looking at the card they pick up from the top of their deck without showing it to their opponent. Right away, they have a decision to make (another thought process): play the card or "take a chance." If they both choose to play the card, the game proceeds as usual. Players would do this if they have a high-number card because they are likely to win (if the rule is that the highest value wins). But, if their card is a low number, they could improve their chances of winning the hand by playing the next card from their deck. However, this risks the possibility of losing both cards. Here's how it works: While both players are holding their cards, Player A says "Take a chance" because she holds a three of circles. Player B holds a ten of squares and so says nothing. They both place their cards face up on the table. (If Player B's card number was the same or lower, the game proceeds as usual.) Because Player B's card number is higher, Player A turns over the top card on her deck and plays that card. If Player A loses (e.g., the next card is a five), both cards go to Player B and the decision to take a chance does not pay off. Of course, both players can choose the "take a chance" option. Twins II can have all the same variations as Twins.

206 ◆ Learning to Think, Thinking to Learn

ThinkinGroups: MENTAL FLOSSERS

Mental flossers are quick, fun mental challenges. They are great for "recharging" between lessons or during breaks. Unlike nearly all the other *ThinkinGroups*, mental flossers are not used for teaching content or to connect to a theme. This is intentional, as they are exercises for the mind, the way recess or gym time is exercise for the body. Some will require a few minutes of preparation between the end of the school day and the beginning of the next day. They engage a variety of HOT skills and can be easily modified to be more or less challenging. Students can work on the solutions to mental flossers individually, in pairs, or in small groups. Here are some examples:

- ◆ Identify two things in the room that are similar but not the same. This could be modified to identify as many things as possible that are all similar but not the same or as many pairs of similar things as possible.
- ◆ Identify something in the room that was not here yesterday. For a greater challenge, the something can be intangible, such as sunlight, excitement, quiet, order, a science lesson, or comfort (room temperature).
- ◆ Identify something that is missing from the room today that was there yesterday. Hints can be given to make it easier.
- ◆ Identify three things in the room that are all different shades of the same color. For a greater challenge, think of something *not* in the room that is a fourth shade of the same color.
- ◆ Think of something that you wish was in the room but isn't. It must be able to fit in the room and be reasonably possible (e.g., wanting a decorative fountain rather than a swimming pool).

Teachers can adjust the level of difficulty so most students are challenged but can still understand the task and not feel too frustrated. Mental flossers should become more challenging as the

HOT Teaching Methods ◆ 207

year progresses and students become more adept. For another level of challenge and fun, students can think up mental flossers for each other and for the teacher. Trying to stump the teacher with really hard challenges is something students will enjoy.

ThinkinGroups: GAME OF STONES (AND SHELLS)

Game of Stones promotes a variety of MOT skills, such as associating/differentiating and categorizing, using aesthetically pleasing, natural materials. It helps build descriptive vocabulary (adjectives) and a variety of social skills. It can easily be made more, or less, challenging.

With a group of four to six students around a table or sitting in a circle, students carefully observe and describe the attributes of each stone and shell among a group and organize them by their attributes. The stones and shells are carefully chosen to be distinct from each other on at least one attribute, such as size, color, or shape. Then the stones are randomly arranged and placed in the middle of the group. One student is the Stone Master, who selects one of the stones to hide in a small box or cup while the other students are not looking. Because it is difficult for many young learners to avoid looking by just closing their eyes—the temptation is too great—it may be necessary to have them turn their bodies to face away from the stones or put their heads down on their folded arms. Then the students look at the stones and shells that remain and try to figure out which one is missing.

When students think they know the answer and can describe its attributes in enough detail to distinguish it from the others, they put their hands on their head. The first student to do this answers first. They always start by identifying it as a stone or a shell. If the student is wrong or cannot describe enough of its attributes to distinguish it, the second student has a turn. The Stone Master is in charge of making the call (with assistance from the teacher if needed). The student who is correct gets to be the next Stone Master.

The first few times this game is played, there should only be a few stones and shells so students can easily learn the game and be successful at the start. The number of stones and shells and the number of attributes vary depending on the age level and skill level of the students. For all grade levels, it is important to continually increase the challenge. More challenging variations include rearranging the stones after a stone or shell has been hid and before students open their eyes, hiding more than one stone or shell, and adding stones and shells to increase the number of attributes. To get the correct answer, students need to use the LOT skills of memorizing and recalling, the MOT skill of associating/differentiating, and the HOT skill of deductive thinking (Figure 9.2).

Game of Stones (and Shells)

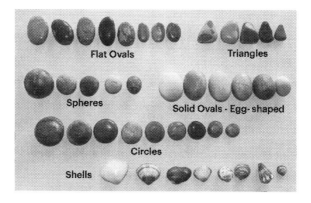

FIGURE 9.2 Game of Stones (and Shells).

Photos by the author. Graphic by Gwendolyn Rodriquez.

HOT Teaching Methods ◆ 209

The following *ThinkinGroups* can use words from any content area. It's a fun way to reinforce new vocabulary and concepts. In the example below, the content area is natural science.

ThinkinGroups: DON'T SAY THE WORD!

This game is played between two teams of about six players, although it could be played with more. The teacher shows a picture or an actual item from nature to one student from Team A so that others on the team cannot see it. This student is called the "scholar." The scholar's task is to describe the item without using its name while her teammates try to guess what it is (HOT skills of infer, induce, and interpret). This is timed with a stopwatch. If the scholar says the name of the item or her team does not guess it in a minute and a half, they are done and Team B has a turn with a different item from nature. (Teachers may need to adjust the amount of time per turn so it is optimal for their students.) If Team A does guess it correctly in the allotted time, they score one point and then Team B has an opportunity to score a point under the same rules. If both teams are not able to guess correctly, the items are revealed and no points are scored. The game continues with two different students, one from each team, taking the role of the scholar. The team with the most points after every student has a turn being the scholar is the winner. Pictures can be of a bird, a bird's nest, a tree, any forest or jungle animal, a river, a mountain, a waterfall, and so on. Actual items from nature can be a leaf, a stone, a flower, an acorn (or other seedpod), an apple (or other fruit), a nut, or other small item.

This game has the additional advantage that it requires few materials. In fact, it can be played with no materials at all. There are many variations to make the game more challenging as students become adept at playing it. Students who can read can be given a word rather than a picture or an item. Students can guess things that are more abstract, such as characters from a story, emotions, or activities like writing, cooking, swimming, and singing. Activities that are specific are even more challenging, such as waiting for a bus, going on a family vacation, or planting a vegetable garden.

The next *ThinkinGroups* is noncompetitive. In fact, it's all about collaboration and communication. Nonetheless, it is one of the more challenging games in the book. It is a game that requires a great deal of practice and teacher assistance at first, but it is well worth the effort. Once they have achieved a reasonable level of competence, students will enjoy playing this game independently and experimenting with variations.

ThinkinGroups: DESCRIBE IT/DRAW IT

Two students sit opposite each other at a table. Each of them has paper and a pencil. In between them is a barrier so they cannot see the area of the table in front of their partner. One partner starts by drawing a number or a letter on his paper. Then he instructs his partner how to draw it, making sure not to say the name of the number or letter (shift perspective). The instructions should be as specific and detailed as possible. Gesturing is highly discouraged! The partner draws on her paper following the directions she is being given (infer, interpret). When this is completed, she states the name of the number or letter. Then they take down the barrier to determine if it is correct. If it is not, they discuss the process and try to determine what went wrong (analysis). (This part of the game may require support from the teacher.) Then they switch roles and repeat the activity. The objective is to get as many correct in a row as they can, which is their "connection score." Teachers help partners keep track of their connection scores so they can try to best them. A student can be a member of several partnerships.

As students begin to master the game, it can be made more challenging. Drawings can have double-digit numbers, two letters, or short words. In one version of the game, all the numbers and letters are written and described as they appear upside down. Additional challenges can entail using mirror image versions of letters and numbers, common shapes, then uncommon shapes, then multiple shapes, then intersecting shapes.

This language- and literacy-focused *ThinkinGroups* is also noncompetitive and collaborative. There are no teams and no scores. The fun is in imagining and in engaging the collective imagination of the class.

ThinkinGroups: CHAIN STORIES

The teacher starts the story by describing a compelling situation or event and modeling formal, literary language. The topic could be related to a theme or a content area. The opening lines establish the main characters and set the plot in motion. Then students systematically take turns contributing to the plot; significant contributions, such as plot twists or new characters, are encouraged. The teacher guides the students with questions as needed. "What is most likely to happen next?" "What could happen that would be surprising? Or funny? Or helpful?" "What do you *hope* will happen?" "Is there another option?" The teacher may also need to help students maintain the tone of the story, to offer ideas that are plausible within the context of the story, and to provide sufficient details.

As a follow-up activity, the story can be recorded and/or key plot elements written down so it can be made into a class book. This will most likely require heavy editing first. Literary conventions like flashbacks, subplots, a narrator, and cliffhangers can be gradually introduced to increase the challenge of the activity and teach new writing skills.

Listed below are the *ThinkinGroups* that have been described in previous chapters:

The Fine Art of Matching, on page 44, focuses on associating and differentiating and addresses art and cultural knowledge.

Shape Shifting, on page 85, focuses on imaginative thinking and addresses math.

Family Groups, on page 127, focuses on inductive/theoretic thinking and can address any content area.

Crayon Physics, on page 198, is a commercial computer simulation game that focuses on creative and logical thinking. It addresses physical science and technology.

ScratchJr, on page 198, is a free app that enables young learners to code and focuses on creative and logical thinking. It addresses art, math and technology.

Conclusion

Collaborating with classmates, using materials that matter, and learning through games, projects, and inquiries that connect to important themes provide a diversity of opportunities for students to learn and practice the full range of MOT and HOT skills. While each of these methods can be effective in and of itself for promoting students' HOT, employing all of them often and regularly over time, increases the effectiveness of each one and infuses HOT throughout the curriculum.

Over time and through many varied experiences, a carpenter's apprentice learns much more than skills. She gains an understanding and appreciation of the unique qualities of each type of wood ("a feel for wood") and of each specialized tool ("a feel for tools"). She begins to internalize the ability to apply an optimal balance of precision and creativity to her physical work and to feel the joy it can bring. In the same way, students learn more than knowledge from teachers who promote HOT with these methods. They begin to get a feel for the value of learning.

They begin to internalize the ability to do intellectually challenging mental work and to feel the joy it can bring.

Key Ideas from this Chapter

1. HOT methods include certain forms or types of social learning, projects and inquiries, themes, case studies, role-plays and sketches, materials, and games.
2. HOT methods align with the four precepts of HOT teaching and foster the development of students' HOT skills.
3. HOT methods give teachers many natural opportunities to teach students HOT skills.
4. Social learning, also called small group or partner learning, requires students to articulate and accurately communicate what they are thinking, adding complexity to thinking tasks and fostering the development of more advanced levels of thinking.
5. Themes that promote HOT, called *HOThemes*, address issues that are compelling to young learners, such as fairness and luck.
6. Projects and inquiries are methods for carrying out *HOThemes* through active learning. Projects occur over time and involve a broad range of activities, including inquiries, in which many subject areas are integrated. Projects often result in a product or set of products. Inquiries are more narrow in scope and are short explorations to answer questions or understand concepts or ideas.
7. Case studies provide students with a relevant problem to solve.
8. Role-plays and sketches enhance and expand students' understanding and appreciation of stories and historic events and figures. They are effective for practicing problem-solving skills and promote creative thinking, particularly improvising.
9. Materials that matter are open-ended, allowing teachers and students to adjust the level of challenge and to

use them in a wide variety of ways. They engage creative thinking and promote flexible thinking (a thinking disposition).

10. Games that promote HOT, called *ThinkinGroups*, are usually tied to a particular subject area such as math. However, some are designed to "recharge" young minds and are intentionally not connected to a subject area, such as "Mental Flossers."

Questions for Discussion

What can teachers do to ensure that when students work in small groups or pairs, they will be productive and have a positive experience?

How can teachers prevent or intervene effectively with typical group dynamics problems such as students who dominate, who don't participate or "pull their weight," who pull others off task, who argue too much, and so on?

What are various ways that technology, including cell phones, tablets, and video games, can be used to promote HOT, if at all?

What are some ways to convince skeptics that games can be an important and effective teaching method?

What other topics or issues for themes would be relevant and engaging to young learners? For cases studies? For role-plays and sketches?

What other materials are potentially effective for promoting HOT skills?

References

Buchsbaum, D., Gopnik, A., Griffiths, T. A., & Shafto, P. (2011). Children's imitation of causal action sequences is influenced by statistical and pedagogical evidence. *Cognition*, *120*(3), 331–340.

Gopnik, A. (2016). *The gardener and the carpenter: What the new science of child development tells us about the relationship between parents and children*. Farrar, Straus, Giroux.

Lionni, L. (2000). *A color of his own*. Random House (Original work published 1975).

Lionni, L. (2011). *Swimmy* (50th anniversary ed.). Dragonfly Books (Original work published 1963).

Lionni, L. (2017). *Frederick*. Dragonfly Books (Original work published 1967).

Pickney, J. (2009). *The lion and the mouse*. Little, Brown.

Sendak, M. (1963). *Where the wild things are*. Harper & Row.

Shannon, D. (1998). *No, David!* Blue Sky Press.

10

HOT Instructional Supports

Sparks, Similes, and Smiles

Instructional supports are teaching practices or techniques that promote a range of students' cognitive abilities and their language skills. *Higher-order thinking (HOT) instructional supports* go a step further. They promote and sharpen students' cognitive abilities to think critically and creatively and the language skills and vocabulary needed to use and express HOT.

Together with HOT precepts and HOT methods, HOT instructional supports constitute the third, and most direct, strategy for promoting and improving students' HOT. Learning to reason with strong logical middle-order thinking (MOT) skills and with the full range of HOT skills can be a long, gradual, and effortful process, even when teachers make it enjoyable. Therefore, it needs to be facilitated, guided, directed, and supported with a high degree of intentionality and effectiveness. This is particularly important for teachers of young learners who are in the best position to prepare their developing minds for the ever more complex cognitive challenges to come, in school and out. Schoolwork gets more demanding by the year, and disinformation gets more sophisticated by the day.

The seven HOT instructional supports covered in this chapter are scaffolding, cuing (nonverbal, verbal, and visual),

DOI: 10.4324/9781032683423-13

demonstrating, prompting, sparking, heating, and conceptualizing. The first support, scaffolding, is a general strategy for implementing HOT instructional supports, rather than an actual support.

Scaffolding

Actual scaffolds are common on construction sites. They allow workers to keep moving higher as floors are added to a building under construction or to support a building that is unstable while under construction. As a metaphor for implementing instructional supports, scaffolding is a fortunate (though unintended) addition to the construction metaphor used throughout this book. Scaffolding simply means helping students act or think at a slightly higher developmental level than they can do on their own. When they no longer require the help given, the teacher stops assisting (removes the scaffold). Often this process repeats so that students' abilities, knowledge, and thinking skills keep developing (more scaffolding is added above). Scaffolds can be verbal, nonverbal, visual, or physical assists. They can range from a supportive nod and smile to a few words of encouragement, to verbal or visual prompts, to offering suggestions, to giving physical assistance. The critical scaffolding skill for teachers is to give students only as much help as is necessary. If more scaffolding is needed, it can always be added. With too much assistance, students will miss the opportunity to independently develop the essential and necessary skills or understandings to move on to the next level. This is akin to working on a building at the fourth-floor level after completing the second floor and ignoring the third floor. Scaffolding is a very useful and effective all-purpose technique for individualizing and for promoting all aspects of students' development, including their HOT. Opportunities to scaffold HOT skills are plentiful during nearly all activities, especially the activities described in the *Cognitivities*, *ThinkinGroups*, and *HOThemes* throughout the book.

Cuing

Cues are reminders. They are a type of mental shortcut for quickly jogging a student's memory to use a HOT skill and to use it effectively. Cues provide a way to communicate with students with minimal disruptions to discussions and activities. Cues can be nonverbal (aka gestures), verbal, or visual or some combination of the three. Visual cues use simple graphics or symbols to remind students to use their HOT skills. They are a form of representational thinking (all cues represent more complete statements or ideas) and require students to infer their meaning, at least at first; responses to cues tend to become automatic after a while. Below are some suggested examples of cues, which teachers should freely change or adapt to make them more responsive to their students' developmental and learning needs. There are also many more cues that teachers can add to each category.

Nonverbal (Gestural) Cuing

There are many simple nonverbal cues that teachers use often from smiling and nodding to a thumbs up, to that dreaded look of disapproval. Many standard sign language signs work well for nonverbal cues, although some of the complex ones can be simplified for the purposes of cuing.

- ◆ Make a small circle with an index finger pointing to the temple: *Think* (American Sign Language or ASL).
- ◆ Tap the head near the temple several times with an index finger: *Think again, rethink.*
- ◆ One hand (with palm down) is placed in front the chest area and moves slowly down towards the waist: *Slow down* (modified from ASL).
- ◆ "Time-out" hand signal as used in sports. One hand is held horizontally on top of the other hand that is held vertically to form a "T": *Pause or stop* (ASL).
- ◆ The palm of the hand is on the head, with a pensive facial expression: *Use higher-order thinking.*

HOT Instructional Supports ◆ 219

- Index fingers of both hands pointing at temples, with a pensive facial expression: *Use critical thinking.*
- Index finger on lips, head slightly tilted, eyes looking up and to the left, whimsical facial expression: *Imagine or use creative thinking.*

Verbal Cuing

Verbal cues are very short, quick reminders; otherwise, they would be directions.

"Take your time."
"Don't hurry."
"Think slowly/deeply/through to the end."
"Use higher-order thinking/deep thinking/creative thinking."
"Avoid thinking errors/faulty thinking."
"That's a thinking error."
"Try again."
"Think again."
"Dig deep."
"Imagine."
"Play with it."
"Run with it."
"Have fun with it."
"Keep an open mind."

Visual Cuing

Visual information in the form of computer icons, emoticons, and all those universal symbols for recycling, handicap parking, restrooms, elevators, and others has become a common form of communication in our world. Simple, clear, easily understood graphics are also effective teaching materials for helping students, particularly nonreaders, remember the meaning and purpose of a concept and for guiding students' behaviors, including their thinking. Each thinking skill can be represented by a simple graphic that suggests its meaning or function. Here are a few ideas (Figure 10.1).

Visual Cues

Logical Thinking Skills

Associate/Differentiate	
Sequence/Pattern	
Calculate	
Connect Causes and Effects	
Represent	2 - TWO - 

Critical Thinking Skills

Query	 ?
Deduce/Induce	
Shift Perspective	

FIGURE 10.1 Visual Cues.

Graphic by Gwendolyn Rodriquez.

(Continued)

Creative Thinking Skills ∞

Imagine	
Generate	
Reframe	
Improvise	

FIGURE 10.1 (Continued)

Demonstrating thought Processes and HOT Skills

Demonstrating is similar to modeling, but it is more overt and closer to explicit teaching than indirect teaching. It entails teachers explaining their own HOT processes to students, as they happen.

The art of demonstrating HOT is to communicate to students the *thinking* that is occurring rather than the subject or result of the thinking. They then are more likely to apply those thought processes and HOT skills to their own actions and circumstances and less likely to just imitate them. One way to do this is to think out loud while using a HOT skill or engaging in a thought process using HOT skills for tasks that are neither academic nor commonly used by students. For example, to model evaluations/decisions, a teacher might say, "I have to decide if I should wear my new coat when we go outside or leave it here. If I wear it and get too warm, I'll have to carry it. If I set it down outside, it will get dirty and I might forget it. But it's too cold to be without a coat … or something. Aha! I can take a sweater instead." Demonstrating, when it is done well, is an effective technique for teaching thinking skills explicitly without being didactic or overly directive. This is particularly helpful for students who are contextual thinkers.

In the *Snap-sHOT, Why It's Hard to Explain Why*, in Chapter 6 (on page 102), the teacher demonstrates ways to respond to "why" questions. His goals are for students to learn the vocabulary that is commonly used to answer such questions and the various types of responses that are possible. This is a bit tricky because the teacher is demonstrating using HOT skills for the same academic task that his students are using. However, he mitigates this problem by giving his responses *after* students have given theirs.

Prompting with HOT Prompts: Roses and Thorns

HOT prompts are usually questions, but can also be requests or suggestions, that elicit students' HOT to the best of their ability. There are two main types of HOT prompts: "roses" and "thorns." Rose prompts spur students to think more expansively, and thorn prompts spur students to think more deeply. As "there are no roses without thorns," students' responses to rose prompts can lead to thorn prompts, and their responses to the thorn prompts can spur additional rose prompts.

Rose prompts reveal students' knowledge and understanding like sunlight and time reveal the petals of the rose inside the bud. Students' responses give teachers important information about how students perceive a problem, issue, or event. They nurture students' awareness of their own thought processes and thinking skills. Often, two or more prompts are given in sequence to expose more layers of "petals." Rose prompts might ask,

"How did you make it?"
"What do you know about it?"
"What more can you tell me about it?"
"What else did you see/hear?"
"What else happened?"
"Where and when was this?"
"Who else was there?"

"What happened next?"
"What problems or challenges did you have?"
"What did you do to solve the problem?"
"What problem are you trying to solve?"
"Where did it come from?"
"How did it begin?"
"How did it end?"

While each question alone can engage students' HOT, a well-improvised sequence of questions reveals the whole beauty of the rose that is a student's mind.

Thorn prompts are sets of questions that challenge students' thinking. While they further reveal how students think, their main purpose is to provoke the use of new or more advanced levels of HOT skills. Thorn prompts might ask,

"What is another way to make it work?"
"How can it be done more effectively/quickly/easily?"
"What might happen next and why?"
"What are all the possible results?"
"What can you change that might change the outcome?"
"What is the worst that could happen?"
"What is the best that could happen?"
"What else could it be?"
"What is another way to get the answer or solve the problem?"
"How do you know that?"
"How do you know if it's true?"
"What is missing or left out?"
"How might someone else answer the question differently?"
"Why did it work/not work?"
"What will/would/could you do differently the next time?"

The following *Snap-sHOT* includes many examples of HOT prompts (roses and thorns) as used by a kindergarten teacher to help a student solve an engineering problem. It also shows how she sequences prompts to scaffold the student's thought process of finding solutions, his use of HOT skills, and his understanding of certain concepts of physical science.

224 ◆ Learning to Think, Thinking to Learn

Snap-sHOT: GO WITH THE FLOW

In early October, Nadia, a kindergarten teacher, borrows a water table from the Head Start classroom down the hall in preparation for a science unit on the properties of water, including flotation and buoyancy. A bag with various types and sizes of funnels, cups, tubes, and bottles comes with it, some of which Nadia puts into the water table.

Over the next few days, Nadia notices that Simon has a keen interest in the water table. Simon is as sharp as he is shy. Although he is the youngest in the class and has a slight speech delay, he reads at the level of a six-and-a-half-year-old. His "uniqueness" may be the reason that Simon has yet to make friends with any classmates. So, one day, Nadia invites Simon to eat his lunch in the classroom with her and use the water table by himself for the whole lunch period. As he rarely talks in class, this gives Nadia an opportunity to get to know him better and learn more about how he thinks.

After a few minutes at the water table, Simon uses a small funnel to pour water from a large plastic container into a clear plastic bottle with a narrow neck. Although the water goes neatly into the bottle, the funnel quickly fills and overflows. Seeing his frustration, Nadia offers rose and thorn prompts with sequences of questions along with other HOT instructional support strategies.

Nadia: "What do you want to happen, Simon?"
Simon: "The water to go in faster. Not spilling."
Nadia: "What makes that happen? What might cause it to spill?"
Simon: "I don't know. Maybe it just *has* to spill."
Nadia: "Maybe. But if you do some higher-order thinking, I'm sure you can think of something to change or do differently that might stop the water from spilling. Any ideas?"

Simon:	(*After a brief pause*) "Well, I can't change that (*pointing to the funnel*) because it's the only one."
Nadia:	"So, are you saying that changing the funnel might fix it? You could be right. If we had lots of different funnels, which would you choose to fix it? How would it be different than this one?"
Simon:	"Maybe a higher one."
Nadia:	"Well, there is a bag by my desk with more funnels and there may be bigger ones, which probably means they are taller. You can get them and use them. Remember, you can always ask for help when you need it, Simon. You don't ever have to be stuck!" (*Simon returns with three funnels.*)
Nadia:	"There is a saying, 'If you don't ask, the answer is always no!' See, there was only one funnel, no other funnels … until you asked! But what if that doesn't work? What can you do if the water still spills?"
Simon:	"Umm, is there more funnels?"
Nadia:	"I don't think so. But there are three other things you are using that you can change: the cup and the bottle are two things. There are also lots of different bottles, cups, and containers in the bag. What do think is the third thing?"
Simon:	"Well, the only other thing is the water and I can't change the water."
Nadia:	"Actually you can in a way. You can change the way you *pour* the water: slower, faster, higher, lower, upside down, in a box with a fox!"
Simon:	"In a house with a mouse!" (*They both laugh.*)
Nadia:	"Exactly! So, I have a question. Which combination of cups, funnels, bottles, and ways of pouring will best fix the problem of the water spilling *and* will make the same amount of water go into a bottle the fastest? Would you like to investigate that question?"
Simon:	"Okay."

> **Nadia:** "Take your time. Try many different combinations. When you are done, we will talk about it. I would like hear about everything you did, the result of your investigation, and what you learned. I'm a pretty good listener. And maybe tomorrow you can write a story about it."

In the above *SnapsHOT*, the first question that Nadia asks is "What do you want to happen?" after seeing that Simon was struggling. The goal of the question is to get Simon's perspective. It is a perfect rose prompt.

The second set of questions Nadia asks are also rose prompts: "What makes that happen?" and "What might cause that to happen?" The answer would entail connecting causes and effects and using deductive and/or inductive thinking. The goal of these questions is to help Simon think more deeply (critically) about the problem by connecting causes and effects. Nadia learns from his response that this is a sticking point. He says, "I don't know. Maybe it just has to spill." The questions may be too conceptual—a little beyond his comprehension. Or he may need help developing or improving cause-and-effect thinking as well as inductive and deductive thinking. To determine this, and at the same time continue the scaffolding process, Nadia asks a question that is contextual and includes directions for action.

She asks Simon for his ideas for changing something that might stop the water from spilling. Embedded in this thorn prompt is a scaffold that helps Simon to focus his thinking on something he can change. Providing such supports along with a challenge is helpful to all young learners, not just Simon. Nadia uses a very effective communication strategy. Saying, "I'm sure you can think of something…" indirectly communicates a positive assessment of Simon's abilities, which is motivating and a boost to his self-confidence. This prompt elicits generative thinking and connecting causes and effects.

Simon responds that he can't change the funnel because there are no others. This reveals that he had already developed a hypothesis of the cause of the problem and how to solve it but believed he could not act on it. His difficulty answering the previous questions was not because of weak conceptual thinking skills or an inability to connect causes and effects, but something else. Perhaps the question itself was too vague and unclear, not the concepts it represented. The reason he said "Maybe it just has to spill" was revealed in this answer. He felt there were no options for changing the funnel. The student's difficulty solving problems, at least this problem, was due to factors that impact his ability to *apply* his HOT thinking skills—perhaps because of his speech delay or shy personality. Nadia realizes this and encourages him to ask for help when he needs it.

Then Nadia gives Simon an intellectual challenge, a thorn prompt rather than a suggestion or directive to help him move forward. She asks him to mentally identify the attributes of a funnel that would be more effective: "If we had lots of different funnels, which would you choose? How would it be different than this one?" This HOT prompt elicits inductive thinking, imagining, and generating ideas.

An exchange follows in which the teacher assists, instructs, and provides content knowledge and a dose of playfulness. Nadia uses another thorn prompt: "What if that doesn't work? What can you do if the water still spills?" His response reveals that he sees the problem to be the funnel and nothing else. To move the process forward and set the stage for a question that will engage Simon in an inquiry (this is also called a "spark"), Nadia provides information and instructions. As the inquiry will entail investigating many causes for an effect and multiple solutions for a problem, Nadia instructs him about the variables he can manipulate.

The next scaffold comes in the form of a very thorny prompt: "Which combination of cups, funnels, bottles, and ways of pouring will best fix the problem of the water spilling *and* will make the same amount of water go into a bottle the fastest?" This investigation will entail a good deal of hands-on connecting of causes and effects, associating and differentiating, deducing, inducing, synthesizing, and, undoubtedly, mopping! By telling Simon that she wants to hear about his investigation, Nadia hopes to prompt him to work more intentionally and remember more. This not only will promote HOT skills but may help him improve his language skills.

By suggesting that Simon write a book about his investigation, Nadia does two effective things at once. She respects Simon's sensitivities and autonomy by not making it an assignment or directive, and she opens up the possibility that the book would show Simon's strengths to his classmates, gaining him more positive regard.

The same types and sequences of HOT prompts are also effective for scaffolding K–3 students' thinking through almost any challenge in any content area.

Sparking

Sparks are special types of prompts. The purpose of a spark is to get students started on a self-directed inquiry. Sparks take the form of a suggestion, idea, challenge, or resource that will engage multiple MOT and HOT skills in the course of an inquiry.

There are two examples of sparking in the *Snap-sHOT, Go with the Flow*, in the previous section. A student is offered the challenge to change something to stop the water from overfilling the funnel and, a little later, the challenge to investigate the combination of cups, funnels, bottles, and pouring strategies that would stop the spilling and fill up a bottle the fastest. The teacher also makes sure the student has the materials to do it.

Why the term *sparks*? Because education is about lighting fires, not filling buckets, as some wise person said. There is even an old expression in the form of a comment to a person deep in thought: "I can smell wood burning." The following *Snap-sHOT* is another example of sparking.

HOT Instructional Supports ◆ 229

Snap-sHOT: NIGHT AND DAY

A third-grade teacher offers a spark to her students during a science unit on the solar system. Although they have seen a computer animation of the planets orbiting the sun, read a short article from a science magazine for children, and watched a demonstration of the earth rotating while orbiting the sun (with a globe and a ball to represent the sun), there had not yet been full and explicit explanations how those events relate to night and day, the length of a year, the seasons, and weather. During one discussion, she tells her students that the sun does not rise and set. After a few students argue with her, she divides the class into three groups, each tasked to either prove that she is wrong or explain why she is right. She provides resources to each group: books, a tablet computer with links to relevant websites, and a flashlight and balls. She gives them a bit of help before they begin: "I said the sun does not rise and set. I did not say there isn't day and night."

The attributes of an effective spark include the following:

- **The right kind of information**: The teacher gives information that is useful, relevant, understandable, actionable, and likely to lead to new knowledge and perhaps new insight, understanding, and appreciation.
- **The right timing**: The spark is given at an opportune moment when students are ready and are motivated and engaged.
- **The right amount of information**: The spark gives only as much information as necessary to ensure that students can run with it with no, or minimal, teacher assistance.
- **The necessary resources**: The teacher provides the materials and resources for students to investigate deeply and thoroughly.
- **Offers of assistance**: The students know that they can access the teacher or other people, such as the school librarian, whenever they need help.

230 ◆ Learning to Think, Thinking to Learn

- ◆ **Follow-up**: By telling students that there will be a "debriefing," the teacher lets them know their processes, discoveries, insights, and results are important and of high interest.

Heating

This is simply the idea of adding an element to an activity or task that uses LOT or MOT thinking skills so that it will also engage one or more HOT skills. (Yes, it's called "heating" because it makes a typical activity a HOT activity; and, yes, the heat often comes from the fire lit by a spark!) This can often be done easily and quickly, such as by adding an element of choice, as discussed in Chapter 6 (on pages 110–113). There are many ways to add creative and critical thinking elements to nearly any activity. For example, in addition to practicing solving math problems (calculating), students can select one problem and respond to the following challenges:

- ◆ Find two different ways to get the answer.
- ◆ Describe two ways that someone could get the wrong answer.
- ◆ Create two other math problems that result in the same answer; for an added challenge, the problems must use two different types of math, both of which are different from the type used in the problem.
- ◆ Describe a real-life situation that would generate the problem such as sports scores, event planning, or building a shelf. Use graphics and text.
- ◆ Develop a recipe that incorporates it.
- ◆ Develop a word problem for it using the characters and setting from a book.

Here is another example of "heating" in the content area of literacy. In addition to reading a story and discussing elements like plot, theme, sequence of events, characters, and setting, students can:

- ◆ Act out the story.
- ◆ Create a new character to add to the story.

HOT Instructional Supports ◆ 231

- Think of another plot element that can be inserted into the story.
- Think of a different ending.
- Place the story in a different time and/or location and make changes to the story accordingly.
- Create a sequel or prequel story.
- Make up a story that is different but has the same theme.

These activities not only engage HOT but help solidify students' understanding of story elements.

Conceptualizing: Maxims, Metaphors, Mottos, and More

All languages have many common phrases that offer sage advice or criticize foolishness, such as "You can't judge a book by its cover." They have a plethora of names: maxims, mottos, proverbs, sayings, idioms, expressions, words of wisdom, and aphorisms, among others. But there is another type of phrase that is just as common. These phrases have a mundane name, "figures of speech," which is unfortunate because they are so colorful and amusing. They succinctly and cleverly describe or explain a person's character, behaviors, actions, feelings, or circumstances. They are typically expressed as similes, metaphors, or analogies: "You are a rock." "That's music to my ears."

These phrases use a few words to convey complex information. They take something concrete and connect it to a broader concept, often with vivid imagery that leaves little doubt about their message. "Look before you leap" is good advice, and thinking about the consequences of *not* following it is a bit frightening. A few well-chosen words can be very impactful and memorable; in fact, some have been in common use for thousands of years: "When in Rome, do as the Romans do."

When teachers use these phrases, they help students develop high levels of the MOT skills of characterizing, representing, and associating/differentiating and HOT skills such as inferring and reframing. They introduce students to conceptual thinking in general, often in an amusing way. In the *Snap-sHOT, Go with the Flow*, earlier in this chapter, the teacher introduces her students to a phrase that conceptualizes a behavior: "If you don't ask, the answer is always no!" Not asking will have the same result as asking and getting a negative answer, although the actual answer might be positive.

These phrases are all mental shortcuts. Some are actually just verbal cues, but because they are very common and well known, they have become maxims, such as "Keep an open mind." Like cues, they can be used as reminders before an action ("Piece it together"), but they are also used to comment after an action ("I just couldn't connect the dots!").

Conceptualizing phrases should always be used in context to help students connect the action and its concept together. For example, when telling students they can write about anything, add the phrase "The sky's the limit." When asking students to work in pairs, add the phrase "Two heads are better than one." Or when a student is dawdling, say "You're going to miss the boat."

When introducing any of these conceptual phrases, teachers may need to help students understand them. One way to do this is to follow the phrase with its explicit meaning or a more child-friendly version while trying to match its tone and cadence: "Don't count your chickens before they hatch" can be followed by "Don't assume you will have something before you have it" or "Don't assume that things will work out perfectly or as you hope" or "Don't invite friends to the victory party before you've won the game."

There is another good reason to use these phrases. Many of them are about the importance of using HOT, particularly critical thinking. The following is a list of phrases categorized to make it easier for teachers to use them as an instructional strategy with intention and purpose. Many common phrases are not included, because their meanings are too obscure or outdated ("A pig in a poke") or their language is too graphic or sophisticated for young learners ("Putting a Band-Aid on an open wound").

Higher-Order Thinking

The pen is mightier than the sword.

Critical Thinking

You can't judge a book by its cover.
Beauty is only skin deep.
There's more than meets the eye.
All that glitters is not gold.
Appearances can be deceiving.
Dig a little deeper.
Look behind the curtain.
Scratch/dig beneath the surface.
Don't believe everything you see/hear/read.
It's all just smoke and mirrors.
Take it with a grain of salt.
It's a house of cards.
 Infer
  Read between the lines.
 Inductive thinking
  Connect the dots.
  Piece it together.
 Shift perspective
  The grass is always greener on the other side of the fence
   (*may not be suitable for many urban schools*).
  One person's trash is another person's treasure.
  One person's ceiling is another person's floor.
  Beauty is in the eyes of the beholder.
  Don't judge people until you have walked a mile in their
   shoes.
  There are two sides to a coin.

Creative Thinking

Think outside the box.
Think for yourself.
The sky's the limit.
Let your imagination run wild.
Think big.

234 ◆ Learning to Think, Thinking to Learn

Think the unthinkable.
Expand your horizons.

Logical Thinking
Connecting causes and effects
What goes up must come down.
What goes around, comes around.
The chickens come home to roost.
Don't put the cart before the horse.
You reap what you sow.
Better safe than sorry.

Thought Processes
Plans/Strategies
Hope for the best, prepare for the worst.
Don't count your chickens before they hatch.
Don't put all your eggs in one basket.
Look before you leap.
Don't miss the boat.
Measure twice, cut once.
You can't put the toothpaste back in the tube.
Let's cross that bridge when we come to it.

Thinking Dispositions
Caution
Think before you act.
Think before you speak.
Before you assume, learn.
Before you judge, understand.
That's a red flag.
Look before you leap.
Curiosity
Keep an open mind.
Patience
Don't eat the marshmallow.
Good things come to those who wait.

HOT Instructional Supports ◆ 235

Don't miss an opportunity
Strike while the iron is hot.
The early bird catches the worm.
Persistence
Don't give up the ship.
Where there's a will, there's a way.
Keep on truckin'.
If at first you don't succeed, try, try again.
Practice makes perfect.

Miscellaneous Concepts
Collaboration
Two heads are better than one.
The more the merrier.
It takes two to tango.
Out of date
This old _____ is a dinosaur.
Prevention
A stitch in time saves nine.
An ounce of prevention is worth a pound of cure.
Out of place/doesn't belong
They're like a fish out of water.
Like putting a square peg in a round hole.
Similarities
They're like peas in a pod.
Annoyances
It's like nails on a chalkboard.
Potential
Like a diamond in the rough
Power
You're just a puppet on a string.
Who is the puppet master?
Enjoyment/happiness
That's music to my ears.
In the cat-bird seat
It's a dream come true.

In seventh heaven
The bee's knees
Milk and honey
Life is a dance, not a race.
Slow down and smell the roses.
Innocence or naivete
You're still a bit green.
Good people
She's a peach.
He's a rock.
You're a gem.
She's the cat's pajamas.
He has a heart of gold.
Not such good people
He thinks he's the center of the universe.
She has a heart of stone.
It's too late
The horse is out of the barn.
That train left the station.
It's futile
You can't get blood from a turnip.
That will happen when pigs can fly.

Making up phrases that are relevant and understandable to students fosters creative thinking. Characters from popular children's literature are a good source:

- ◆ "You are kinder than the lion who didn't eat the mouse!"
- ◆ "You two are the best friends since Frog met Toad!"
- ◆ "I got dirtier than Harry on a bad day!"
- ◆ "This room looks like the Cat in the Hat and Curious George had a party!"
- ◆ "How old am I? If I was a turtle, I'd be more Morla than Mutant Ninja."

Students can also make up phrases. A good place to start is to have them think of new terms for common phrases:

Quiet as _____
As smooth as _____
Silly as _____
As deep as _____
Strong as _____
Sharp as _____
Happy as _____
Sweet as _____
As far as _____
As scary as _____

Conclusion

To ensure that HOT instructional supports will develop students' HOT, they must be used cumulatively, often, and with intention. Their power is enhanced when they are used while students engage with activities that align with HOT precepts and HOT teaching methods discussed in the previous two chapters.

The issue of assessing HOT is beyond the scope of this book; it would take another entire book to address it properly. But it is an important issue for several reasons.

There is a common maxim among educators: "assessment drives curriculum." (This is a phrase that could have been placed under the concept of "connecting causes and effects" in the above section on conceptualizing.) Assessments that only tax students' LOT and MOT abilities are major obstacles to making critical and creative thinking a prominent part of every curriculum. Skills that are not assessed are too often and too easily dismissed as unimportant. After all, if they were important, they would be assessed!

Assessing HOT skills is not easy or straightforward. Paper-and-pencil tests are problematic for young learners, many of whom are not yet reading and writing. And among those students who can read and write, many do so at a level much lower than their level of thinking. Accurate assessments of HOT skills require careful and informed observations of students engaging in challenging tasks.

238 ◆ Learning to Think, Thinking to Learn

The biggest obstacle to observational, authentic assessment of HOT has less to do with the time and effort needed to conduct it and more to do with a lack of understanding of it as well as its value. As discussed in Chapter 8, a difficult or complicated task is not the same as a challenging or complex task. Nevertheless, students with HOT skills are usually good at taking tests of any type, because they can transfer HOT skills, such as inferring, deducing, shifting perspective, and reframing, and apply them across a wide variety of cognitive tasks, irrespective of content. Compared with students who have weak HOT skills, students who have strong HOT skills, but have the same level of knowledge, are better able to figure out the correct answer when they are unsure or do not know it. One of the advantages they have is the ability to shift perspective to determine the answer the test developer is looking for.

Key Ideas from this Chapter

1. HOT instructional supports promote and sharpen students' cognitive abilities to think critically and creatively and the language skills and vocabulary needed to use and express HOT.
2. HOT instructional supports include scaffolding, cuing (nonverbal, verbal, and visual), demonstrating, prompting, sparking, heating, and conceptualizing.
3. Scaffolding is a general strategy for implementing instructional supports. Teachers help students act or think at a slightly higher developmental level than they can do on their own. The teacher stops assisting (removes the scaffold) when the student no longer needs assistance.
4. Cuing gives students quick reminders to use HOT.
5. Nonverbal cuing uses gestures that can include standard sign language signs.
6. Verbal cuing uses short statements such as "Try again."
7. Visual cuing uses pictures or icons to represent MOT and HOT skills.

HOT Instructional Supports ◆ 239

8. Demonstrating entails teachers describing and explaining their own thought processes and uses of HOT to students.
9. Prompting uses statements and questions to expand and expose students' thinking (rose prompts) and to provoke critical and creative thinking (thorn prompts).
10. Sparking gives students suggestions, ideas, challenges, or resources that will engage them in a self-directed course of an inquiry.
11. Heating entails adding an element to an activity, or modifying it slightly, to engage HOT.
12. Conceptualizing involves using short phrases to convey complex information. They can be proverbs or maxims or phrases that cleverly describe or explain people's characters, behaviors, actions, feelings, or circumstances. They take something concrete and connect it to a broader concept, often with vivid imagery that leaves little doubt about their message, such as "Don't put the cart before the horse."
13. Assessing students' HOT skills is challenging but it is necessary because "assessment drives curriculum." The biggest obstacle to effective and accurate assessment of HOT skills is a lack of understanding of HOT and its purpose and value.

Questions for Discussion

What are some ways you have scaffolded students' learning? Share any examples that involved scaffolding their thinking. What thinking skills were promoted? Did the scaffolding sharpen an existing thinking skill or introduce a new one?

What proverbs or maxims have you said or do you say to your students? Was it planned or spontaneous? What were your students' reactions or responses, if any?

What proverbs did you hear as a child and student from parents and teachers? What did they attempt to communicate? How did they influence your thinking? If you have children, do you repeat the same aphorisms to them? Do you use new ones?

How have you used demonstrations in your teaching? How did you promote the transfer of the lessons of the demonstrations to avoid imitation?

Are there other instructional supports that you have used or that you think could be used to promote HOT skills that were not covered in this chapter?

Describe and discuss any experiences you have had with assessing HOT. What do you think are some effective ways to do it?

11

Teaching Reading and Writing with Higher-Order Thinking

Yearning to Learn

This concluding chapter culls the ideas and practices described in the previous ten chapters and applies them to a major aspect of teaching and learning in early primary education. It is also, arguably, the most contentious issue in all of education. How students should be taught to read and write has been so politicized for so long and subjected to changes in "best practice" so often and so extreme that K–3 teachers—the people in the line of fire from all sides of this war—should receive hazard pay and be awarded Purple Hearts.

In many schools, a literacy goal for their youngest learners is to read fluently by the end of third grade. However, to be literate requires more than the ability to read fluently. If fluent readers cannot understand what they read, then they are just decoding and memorizing. If they misinterpret what they read, then they can technically read but they are not literate. Third-graders who fluently read that their favorite pop star is really an alien from another planet who wants to take over Earth, and believe it, lack the ability to infer that this may be satire or to parse the truth of the statement using critical thinking skills such as querying, deducing, and inducing. Also, their dispositions to be cautious,

DOI: 10.4324/9781032683423-14

curious, and persistent may be weak or lacking. If students are to be literate by third grade, these higher-order thinking (HOT) skills and dispositions must be taught and encouraged, along with decoding and other reading strategies, as soon as students start learning to read, if not before.

For fluent third-grade readers to be literate, they must have the ability to ask questions and seek answers about a story or text that go beyond descriptive. "Why did the author write this book?" "What does the author want me to learn, believe, and feel?" "How do the events or characters relate, or not relate, to things in my life?" "If I could talk to the author, what would I want to say or ask?" Reading fluently *and* thinking critically—to fully understand what is written and to be able to analyze and evaluate it at a basic level—close the circle on what is required to be literate in this disinformation age, even for third graders.

Is it possible to teach complex cognitive and technical skills like reading, or complex cognitive and mechanical skills like writing, with HOT? After all, practicing writing the letter "*e*" is necessary and is a motor task for which HOT is largely irrelevant. And tasks like learning to recognize and know the sounds of blends or memorizing sight words are necessary to learn to read, but primarily require lower-order thinking (LOT) skills. Learning to read takes a great deal of practice and effort. It involves struggling with long and unfamiliar words, losing and finding one's place in the text, and other not-so-fun LOT tasks.

> **On the road to reading, there is no avoiding those mundane, repetitive, joyless, drill and practice potholes, stop signs, detours, and speed bumps. However, this is the very reason why everything about learning to read that can possibly involve critical and creative thinking needs to involve critical and creative thinking. By doing this, the potholes, stop signs, detours, and speed bumps will be minor inconveniences on an enjoyable journey full of adventure.**

Of all the things that can and should involve HOT skills, perhaps the most important and impactful is the quality of the texts with which students learn to read. (This was also discussed in Chapter 9 in the section about materials that matter on pages 199–200.) Students need to work with materials developed by adults who used HOT skills to create them. Inauthentic texts, commonly found in commercial reading curricula, sacrifice meaning for some notion of instructional value, which is another way of saying that they engage LOT skills at the expense of HOT skills. They are not benign. They stifle students' motivation to want to read. Quality texts, on the other hand, engage LOT, MOT, and HOT skills *and* motivate students to want to read. With so much great children's literature available, both classic and contemporary, it is difficult to justify not using high-quality texts. Quality texts are not only for students to read for themselves but for teachers to read to students. At every grade level, students need to hear wonderful stories read to them from books that are several reading levels more advanced than their own.

Authors of excellent children's literature have advanced critical thinking skills. This is reflected in their deep understanding of children's emotional and cognitive needs, concerns, and interests. But it is their advanced creative thinking skills that enable them to use this understanding to create stories that children can comprehend, connect to, and delight in—stories that children want to hear over and over again.

Throughout the book, there have been examples of many activities in which students both develop literacy skills and practice HOT. They include HOT methods, instructional supports, and games. They are categorized below and include a few new activities.

Writing That Is Meaningful and Learner-centered

Scaffolded writing is discussed in Chapter 4 in the section about representational thinking (on pages 58–59). Developed by Bodrova and Leong (2019), scaffolded writing is a literacy development strategy in which preliterate children use lines to represent words to "write" meaningful and purposeful messages. This is also a tool that teachers can use as a bridge to conventional writing.

Students who are able read and write should have many opportunities to create their own messages and stories. HOT skills are engaged when the messages and stories have a real purpose rather than just an academic exercise. For example, they can be messages to parents, friends, or "my future self." They can be stories about things that they did or that happened to them that were scary, surprising, funny, or sad. These can become a collection of stories that comprise their autobiographies….so far! Stories can also reflect or complement the style or genre of a recently read story. For example, after reading *Horton Hatches the Egg* (Seuss, 1940/2013) and *Horton Hears a Who!* (Seuss, 1954/2013), second- and third-grade students can research whether elephants actually are faithful, empathetic, and protective. They can write about the social traits of elephants and give presentations on the topic. They can also write stories in the style of Dr. Seuss. What if Dr. Seuss had written more books about Horton? (This is a good example of a Spark.) In response, students can create stories in which Horton has more adventures.

Another type of book that students can write is the guidebook, which entails critical reflection (a type of analyzing). Near the end of the school year, third graders create a Survival Guide for current second graders to help them be successful in the third grade. Second graders can do the same for first graders, and first graders for kindergartners.

Author and Theme Studies

A study that is both an author and theme study is described in Chapter 9 (on page 188). The theme is "Me and We," and the author is Leo Lionni. Most of his books are about the many ways that an individual can have a unique identity but still be a vital member of a group. *Frederick* (1967) is mouse with a unique personality who is finally able to find a role in the mouse community as a storyteller and poet. *Swimmy* (1963/2011) is the only black fish among his red schoolmates. But, when they all swim together in the formation of a large fish to scare off predators, his unique color makes for the perfect eye.

Other themes found in children's literature include friendship in the Frog and Toad series by Arnold Lobel; parents' unconditional love for their children in the David books by David Shannon and in many of Maurice Sendak's books; and the up-and-down relationships between students and teachers in the Ramona books by Beverly Cleary, the Miss Nelson books by Harry Allard, and the Lilly books by Kevin Henkes.

Word Games

Rhyme Time, in Chapter 9 (on page 184): This is a game played in teams in which students from one team need to determine the two or more words that rhyme from pictures or actions created by the other team.

Chain Stories, in Chapter 9 (on page 211): In this activity, everyone contributes sequentially to spontaneously making up a story.

Don't Say the Word! in Chapter 9 (on page 209): This is a game played in teams in which students need to determine the name of an object or idea from its description.

Conceptual Phrases

The instructional support of conceptualizing in Chapter 10 (on pages 231–237) includes a number of phrases that are literature-based. Among them are "You are kinder than the lion who didn't eat the mouse!", "You two are the best friends since Frog met Toad!", "I got dirtier than Harry on a bad day!", "This room looks like David and Curious George had a party!", and "How old am I? If I was a turtle, I'd be more Morla than Mutant Ninja."

Here is another that plays off the theme in Lilly's Big Day (Henkes, 2006). It describes wishful thinking as "The flower girl at Mr. Slinger's wedding." A variant is "Throwing flowers at Mr. Slinger's wedding." This is a combination of "Don't count your chickens before they hatch" and "Building castles in the sky." Given some prompts, students can create expressions based on the personalities and actions of characters in the books they read: "This is funnier than (character / character's action or situation)" and "You are as clever as (character / character's action or situation)."

Heating a Literacy Activity

Heating, as discussed in Chapter 10 (on pages 230–231), involves adding an element of creativity to lessons or activities. The heating ideas related to a book or story include the following: acting out the story, creating a new character for the story, thinking of another plot element that can be inserted into the story, thinking of a different ending to the story, rewriting the story to place it in a different time and/or location, creating a sequel or prequel story, and making up a story that is different but has the same theme.

Supporting Every Unique Reader

Learning to read requires a great deal of time just practicing. A key to learning to read is to spend many hours reading aloud with an attentive adult who judiciously and kindly offers individualized assistance, corrections, and suggestions for reading strategies; who helps keep the focus on the meaning and the enjoyment of the story; and who, most of all, gives copious amounts of encouragement.

Every student seems to have their own unique approach to learning to read, regardless of the instructional method. It's like teaching handwriting—no matter what style you teach or how you teach it, every person's handwriting will be different. The students who are naturally phonetic readers need support and guidance to use contextual cues and to keep their focus on meaning. Contextual or sight readers need assistance to slow down and read the words they skip over and to sound out the words they misstate. Often these are words like *has/had* because they are short and easy to glance over quickly, they have similar meanings, and the difference between them is at the end of the word. Students who are equally contextual and phonetic readers need help to strengthen any weak areas, but they mostly need a patient and appreciative listener.

The individual nature of learning to read is a contributing factor to the "reading wars." No single approach is going to work for all students, and the effectiveness of any approach is limited without many additional literacy activities and supports and other activities that develop HOT skills, such as those in this chapter and throughout the book.

Even a combined approach, as discussed in Chapter 7 (on page 147), is not a panacea, because learning to read in a large group is antithetical to individualizing. Nevertheless, it is still the most sensible approach and the one most likely to reach the most students. The effectiveness of the combined approached would be greatly enhanced if parents, community members, retired friends and relatives, office staff, middle and high school students, volunteers, and others received training and support to guide students one-to-one as students read aloud.

The following poetic saying has been attributed to the author Antoine de Saint-Exupéry, but it is apparently an amalgam and paraphrase (by an unknown person) of things he wrote in *Wisdom of the Sands* (de Saint-Exupéry, 2003) and not a direct quote (Quote Investigator, 2015). It expresses a concept that has important implications for teaching reading.

> *If you want to build a ship, don't drum up the men to gather wood, divide the work, and give orders. Instead, teach them to yearn for the vast and endless sea.*

This saying, which is not to be taken literally, is an eloquent statement about the power of the desire for something grand, inspiring, and mysterious to motivate people to do hard work. The same holds true for the version of this saying below.

If you want to teach children to read, don't make them decode nonsense. Instead, teach them to yearn for places where wild things roar, elephants hatch eggs, pigs talk, mice drive motorcycles, and where sidewalks may end, but stories never do.

Conclusion

There is a topic that has not been directly addressed in this book but is something you have likely considered while reading: What about our own HOT skills? It is helpful to know where our own strengths and weaknesses are, so we can more effectively teach others. What are the thinking errors that we make most often or that trip us up the most? How good are we at recognizing, parsing, and rejecting disinformation and other deceptions? Which thought processes are we good at and which do we try to avoid? Because these things are very difficult to self-assess, it is helpful to have people who know us well and whom we trust to answer these questions about us.

Knowing this and having greater self-awareness are just the first steps. We all need assistance and support to improve skills.

How do our school administrators and colleagues support and/or suppress critical and creative thinking for the staff and for the students? As disinformation gets more sophisticated, the HOT skills to counter them have to get sharper. This puts the onus on school systems to provide teachers with ongoing support, resources, professional development, and discussion groups on all aspects of developing and teaching HOT skills. But, as teachers, we also have a responsibility to do this with or without support.

Among the organizations that provide professional development for educators and teaching resources and materials for promoting critical thinking are the Critical Thinker Academy (https://criticalthinkeracademy.com) and the Critical Thinking Consortium (https://tc2.ca), which is based in Canada.

For resources on teaching creative thinking, check out the Massachusetts Institute of Technology's Learning Creative Learning (https://lcl.media.mit.edu), the Creative Learning Foundation (https://www.creativeeducationfoundation.org), and the Global Institute of Creative Thinking (https://www.gioct.org).

There are organizations that provide online resources for adults to improve their HOT skills, through courses, conferences, webinars, videos, self-assessments, and research articles, though they are more focused on critical thinking than creative thinking. These include the Foundation for Critical Thinking (https://criticalthinking.org) and the Reboot Foundation (https://reboot-foundation.org). "Bad News" uses a clever game format to convey information about the techniques used to deceive people in media disinformation campaigns (https://www.getbadnews.com/en#intro).

Other organizations focus on keeping the public apprised of disinformation in general but also track and expose specific disinformation campaigns in the media as they come up. They also have helpful exercises that test our ability to distinguish fake news from real news, online postings that are propaganda from postings that are factual, and computer-generated photos from real photos. These include Snopes (https://www.snopes.com), FactCheck.org (https://www.factcheck.org), PolitiFact (https://www.politifact.com), the News Literacy Project (https://newslit.org), and the European Disinformation Lab (http://www.disinfo.eu).

The website for this book also has information, resources, and links to these and other organizations that help adults develop their HOT skills and stay informed about media disinformation: **https://higher-order-thinking.com**

Final Thoughts

A year from now, you will likely remember just a few ideas from this book. They may be concrete ideas such as certain activities or instructional supports or the three levels of thinking skills as illustrated on Saifer's Taxonomy. But, in addition, I hope you

250 ◆ Learning to Think, Thinking to Learn

will have retained things from this book that are not ideas. They are feelings you will still hold inside.

- ◆ A sense of your value and importance as a person who, in your role as a teacher, promotes the well-being, knowledge, abilities, and thinking skills of young learners.
- ◆ A sense of urgency to help learners also be thinkers and a feeling of responsibility to do so.
- ◆ A feeling of confidence that you have the knowledge, skills, and resources to teach young learners to think in many different ways at the highest levels of which they are capable.
- ◆ Feelings of pride and accomplishment that you have made and continue to make a difference in the lives of young learners—a difference that will positively affect their futures and the future of society.

Key Ideas from this Chapter

1. To be literate requires the ability to read, to understand what is read, and to think critically about it.
2. Every aspect of learning to read that can include critical and creative thinking should include critical and creative thinking as a counterpoint to all the aspects of learning to read that use LOT but are necessary.
3. High-quality texts, including classic and current children's literature, are important for teaching reading with HOT.
4. A combined approach to teaching reading incorporates phonics, sight reading, and other strategies with contextual strategies and with HOT activities.
5. A combined approach is necessary but insufficient for reaching all learners because every child has a unique way they learn to read.
6. Students need ample time to practice reading one-to-one with an adult or an older student who can provide guidance and encouragement.
7. Teachers need support and resources to assess and hone their own HOT skills.

Questions for Discussion

Reflect on, share, and discuss your own experiences learning to read. What aspects were challenging? What individualized supports, if any, did you get?

Discuss experiences you have had using various approaches to teaching reading. How often did they change? What precipitated those changes? Which worked best for you?

What strategies, if any, have you used to engage students' HOT in the process of teaching reading or improving students' literacy skills?

What literacy-related methods, activities, instructional supports, and so on from this book are most appealing to you and why? What adaptations, if any, would you make to better meet the need of your particular class of students?

References

Bodrova, E., & Leong, D. J. (2019). *Tools of the mind: The Vygotskian approach to early childhood education* (2nd ed.). Pearson.

de Saint-Exupéry, A. (2003). *Wisdom of the Sands*. Amereon Press.

Henkes, K. (2006). *Lilly's purple plastic purse*. Greenwillow Books.

Lionni, L. (1963/2011). *Swimmy*. Knopf Books for Young Readers.

Lionni, L. (1967). *Frederick*. Pantheon.

Quote Investigator. (2015, August 25). *Teach them to yearn for the vast and endless sea*. https://quoteinvestigator.com/2015/08/25/sea/?amp=1

Seuss. (2013). *Horton hatches the egg*. Random House (Original work published 1940).

Seuss. (2013). *Horton hears a Who!* Random House (Original work published 1954).

Index

Pages in *italics* refer to figures.

Abrami, P. C. 165
Acs, G. 116
Activities 4; challenging and enjoyable (a HOT teaching precept) 172–173; meaningful and relevant (a HOT teaching precept) 167–172
Aesop's fables 25
Allard, H. 245
ambiguity (discomfort with) 138–139
analyses (a thought process) 100–104
Ansar, M. R. U. 167
Aristotle 15
art: creativity 82; improvisation 91; Metkids 197; Metropolitan Museum of Art 42; National Gallery of Art 42; ScratchJr 198; ThinkinGroups: Describe It/Draw It 210; ThinkinGroups: Rhyme Time 184; ThinkinGroups: The Fine Art of Matching 42
assessment (of HOT) 237
associate/differentiate (a MOT skill) 41–43

Bartels, L. M. 16
Beishuizen, J. 68
Blanch, A. 120
Bodrova, E. 58, 59, 243
Bouygues, H. L. 11
brain development and functioning: effect of stress 13,

154–155; aversion to critical thinking and intellectual work 12–15; "us vs. them" thinking 13–15, 49
Brannon, E. M. 35
Breslin, F. 11
Buchsbaum, D. 185
Buller, R. 14
Butler, H. A. 11

Cadima, J. 173
calculate (a MOT skill) 50–51
case studies (a HOT teaching method) 195
categorize (a MOT skill) 43–49
Celli, L. M. 167
Chalkiadaki, A. 10
characterize (a MOT skill) 40–41
Cleary, B. 245
Cognitivities 4; Brain Baits 155; The Case of the Unknown Bully 195; Inventors Inventing Inventions 83; May the Best Map Win 111; Orchestra Conductor 58; Same Words, Different Meanings 70; What Makes a Good Map? 108; Who Knows? 140
Collins, R. 165
conceptualizing and conceptual phrases (an instructional support) 231–237
conceptual thinking 12, 22–24, 167
connect causes and effects (a MOT skill) 51–55

contextual thinking 167–168,
171–172, 177, 184, 200
Copernicus 122
copy/imitate (a LOT skill) 32
Córdova, A. 154
creative thinking (a HOT skill
category) *23*, 80–92; resources
for teachers and adults 249
critical thinking (a HOT skill
category) *23*, 65–79; resources
for teachers and adults 249
cuing (an instructional support)
218–221; nonverbal cuing
218–219; verbal cuing 219;
visual cuing 219, *220*–221

da Vinci, L. 15
deceptions *see* disinformation,
thinking errors
decisions and deciding (a
thought process) 104–107; *see
also* evaluations; developing
students' abilities to decide
110–113
deduce and deductive thinking
(a HOT skill) 72–76; *see also*
induce and inductive thinking
(a HOT skill)
Dehry, I. 116
democracy (role of HOT) 15–16
demonstrating (an instructional
support) 221–222
de Saint-Exupéry, A. 247
differentiate (a MOT skill) 41–43;
see also associate/differentiate
(a MOT skill)
discrete thinking 167–168
disinformation: in relation to
HOT skills 10–11; in relation
to reading 242; resources for
teachers and adults 248–249;
teachers' role in countering
159–160; verbal deceptions
152–159

dispositions and thinking
dispositions 27–28, 137–141,
234–235
Donovan, C. A. 58
Doyle, A. C. 72
Dubuc, M. 155
Dunn, D. S. 11
Dyer, F. 84

Early Childhood Learning and
Knowledge Center (ECLKC)
173
Einstein, A. 15, 64, 124
Ellerton, P. 164, 165
estimating 43, 122–123
evaluations and evaluating (a
thought process) 104; *see also*
decisions and deciding (a
thought process); developing
students' abilities to evaluate
107–110

Fairless, T. 16
Fauth, B. 173
field-dependent/field-
independent thinking 167–168
Filiatrault-Veilleux, P. 69
follow rules and directions (a
LOT skill) 32–33
Food Marketing Institute 117
Furey, W. 167

games (a HOT teaching
method) 202–212; *see also*
ThinkinGroups
Ganesh, M. P. 167
Gardner, H. 167
generate (a HOT skill) 27, 81–86,
117
Giffens, G. 120
Gobet, F. 120
Golding, W. 56
Goodwin, B. 165
Gopnik, A. 185

254 ◆ Index

Gorman, J. M. 13
Gorman, S. E. 13
Gross, J. 2
Grossman, I. 2, 5

Haden, C. A. 68
Haggard, S. 16
Halpern, D. F. 11, 150
Hamlin, J. K. 13, 77
Hanna, P. R. 147
Hardwick, J. 15
Hawking, S. 15
heating an activity (an
    instructional support)
    230–231
Henkes, K. 52, 245, 246
Heppt, B. 173
higher-order thinking (HOT)
    23, 63–96; as an educational
    imperative 11; benefits
    to students 9; for gaining
    insight, understanding, and
    appreciation 174–176; *see
    also* teaching precepts; how
    it should be taught 164–166,
    185; importance of starting
    early 11–12; *see also* brain
    development and functioning
Hines, M. 150
history and social studies:
    Cognitivity: Who Knows? 140;
    Snap-sHOT: Harriet 'Round
    the Mountain 174; Snap-sHOT:
    Lincoln Thinkin' 157
Hofstede, G. 168
Howard, B. 150
Huguet, A. 14
hypotheses and hypothesizing (a
    predictions thought process)
    123–124

identify/quantify (a LOT skill)
    35–36
imagine (a HOT skill) 81–83

imitate/copy (a LOT skill) 32
improvise (a HOT skill)
    91–92
induce and inductive thinking
    (a HOT skill) 72–76; *see also*
    deduce and deductive thinking
    (a HOT skill)
infer and make inferences (a HOT
    skill) 69–70, *71*
infusion approach to teaching
    HOT 164–165, 172, 185
innovations (a solutions thought
    process) 115–116
inquiries (a HOT teaching
    method) 191–194; *see also*
    projects (a HOT teaching
    method)
instructional supports and
    HOT instructional supports
    216–240
interpret (a reframing HOT skill)
    89–90
investigating (an analyses
    thought process) 100–101
investigations 191

Joshi, R. M. 147

Kahneman, D. 13, 141, 150
Katz, L. 173
Kaufman, R. 16
Kelemen, D. 12
King, S. P. 167
Kinzie, M. B. 68
Kitayama, S. 2, 5
know or do by rote (a LOT skill)
    34
Kolbert, E. 13
Kulke, H. 120

Lantian, A. 11
Lee, K. S. 2, 5
Lee, Y. 68
Leong, D. J. 58, 59, 243

Index ◆ 255

Leppink, J. 164
Lionni, L. 188, 244
literate (to be in the disinformation age) 241–242
Lobel. A. 245
logical thinking *see* middle-order thinking
lower-order thinking (LOT) 23, 31–37

Mahajan, N. 13
Martin, T. 84
Maslow, A. H. 21
Mason, B. A. 167
materials that matter (a HOT teaching method) 197–202
math: calculate 50–51; HOTheme: No fair! 186, 192–193; HOTheme: Skill or luck? 187; math playing cards 200–202; quantify 35
McGrew, S. 11
media literacy: critique of 14; in Finland 2
Melville, H. 56
memorize/recall (a LOT skill) 33–34
mental shortcuts 148–152; assumptions 148–149; false associations 150; stereotyping 150–152
Mercier, H. 13, 15
Merkley, E. 15
middle-order thinking (MOT) 23, 38–62
MOTivations: Beads 46; Drought 54; Free the Trees! 47; Lilly 52
music: Cognitivity: Orchestra Conductor 58; Snap-sHOT: Harriet 'Round the Mountain 174

Na, J. 2, 5
Newton, I. 124, 125

Nisbett, R. E. 2, 5
Norman, L. 16

Organization for Economic Co-operation and Development (OECD) 2, 5
Orhan, Y. E. 16
Orwell, G. 56

Park, J. 35
parsing (an analyses thought process) 101
pattern/sequence (a MOT skill) 49–50
Pickney, J. 189
plans and planning (a thought process) 117–118; *see also* strategies
predictions and predicting (a thought process) 121–124; *see also* theories
Pritchard, A. 167
problem-solving *see* solutions
professional development and teacher resources 248–249
projects (a HOT teaching method) 191–192; *see also* inquiries (a HOT teaching method)
prompting with HOT prompts (an instructional support) 222–228

quantify/identify (a LOT skill) 35–36
query (a HOT skill) 65–69
questions 26–28, 34, 102–103; *see also* prompting; query
Quote Investigator 247

reading 241–248; books and texts 199–200; combined approach 147; contextual and phonetic readers 247
Reboot Foundation 11, 249

256 ◆ Index

recall/memorize (a LOT skill)
33–34
reframe (a HOT skill) 86–89
represent (a MOT skill) 55–59
role-plays and sketches (a HOT
teaching method) 196–197
rote knowledge *see* know or do
by rote
Rothermund, D. 120

Saifer's Taxonomy of Thinking
Skills 21–26, 31, 249
Sala, G. 120
Saracho, O. N. 167
scaffolding (an instructional
support) 217
Schwabe, L. 13
science 12; Cognitivity: Inventors
Inventing Inventions 83;
Cognitivity: Who Knows! 140;
connect causes and effects
51–55; Crayon Physics 198;
HOTheme: Changes 186;
HOTheme: No Fair! 186,
192–193; MOTivation: Drought
54; Snap-sHOT: Float Your Boat
73; Snap-sHOT: Go With the
Flow 224; Snap-sHOT: Night
and Day 229; Snap-sHOT: Wild
and Tame 189; ThinkinGroups:
Don't Say the Word! 209;
ThinkinGroups: Game of
Stones (and Shells) 207–208, *208*
Scott-Weich, B. 58
Sendak, M. 189, 245
sequence/pattern (a MOT skill)
49–50
Seuss 244
Shakespeare, W. 24, 80, 89
Shannon, D. 189, 245
shift perspective (a HOT skill)
76–80; interpersonal shifting
76–77; social shifting 77–80

Skelton, A. E. 49
Snap-sHOTs 4; "Cheetah'ed" 156;
Float Your Boat 73; Go With
the Flow 224; Harriet 'Round
the Mountain 174; Is the Sky
Falling? 165; It's Time to Party
88; Lincoln Thinkin' 157; My
Family Feeds the World 68;
Night and Day 229; Questions
for an Author 66; Reframing a
Parent/School Conflict 86; A
Special Lunch 168; Why Can't
Jordan Read? 106; Why It's
Hard to Explain Why 102; Wild
and Tame 188
social learning and collaboration
(a HOT teaching method)
183–185
solutions (a thought process)
113–115; *see also* innovations
sparking (an instructional support)
228–230
Sperber, D. 13, 15
Stenner, K. 16
Stern, J. 16
strategies and strategizing (a
thought process) 118–121; *see
also* plans
student achievement 2
Swartz, R. J. 165
Sweller, J. 164

teaching methods and HOT
teaching methods 183–214
teaching precepts and HOT
teaching precepts 163–180
Teachstone 173
technology & electronic materials
197–199; Crayon Physics 198;
role in generational differences
125–126; ScratchJr 198
Teemant, A. 173
The Numbers 15

themes and HOThemes (a HOT teaching method) 185–194; *see also* inquiries (a HOT teaching method); projects (a HOT teaching method)

theories and theorizing (a thought process) 121–122

thinking errors 141–159; *see also* mental shortcuts; confirmation bias 143–145; either/or thinking 146–147; illusory truth effect 145–146; optimism bias 143; teaching students to avoid and correct 159–160

ThinkinGroups and games (a HOT teaching method) 4, 202–212; Chain Stories 211; Crayon Physics 198; Describe It/Draw It 210; Don't Say the Word 209; Family Groups 127; The Fine Art of Matching 44; Game of Stones (and Shells) 207; Mental Flossers 206; Rhyme Time 184; ScratchJr 198; Shape Shifting 85; Twins 203

thought processes 23, 98–133

transfer (a reframing HOT skill) 90–91

Turner, G. T. 174

Twenge, J. 125–126

Twenty-first Century Skills 10

Tylor, J. 11

uncertainty (discomfort with / acceptance of) 138–139

van de Pol, J. 68

Varnum, M. E. 2, 5

Viereck, G. S. 64

Volman, M. 68

Weisberg, D. S. 68

Wiggins, G. 11

Williams, V. B. 77

Willingham, D. 164

Wineburg, S. 11

Witkin, H. A. 167

Wolf, O. T. 13

writing 241–243; scaffolded writing 58–59, 243

Wynn, K. 13, 77

Yaden, D. B. 58

Young, N. D. 167

Yu, R. 154

Yu-Lin, Y. 2, 5

Printed in the United States
by Baker & Taylor Publisher Services